Men and Gods in a Changing World

JUDITH M. BROWN

=

MEN AND GODS IN A CHANGING WORLD

=

Some Themes in the Religious
Experience of Twentieth-Century
Hindus and Christians

SCM PRESS LTD

334 01002 0

First published 1980
by SCM Press Ltd
58 Bloomsbury Street, London WC1

Photoset by Input Typesetting Ltd
and printed in Great Britain by
Richard Clay Ltd (The Chaucer Press)
Bungay, Suffolk

To Peter and Sonya

Those who believe they believe in God, but without passion in the heart, without anguish of mind, without uncertainty, without doubt and even at times without despair, believe only in the idea of God, not in God himself.

Unamuno

Contents

Foreword

A book of this nature is built on innumerable debts of gratitude, not least because it is the result of many different kinds of journey, in the course of which I have received much and varied help from friends and colleagues in India and Britain. To them all, and particularly those who read parts of the book in the making, I offer deep thanks.

I must, however, make special mention of the generosity which enabled the academic research for and delivery of the Teape Lectures in India in the winter of 1979-80: to the Teape Committee in Cambridge for their invitation to lecture; to the British Academy for a grant for research in India in 1978; to the University of Manchester for three weeks' leave of absence at the end of 1979 and to the staff and students who cooperated in my questionnaires; to my generous hosts in India during the Teape Lectures, at St Stephen's College, Delhi, Bishop's College, Calcutta, the Christa Prema Seva Ashram and the Pontifical Athenaeum in Pune. Mrs Bridget Johnson and Mrs Pat Moorcroft have borne with me and my typescript with great humour and professional expertise, and my family's encouragement has been, as always, unfailing.

Introduction

==

Books, like people, have biographies. To understand and relate to a book, as to a person, it helps to know something of its background, formative influences and goals.

Men and Gods in a Changing World is a leap in the dark for me. Before I started it I had worked in and observed India as an academic historian, specially concerned with India's recent political history and the career of its foremost nationalist leader, Mahatma Gandhi. Studying such an enigmatic man, reputed to be a saint in politics, took me deep into his ideas and religious beliefs, and those of the society in which he worked and exerted such a singular appeal. But my professional skills were not and are not those of a theologian or a student of comparative religion. Then an invitation came to do *Thought for the Day*, BBC Radio 4's breakfast-time moments of reflection: the brief was to say how my experience of India had affected my own beliefs. As illustration, I used some of the poetry of Rabindranath Tagore, a poet and educator, who like his compatriot and contemporary, Gandhi, wrestled with the meaning of his religious tradition in the modern world. The reaction of listeners to these brief talks ranged from the violently hostile to those who said that Tagore, though a foreigner and a Hindu, spoke to them in terms Christianity seemed to fail to do. It became clear to me that people in the West are often profoundly ignorant of faiths other than Christianity, despite this century's revolution in communications, and that they are the poorer for it.

At that point I would probably have ended my excursion into strange territory, had it not been for a request to lecture in India. The benefactor who endowed these lectures, W. M. Teape, was an Anglican parson who never visited India but developed a consuming interest in Hinduism. His point of entry into the world of Hinduism was the great scriptural texts of the Upanishads.[1] My interest, which his generosity permitted me to pursue in the lectures

and now in this book, is religion as a contemporary reality, lived
or abandoned by twentieth-century men. No religious tradition or
institution can stand still for long, however much its adherents
look to the past for authority and inspiration, however stridently
they claim to maintain orthodoxies hallowed by time. All religious
beliefs and structures have to be reinterpreted and adapted in
response to changes in the surrounding society and climate of ideas,
if they are to ensure their continuity and attract successive generations with a message which seems to have contemporary relevance.
Survival demands change. The intention, therefore, of this book is
to investigate some aspects of religion in today's changing world,
through specific comparison of Hindus in India and Christians in
Britain. The one is an environment where imperial rule and then
conscious modernization by an independent government have precipitated more rapid and significant social and economic changes
than in any previous era of the subcontinent's recent history. The
other is a society refashioned out of a stable, agrarian order, by
two centuries of industrialization and urbanization, now facing the
material and ideological dilemmas of industrial decline in the aftermath of two debilitating world wars.

Immediately I found that although much had been written by
theologians, historians and sociologists about contemporary
Christianity in Britain, there was virtually nothing to be found on
how educated Hindus perceive and act out their religious tradition
in India. There are studies of Hindu scriptures, and
anthropologists' enquiries into the small-scale village communities
of the subcontinent, of which observation of religious practices is
a part. But almost nothing has been written on the religion of
educated Hindus who live in towns and engage in modern professions, whose world has changed more markedly than that of many
other Indians, and who are consequently most exposed to the
strains which change produces.

This enquiry therefore focuses on educated, urban Hindus and
their world, asking questions prompted by the experiences of their
Christian counterparts in Britain. It may provide few answers. But
that will not matter, as my hope is to open a door into an area of
human experience which is of more than academic interest. It is
significant not only for an understanding of modern India and
Britain but for insight into the turmoil into which believers within
any religious tradition are plunged by the uprooting of old social
orders, and the challenge to traditional beliefs and standards posed
by new and increasingly secular ideas. The different parts of the
twentieth-century world are increasingly drawn closer together.

Now it is far less possible for sensitive people to grapple with problems without being aware of the similar experiences of others, even though they may be far removed by geography and tradition. Moreover as society in Britain becomes more heterogeneous it becomes the more urgent for teachers of religious studies and those with Hindu neighbours to understand the strains change imposes on people outside as well as within the Christian religious and cultural heritage. The appearance of Hindu and allegedly Hindu teachers and cults in the West also calls for understanding and evaluation, which must in part be based on knowledge of their background and place within India's own religious tradition. This book is intended for readers in such diverse situations of encounter and change.

The plan of the enquiry is simple. The first chapter surveys the pitfalls in undertaking such a comparative study. Obviously there are immense problems of method and evidence in comparing the experiences of people from such widely different societies and religious backgrounds; these must be honestly stated. (The sketch of some of the main features of Hinduism and the Indian society so largely moulded by it may well be omitted by readers already familiar with the subcontinent.) There follow two factual chapters, based where possible on empirical enquiry and statistical evidence. These assess how far change has produced either in India or in Britain a 'secular society', and the extent to which people in both societies feel that the gods of their fathers have 'died' for them. The study then moves to closer consideration of a limited number of themes in the response of those who retain some religious beliefs to the threats and opportunities proffered by a changing world. Radical questioning of religious authority and the search for an authentic, modern spirituality are two interwoven problems which seem particularly urgent in the experience of Christians. These are traced in the Christian and Hindu contexts, to see whether in both there are similar issues at stake and whether comparable resolutions of these dilemmas have been found. I conclude on a more personal note, indicating what our comparison seems to say to one educated believer within the Western Christian tradition, caught up in the turmoil of a changing world.

Precisely because religion impinges on so many aspects of people's life in society such an enquiry must use many different tools and materials. It is impossible to compartmentalize study of religion and its ramifications into one tidy, academic discipline, and to specialists in fields other than my own I apologize for my novice's entry into their worlds of evidence and expertise. For

Indian evidence I have used what secondary literature exists. Generous Indian friends also showed me results of surveys into the religious attitudes of various groups of students and professional people. These are listed in the bibliography. However, I have relied heavily on personal observations and interviews with educated Hindus in 1978 in four widely differing cities of India. These were Varanasi (formerly Banares), the heart of Hindu orthodoxy in northern India; Pune (formerly Poona), in western India, where a Hindu renaissance occurred in the late nineteenth century and now modern education goes hand in hand with a living urban religious tradition; Bombay, a cosmopolitan port long exposed to foreign influence; and Delhi, India's capital, where foreigners throng with the country's administrative and political elite, where social customs have changed to a marked degree among many Indian groups, and where opportunities for higher education are among the finest in the land.[2]

For the study of contemporary Christianity in Britain the published evidence was far more plentiful. I supplemented this with a continuous watch on religious broadcasting, publishing and related articles in the press over a two-year period in the late 1970s, and I conducted two surveys of the religious world of students and lecturers in my own university, to match as nearly as possible the survey material provided by Indian colleagues. I am well aware that such people are a limited segment of the total educated population in both countries; but they are by virtue of their education and professional training among the most geographically and socially mobile, the most exposed to social and intellectual pressures to change their life-styles and attitudes. Their experiences and attitudes will be a window through which we can begin to see what our two educated groups make of their religious inheritance, and how they experience their gods in a changing world.

The general reader need bother no further with the nature of the sources on which this study is based. A full bibliography is provided. But footnotes have been kept to a minimum and tables of statistics are placed at the end of each chapter.

Chapter One

The Religious Experience:
Problems of Comparison

===

Redundant churches, a Pope with an actor's skills and charisma, vibrant black congregations in decaying industrial cities, Buddhist monks and Hindu *ashrams*: these are some of the religious signs of the times in late twentieth-century Britain. But what do they mean? The evidence is ambiguous. So it is in India, where some Hindus abandon belief and ritual, but wandering holy men storm the streets of the capital, the saintly ascetic is assured of veneration and material support, and thousands go on pilgrimage to the country's sacred rivers.

Anyone who asks questions about religion finds there are few subjects more explosive. Enquiry into people's religious beliefs and practices elicits replies of commitment, enthusiasm, dogmatism, prejudice, contempt and fear, but seldom of apathy or neutrality. The reactions triggered depend on the person's position in relation to his own religious tradition, his own specific experience of it, and the constructive or destructive part it has played in the formation of his own personality. Such individual experience partly explains why there are so many possible answers to the question, 'What is religion?' – 'the truth about God', 'myth', 'old-fashioned superstition', 'delusion', 'class ideology', 'a woman's hobby', 'the weakling's prop', 'social habit' – these are but a few. So we must stake out the territory to be explored, and define with particular care the phenomenon and experience to be observed and compared.

The conceptual and analytical tools for defining religion have been refined principally through the work of sociologists, who by over a century of study and controversy have removed religion from the preserve of the theologian and the historian of religious institutions and placed it squarely in the purview of all who study aspects of man in society, past and present.[1] Analysis of great religious texts, familiarity with lives of founders and prophets of religious traditions, and knowledge of religious institutions reveal but a small part of the reality and power of the religious experience. All religions, however much they differ in content and outward expression, are essentially total world views: visions and explanations for the believer of the fundamental nature of man and the world he experiences. Most have great accounts of the origins of man and his world, enshrined in myth, legend or written scripture. Through powerful symbols as well as words all carry a 'gospel', a message which enables man to deal with the known and unknown, the everyday experience and the apprehension of the totally 'other' which threatens to engulf man with its immensity and incomprehensible nature and to obliterate the stable sense of identity which he craves. Religions also teach men the correct orientation towards the fundamental realities of existence, which may or may not be understood in terms of one God or a multiplicity of deities. They prescribe the right behaviour with which to demonstrate this orientation, in the context of social and personal relations, and almost unfailingly through certain specifically 'religious' activities, such as sacrifice, worship and prayer.

Such world views and their corresponding patterns of appropriate behaviour in cult and life-style are grounded in a variety of 'authorities'. The most common are what is accepted as authentic revelation mediated through a founder or prophet whose actions and teachings are recorded in oral tradition or written scripture, or teachings transmitted by an institution and/or individuals believed to receive peculiar sanction by the very nature of ultimate reality. All such ways of understanding ultimate meaning have of course to be handed down to succeeding generations. Consequently religions develop ways of communicating their message to believers' children, and in some cases to 'outsiders', too. But because men and women alone can rarely sustain belief, and cannot in isolation adhere to patterns of religious practice, each religious tradition over time constructs a supportive community. This encourages and disciplines those within it, helps to socialize their young, and either seeks to attract those outside or draws rigid boundaries between them and its own members, to preserve its message and appropriate behaviour patterns. The Hindu caste system is an extreme example of the latter strategy, although, as we shall see, this rigid boundary-drawing through social separation is weakening, and some Hindus are seeking for a strategy more like that which Western Christianity has followed for the past three centuries, of seeking to attract the outsider and reform the deviant, rather than persecute or obliterate them as infidels or heretics, which was done in the centuries when Christendom coincided with distinct political boundaries. Almost all communities of faith and practice have been tied to a specific political order. Where religious identity and obedience to an earthly power structure were coterminous, both reinforced each other. The one helped to legitimate the earthly power by the supposed approval of ultimate reality, the other supported with physical might the claim of the religious order to bear the message of life's meaning.

The religious experience is therefore never solely one of belief in and relation to what is perceived as ultimate reality. For religions are intimately connected, though in different ways, to the social, political and intellectual environments in which they function. All stand within a particular historical context, and the 'religious' experience of their adherents is inevitably shaped by it. Because of this interweaving, religions are exceedingly vulnerable to change; and their adherents are subjected to the tensions change generates, wherever this occurs in man's life and society. As we shall see, new forces in society and the economy can undermine religious institutions and break up the supportive community of faith and practice. New ideas can threaten the credibility of religious authorities, while the means of transmitting ideas and knowledge may change so much that older religious forms of instruction become outdated and ineffective, leaving the field wide open to proficient communicators who may well have a different message to purvey. But equally, change may provide the context for new vision, new styles of worship, and new communities of faith.

Confronted by changes in their environment, all religions have to adapt; the blunt necessity for survival forces this on them. Somehow in the changed situation they must ensure their own continuity. All major religious traditions have, piece-meal and over time, modified their messages, their institutions and their lines of communication, in order to retain adherents and buttress the community of the faithful in a changing world. The muezzin who uses microphone or record to call the Muslim flock to prayer is a tiny piece in a larger pattern of adaptation. Christian churches acknowledge that the pulpit can no longer be the only place from which to preach their gospel, and they send their preachers to exploit the potential of radio and television. At a deeper level of intellectual adaptation Christianity has come to terms with the discoveries and claims of modern science. Thus only could believers be liberated from the destructive effects of a direct confrontation between the claims of religious and scientific authorities. Moreover the standards of a sharpened historical and textual analysis have been incorporated into biblical studies, to safeguard their intellectual integrity and respectability in the changing world of scholarship. Even religions which have been described as 'unchanging', on close inspection prove to have adapted in the course of time in the realms of thought and outward observation, and to have accommodated movements for social change. Although Hindu tradition is often called 'static' or 'timeless', historical study of the Hindu religious experience shows clearly this sort of adaptation.[2]

Studies of this adaptive process bring together the history of ideas and institutions, analyses of social and economic change, and understanding of the pervading influence of politics. A mature literature deals with religious adaptation in the Western Christian experience.[3] But writing on the Hindu experience has tended to be starkly divided into study of religious texts and observation of the religion of villagers in the context of small communities sheltered from the strongest forces of change. There has been little attempt to portray and understand the religious experience of Hindus exposed to the full blast of new ideas, thrust by their education and occupation into new social relations, and consequently uprooted to a significant degree from the communities which had enshrined older beliefs and helped to mould and maintain life-styles in accordance with them. Little is known of the effects of such people's experience of change on their beliefs and religious observation. Nor is it clear whether Hindus are adopting or constructing new means of communication now that mass media have come to India as to the West. These unknowns must be part of our comparison.

However, the pitfalls are many, both in analysing and comparing religious experience in a changing world. The rest of this chapter examines some of the major ones. We shall then at least be warned of the difficulties in acquiring and collecting the necessary evidence; and reminded that there are no simple answers to questions about man's experiences in society, least of all where religion impinges upon them.

The first hazard is the evidence itself. Since the phenomenon of religion has such wide ramifications, the range of evidence from the environment in which it functions must be as reflective of this width as possible. But there must also be a precision of observation capable of sustaining an analysis which goes beyond the most obvious and superficial. This means the collection of hard facts and figures; not only about what people say they believe, but what they actually do in response to the demands of their religion. Statistics are fairly plentiful for the Christian part of our comparison.[4] For the Hindu part they are much scantier, and amount to a few surveys by academics of selected, local groups.[5] But even where reliable statistics exist it is difficult to interpret them, let alone use them comparatively. In the Christian context, for example, figures for church membership will reflect different levels of commitment to belief and practice, because the various denominations use dissimilar criteria for 'membership'. Or where figures indicate a decline in certain practices, like attendance at Sunday school or church, it would be superficial to conclude simply that they indicate a flight from faith. They must be interpreted within a wider context of evidence. Such declines may reflect changes in age structure, migration from an area, or increase in Sunday working; or the rise in car ownership enabling the habit of week-ending and the family outing on Sunday.[6] Strictly statistical comparisons across two continents and religious traditions are even more problematic. It is impossible to count 'membership' in the Hindu setting. The idea is meaningless there, as there is no church or equivalent religious institution to which one gains admittance by a specific, individual act, the sum total of which can then be enumerated. Moreover temple-going in the Hindu tradition plays a totally different part and has a different value compared with church-going within Christianity. Nor are figures for ownership of scriptural texts comparable, because the Bible has a far more significant place in the life of a practising Christian, at least in the Protestant traditions, than do Hindu scriptures in the life of a Hindu. Statistical evidence for religious reading or broadcasting, moreover, has to be seen against the contrast of a society which is almost totally literate and sufficiently prosperous to afford books and radios; and one where many still cannot read, and books and radios are luxuries rather than casually accepted pieces of domestic clutter.

More subtle problems, however, arise from the assumptions and conceptual tools with which observers may approach a comparison between the Hindu and Christian religious experiences in this century. One is the still widespread belief that Indians are more 'spiritual' than their Western contemporaries. This notion – one might call it a social myth – has a long history.[7] Early images of India in the Western mind had been of a land of fabulous wealth, and later of the home of benighted heathens who were in sore need of rescue from idolatry and moral turpitude. By the early nineteenth century the work of a group of European scholars, the 'Orientalists', had displayed to Western audiences some of the wealth of Hindu scriptures and spiritual teaching. Indian writers and publicists such as Vivekananda then built on this foundation to propagate the idea of Hindu spirituality in contrast to the sup-

posed materialism of the West. Mahatma Gandhi continued this
theme in his assertion and redefinition of Indian nationality early
in this century. Writing after a visit to England in 1909 he
proclaimed,

> Looking at this land, I at any rate have grown disillusioned with
> Western civilization. The people whom you meet on the way
> seem half-crazy. They spend their days in luxury or in making
> a bare living and retire at night thoroughly exhausted. In this
> state of affairs, I cannot understand when they can devote them-
> selves to prayers. . . . While Western civilization is still young,
> we find things have come to such a pass, that, unless its whole
> machinery is thrown overboard, people will destroy themselves
> like so many moths.[8]

Later generations of a broad spectrum of Westerners contributed
still further to this idealized dichotomy between a spiritual East
and a material West. They ranged from the distinguished sociologist, Weber, who portrayed Hinduism as inherently other-worldly
compared with the bustling, earthy spirit he saw in Protestant
Christianity; to diverse ideological refugees from Europe and
America who glimpsed in Gandhi's teaching of non-violence a
spiritual replacement for war, or in various cult movements and
leaders originating in India a possible religious alternative to belief
within the Christian tradition. Images must be tested against reality, and this is part of the object of this book.

Yet another assumption which colours all work on religion in
the twentieth century is that which goes by the shorthand,
'secularization'. Once this word was simply descriptive, not emo-
tive or ideologically charged: it referred to the removal of property
from the church authorities and to the return of a person in religious orders to his or her previous state in 'the world'. Now it is
a routine and often ill-considered part of ordinary and scholarly
language. Behind it, too often, lies a barely conscious story or
theory of modern man's religious experience, which runs something
like this. Traditional society was in a real sense religious: religious
belief moulded men's minds while religious institutions played a
crucial and powerful role in public and private life. However, the
industrial revolution with its attendant economic and social up-
heavals, and the emergence of modern science as a discipline and
authority on the nature of reality, eroded faith and the power of
religious leaders and bodies. Twentieth-century man has therefore
come of age as a secular man, able to cope with himself and his
environment without reference to any idea of divine power. The

society he builds is secular in the sense that it has been liberated from clerical control and religious norms, and is ordered on rational criteria by politicians and planners who discount religion in their decision making. Put this way the notion of 'secularization' cries out for demolition by those with knowledge of history and contemporary society. One eminent English sociologist, David Martin, has with wit and irony conducted just such a campaign against 'secularization' as a bogus artefact.[9]

For our purposes the idea has severely limited use, because it rests (in as far as it is historically proven) on evidence from the experience of the Christian West, where religion has the particular institutional form of church structures, and where economic change took the form of industrialization overturning the old society. As a conceptual tool secularization makes far less sense in the study of India, where economic change has been of a different kind and degree and where the whole idea of specific religious institutions and doctrines distinct from the social order and its values is alien to the Hindu religious tradition.[10]

Even within the Western context the idea must be treated with extreme caution. It must be measured against evidence, and this means historical research as well as contemporary observation. (How 'religious' were our medieval ancestors in the so-called age of faith? Lack of faith and disregard for Christian moral standards do not appear to be a twentieth-century prerogative, judging by the number of brides, for example, who three hundred years ago went pregnant to the altar.[11] How persistent is religious belief and practice today, whether in traditional or novel forms, inside and outside the churches? There is plentiful evidence that modern men are still capable of 'irrational' groping towards and belief in the non-material, that they willingly participate in bizarre as well as more staid manifestations of this, while few have entirely jettisonned the values of Christianity, whatever they may make at a conscious intellectual level of its theological formulations.) Moreover, this idea often seems to include the assumption that the changes to which it refers are an irreversible and inevitable process, and that those changes occur uniformly throughout society. It may well be part of a larger historical pattern of ebb and flow in intellectual change, social practice and institutional influence. It is undoubtedly patchy even in so small a society as Britain's, having no uniform effect on the various geographical regions and social levels which compose that society. But once the word 'secularization' is hedged around with warnings against misuse, it remains a useful shorthand for certain major changes in the role of religion in Western society, some of which will be part of the subject matter of the next chapter. It refers to the broad range of changes which have resulted in a situation where religion has become far more a private and optional matter for each individual, where religious practices are less prevalent, and religious norms and institutions less authoritative and powerful in society.[12]

An allied problem occurs in the idea and definition of the secular state, which is part of any comparison of contemporary religious experience across countries. Here we have a different definition and usage of the same combination of words by people who speak the same language, English, but have learnt to use it in the context of different historical backgrounds and present situations. In Western usage the secular state is one which is officially separate from any religious belief or institution. This stems from the historical experience of Europe, where there were in the churches specifically religious institutions once bound into the structures of temporal authority and power which could be separated off from them when ideas and political experience demanded this. Indians have taken over the phrase. But as it reflects little in their historical experience they use it in a different way. In their religiously plural society, life-style and social groups are the bearers and embodiments of religious tradition, rather than country-wide religious institutions and hierarchies of religious specialists. Consequently governments cannot make neat distinctions between secular and religious actions and institutions. In Indian English the secular state is one which does not divorce itself from religion, but treats all religious traditions with cordial impartiality.[13]

The meaning of 'secular state' may seem just a semantic question, answered easily by reference to the context within which the phrase is used. But it raises the crucial issue whether the contemporary Hindu and Christian religious experiences are indeed comparable. Are we comparing like with like, or is the comparative enquiry this book seeks to open up an impossible enterprise? At a deep level the answer must be 'yes': such a comparison is possible because the substance of both experiences is what it is like to live in a time of change within a religious tradition which provides a total cosmic view, a message of ultimate reality and its relationship to men and women in their everyday lives. But there must also be a 'no' to the question of comparability. There are vast differences in the two cases between the ways in which ultimate reality is perceived, and news of it communicated and supported by communities of those who accept it. Moreover the sorts of changes with which these religious traditions are confronted and through which their adherents have to live are very different. We must therefore consider some of these differences if we are to put the empirical evidence into its proper context, and evaluate the different significance for each religious tradition of various aspects of change.

At this point it is right to underline the fact, obvious to the 'believer' within any religious tradition, that it is really necessary to live *within* that tradition to get its feel and flavour, to appreciate its subtle nuances and to understand both the pain and exhilaration which changes in the environment make inevitable, whether one abandons or adapts one's tradition in response. In a real sense religions cannot be studied. They must be experienced, and lived as religious acts.[14] Our analysis can therefore only be an imaginative approximation to the living reality.

Probably the greatest difference between the Hindu and Christian religious experience lies in that complex of issues which could be labelled 'orthodoxy' and 'authority'. What is it that marks out the Hindu or Christian? What is distinctive about his experience? It is much easier to define the area of the Christian religious experience, and to formulate a working definition of a Christian on objective criteria. (I purposely leave aside here the subjective criteria, that inner judgment whether an outwardly professing Christian is necessarily a 'real Christian' which has tortured some groups, and individuals of a particular temperament, through the centuries, but more markedly in the Protestant tradition since the collapse of an outwardly universal church.) The hall mark of the Christian is profession of belief in one God as the source of all being, the heart of ultimate reality, who has revealed himself in human history and thereby made himself knowable by his human creation in personal terms, first in his dealings with a chosen people, the Israelites, then supremely in Jesus of Nazareth. Experience of him by his contemporaries during his life-time, and then by them and others drawn into the experience after his death, forged a new religious realization and formulation, utterly unexpected in the context of Jewish monotheism – that this man was so uniquely close to God that in some mysterious way he shared in the very being of God, a sharing described as 'sonship'.

From this experience of Jesus flowed two streams of development. There emerged a distinctive life-style and a pattern of specifically religious actions through which believers felt they were living in conformity to his commands, and enabled to enter the right relationship with God to which his own life and death as well as his teachings had pointed. But of crucial importance was their conviction that he had not just been a Godward signpost in one

brief life-time. He was felt to have triumphed over death and all
that separates man from God, and to be a continuing vibrant
presence still at work in them, still enabling that right relationship
with God by bestowing on them and incorporating them into his
divine life. The most potent means for this new life-sharing process
were the outward sacramental symbols of baptism and eucharist
which the community of believers celebrated as their distinguishing
religious rituals. As it seemed that the very breath of God was
moving them in a movement as mysterious as wind they began to
talk of Holy Spirit. The need to describe and make intellectual
sense of this new range of religious experience gave rise to a new
theology. Its roots were the need to understand and cast into
communicable form what was essentially a 'gut reaction', an overwhelming conviction that in the life and death of Jesus there was
a new revelation of the truth about the world men experienced and
its real meaning.

Behind this new belief which marked out the Christian as distinctive in a Jewish, Roman or Hellenic environment, were two
grounding authorities, scripture and the church as the formal,
outward structure of the community of faith. These have remained
the two undergirdings of Christianity, despite the difference in
importance and dependability placed upon them at various historical times and by different groups of Christians. In scripture was
the written record of the experience of those nearest to Jesus in
time, as they remembered that experience, wrestled with its meaning, strove to hand it on and to build communities which would
reflect that experience and enable its replication. Acceptance of the
teachings enunciated in scripture and conformity to its precepts for
living were consequently one touchstone of Christianity. The other
was life within the church. This gave the believer the supportive
community he needed for survival in a hostile world, and ensured
the continuity of the faith. It did this in two distinctive ways. It
provided mechanisms, accepted as divine in origin, for the transmission of the new life in Christ, particularly the sacramental
rituals. It also selected and trained a hierarchy of religious specialists, whose essential function became a dual one of teaching the
faith and conducting the major rituals in which the faith was
symbolized and dramatically made real in the present. Over the
centuries of course the early simplicity was overlaid as Christians
and their faith became respectable. Once the faith became 'official'
throughout the Western world the churches' institutions grew in
size, complexity and power, and became inextricably involved with
the surrounding social and political structures. But whatever the

contradictions and ambiguities these developments brought, however great the body of Christians who drifted into the churches through birth, social custom or political pressure rather than active conviction of the reality of the 'Christ experience', the distinguishing mark of Christianity remained a cluster of beliefs about a specific revelation of God in human history, while its sources and structures of authority remained those essential to safeguard a significant degree of credal orthodoxy.

No contrast could be more striking than with the Hindu religious experience. Here is no clear beginning in an overwhelming historical experience of the revelation of divinity as ultimate reality. Indeed one can be a Hindu and an atheist; for belief in the existence of God is not at the core of religion as the Hindu experiences it. In contrast with the Christian vision, the Hindu cosmic view of the world and its meaning has grown and is still growing piece-meal, by a steady accretion of insights, all of which are but partial glimpses of truth. There are certain major philosophical themes which most Hindus know of, and which many would accept as central in their religious experience. Their source is the Veda, the oldest Hindu scriptures; and acceptance of Vedic authority is the nearest approximation to a credal definition of 'Hinduness'. Outstanding among these concepts are *brahman* (the eternal ground of the universe), *atman* (the self), *dharma* (duty), *karma* (the inexorable law of ethical causation), *samsara* (the cycle of cause and effect to which all phenomenal existence is subject and which ties men by the working of *karma* to a succession of rebirths), and *moksha* (liberation from this cycle).[15] But these are in no sense obligatory orthodoxies, credal beliefs without which a person is not a Hindu. At the core of religion for the Hindu is not a revelatory experience enshrined in a credal statement, but a persistent and practical obedience to *dharma*, which is generally translated into English as religious duty. This means far more to the Hindu ear and heart than the phrase conveys in translation. *Dharma* is the fundamental and eternal law which governs all existence, human and non-human: it is the way the world functions, its essential morality. Man's *dharma*, by extension, is obedience to this fundamental law. His knowledge of it comes through conscience, the teaching of scripture, and prescriptions of society which are believed to enshrine *dharma*. For the Hindu, therefore, religion is something to be done rather than believed and there is no division, so common in the West, between belief and life.[16]

The consequences of this central difference between the Hindu and Christian experience are clear in the realm of orthodoxy and

authority. In place of a credal core of necessary theological orthodoxy there are diverse schools of philosophical speculation and
theological formulation, which have emerged over the centuries
within the framework of Hindu practice. They vary widely on
numerous important issues; and within them occur monism, dual-
ism, pantheism and agnosticism.[17] This offers the Hindu a wide
range of belief systems to choose from, giving the Hindu religious
experience a flexibility which is significant for its survival in a time
of change. But it does make any definition of 'Hinduism' in terms
of orthodoxy in belief quite impossible.

This absence of credal orthodoxy relating to a central revelatory
experience crucially affects scriptural and institutional authority.
This will be dealt with in more detail in Chapter 4. At this point
it is enough to say that the great corpus of Hindu scripture has a
significance and function for the Hindu very different from that of
the Bible for the Christian. At the root of this difference is the fact
that the Bible is believed to contain crucial witness to a unique
action of God, knowledge of which is essential for man's proper
relationship with God. Much biblical writing bears witness to
historical events, comments on these events and wrestles with their
interpretation; though the Old Testament has its share of myth,
song and drama, while the New Testament concludes with a mystical vision. Hindu scripture by contrast enshrines no one revelatory
experience in time, and is far more diffuse in content and genre. In
it there are two grades of sanctity and authority. *Sruti*, 'what is
heard', is the crucial part, through hymns, formulae, sacrificial
texts and treatises handing on eternal truth and wisdom heard by
ancient holy men. *Smriti*, 'what is remembered', is less rigorously
defined, but includes a patchwork of truths remembered cumula-
tively over many generations, which take the form of laws, philosophical aphorisms and mythological poetry of great length,
describing and extolling the lives and times of numerous gods and
goddesses. There are also practical differences which contribute to
the contrast in the nature of Hindu and Christian scriptural authority. Whereas the Bible is moderately manageable in size for a
fairly persistent non-specialist reader, and is freely available in
vernacular languages, Hindu scriptures are too vast to be known
in detail by ordinary people, and for the most part they remain in
Sanskrit.

The very idea of a specifically religious institution bearing religious authority is difficult for a Hindu to comprehend. Because
there is no Hindu orthodoxy to be guarded against heresy, no
divine life to be fostered and transmitted through sacrament and

the fellowship of believers, there are no church structures with centrally controlled hierarchies of religious professionals. There are in contrast many different types of religious leaders and many centres of religious authority. Certainly among these are temples. Some are of regional and even continental significance, buildings of great beauty and large endowments. Their priests cater for worshippers and pilgrims from a wide geographical area: their role being essentially ritual, enabling the performance of *puja*, worship, rather than teaching or offering spiritual guidance. Other temples are purely local structures, where people drop in during the day to make an offering before the deity. Here the priest or *pujari* would be little more than a shrine attendant, having an insignificant ritual function and little authority or standing in the community. Others accredited with religious authority include the man who renounces worldly life and becomes a hermit or wanderer: the 'realized' man whose experience of *moksha*, salvation, is a pledge of its reality for those who are still entwined in *karma*; the leader of an *ashram* or community of devotees who acts as guide both to them and to those who choose to place themselves under his care while remaining in their ordinary occupations: the man or woman who is thought to be in touch with the supernatural and to have powers of healing and exorcism in the small world of the village where folk custom and popular belief are often far removed from the austere perceptions and precepts of the Vedas. Regular ritual specialists preside at the ceremonies normally conducted in the home to mark significant times in the lives of individuals, families and communities. Birth, puberty, marriage, death are the obvious examples. Such men are those of the Brahmin or priestly caste who have actually been trained by study and apprenticeship to a working priest in the performance of ritual and knowledge of the Sanskrit texts essential to that ritual.

The diversity of religious authority in part reflects the *spread* of religious duties in Hindu society. Each person in his particular caste has his own *dharma* to perform; and this includes the performance of personal and family *puja* in the home, at which time the presiding member of the family has an authoritative role. Religious experience for the Hindu can never be dominated by the religious specialist. Its holding framework is not an ecclesiastical institution and hierarchy but the way of life and the social order developed to a fine sophistication in the caste system. Hindu society is composed of interdependent castes into which people are born: the *dharma* peculiar to each caste is the main way in which the religious experience of each individual is moulded and manifested.

The essential expression of the Hindu experience is *orthopraxis* in the way prescribed by caste rather than *orthodoxy*. The interlocking community of castes and their respective behaviour patterns and life-styles, rather than creed and church, are therefore the primary means for maintaining the Hindu vision of reality.

The sheer size of the Indian subcontinent and the diversity of its regions also makes comparison difficult. Every region has a distinctive geography and historical experience: they were only welded into a political and economic whole by the British imperial presence in the nineteenth century. Consequently not only are there the great variations at the 'theological' level of Hindu thought referred to earlier: each region has tended to produce a religious style and flavour peculiar to itself. In western India Hindus from Maharashtra, for example, have a great local religious heritage on which to draw, created from mediaeval times by the presence of striking saint figures and their teachings. This gives the regional religious experience a mood and manifestations quite different from that of Bengal, on the eastern side of India, where veneration of Kali, the mother and destroyer goddess, is prominent; or from that of the Punjab, where the constant stream of foreign invaders and migrants with their own religious background not only attracted converts and precipitated the Sikh reform movement, but made its impact on those who remained within the Hindu community.[18] Such variations are not dissimilar to those found, for example, in Orthodox as compared with Western Catholic Christianity, or in the religious experience of the Spanish Catholic compared with that of a Swedish Protestant.

In the Western Christian experience, however, there is far less variation in religious experience and expression according to level of culture than there is in India. In Europe the 'standard' patterns of belief and worship gradually prevailed not only over pre-Christian paganism, but over local varieties of Christianity such as those of the Celtic people, partly because the church was firmly supported by temporal powers. The triumph of a new orthodoxy took time, and often had to incorporate into the new faith pagan festivals and customs. But it occurred; to a far greater extent than in the Hindu experience, where different levels of that experience still differ markedly. The Great Hindu Tradition, rooted in the Sanskrit texts, with their social prescriptions and their all-Indian pantheon of deities, constantly interacts with the Little Traditions of each region, in which local cults, supernatural manifestations and appropriate rites of propitiation and celebration are still very strong. This interweaving of the great continental textual tradition, preserved in the life-style and rituals of higher castes, and the local, earthy, less philosophical perceptions more common among the lower castes, is symbolized, for example, in Central India by the complementary roles of the Brahmin priest and the non-Brahmin Baiga. The former has the qualifications of purity, prestige and ritual skill associated with the Sanskrit tradition: he stands at the interface between villagers and the great Hindu pantheon. The Baiga is an exorcist and healer whose role is to mediate between people and the local deities and to help them cope with supernatural incursions into ordinary life which have no place in the Great Hindu Tradition. People accept their ministrations on different occasions and for different purposes, but there is no sense of dichotomy, as the two together are essential in local religious needs and their fulfilment.[19]

At this point the reader may be tempted to ask whether there is anything which can be called 'Hinduism' amidst such variety, and if so, what is its essence. I have deliberately avoided using the word 'Hinduism' in the discussion so far, because that word originated in the minds of Westerners in their attempt to describe what they saw as the religion of the people of India. It reflects the ideological baggage they carried east with them, particularly the association of religion with a central belief system. The word raises at once problems of definition which deflect attention on to an abstract construct, an '-ism', away from the very real religious experience of people brought up in the Hindu community, which is the subject of this investigation. Scholars, once landed with the word, have disputed at length about the definition of Hinduism. Some have argued that there is an essential core and a continental unity, which justifies the use of the word 'Hinduism': it is thought to be found in the Sanskrit texts and the Brahminical life-style and worship– patterns associated with them, which have gradually been accepted as normative by wider social groups. Others emphasize the continuation of non-Sanskritic texts, life-styles and rituals as evidence against such a definition resting on the idea of a normative core.[20]

The problem of definition is raised repeatedly in different contexts by Indians themselves, outside the sphere of academic observation and controversy. It came up in my discussions with Hindus when we considered whether it was possible for a non-Indian, not *born* a Hindu, to become a Hindu. Can you be 'converted' to Hinduism by accepting certain beliefs? Can you become a Hindu by adopting a Hindu life-style? If so, do you have to conform to the *dharma* of a particular caste; and if you do this, is there any

chance that the caste in question will accept you and your children
into its social and marriage network?

To such questions there were no ready answers. Most people
began to talk in terms of a double definition of what it meant to
be a Hindu. First, they saw the easy working definition, accepted
by the state and society in India. A Hindu is one who is born into
the Hindu caste-ordered society. Then there emerged in their conversations the idea of a 'spiritual Hindu' who held certain beliefs,
but would probably not be accepted socially as a Hindu. Among
the 'essential' beliefs mentioned were faith in a supreme deity and
acceptance of the Vedas and Upanishads. The confusions of such
ordinary Hindus with no public reputation or platform are paral-
leled in the writings of prominent Indians who in the past century
have wrestled with the need to clarify what is essential to being a
Hindu. Almost all of them have groped towards a credal definition.
Radhakrishnan is one of the best known proponents in English of
the idea that there are essential Hindu beliefs which can be adopted
and transported outside the Indian social milieu, while K. M.
Pannikar has argued that Hindu belief and society must be separated, and Hinduism *become* a credal belief. Gandhi himself veered
towards such a definition of Hinduism when he rejected the practice of treating the lowest of Hindu society as literally untouchable
and the ideological underpinning of the practice in the concepts of
purity and pollution. He declared in 1915:

> If it was proved to me that this is an essential part of Hinduism,
> I for one would declare myself an open rebel against Hinduism
> itself. . . . But I am still not convinced that it is an essential part
> of Hinduism.[21]

Such groping for definitions was perhaps an inevitable development once Indian society was opened in the nineteenth century to
the curious eyes of Western administrators and scholars. Not only
did they try to label what they saw in terms familiar from their
own experience. Indians themselves began to use Western concepts
to explain and defend their own religious experience. In a very real
sense, therefore, it is possible to speak of 'Hinduism' as a religion
invented in the nineteenth century. As the 'Orientalist' scholars
explored the world of the Sanskrit scriptures they naturally emphasized these as the core of the Hindu religious experience regardless of the practical ignorance of these scriptures among most
Indians, and with little knowledge of the living force of the numerous Little Traditions which left few texts for scholars to study.
Some Indians, conscious of the need to present their religious

heritage as a 'religion' in terms acceptable to foreign audiences, complemented the Orientalists' work by claiming for a particular philosophical-theological strand in Hindu thought the status of 'true Hinduism'. This strand was the Advaita Vedanta philosophy, as expounded by the eighth-century commentator, Sankara.

Vedanta, 'the end of the Veda', rests on the Upanishads. According to Sankara's interpretation of their teaching, the supreme reality is Brahman, the source of all consciousness. The apparent individuality and existence of the self and material objects is false knowledge, and man's true goal is knowledge of the oneness of reality which matter *veils*. Such knowledge is not basically intellectual; it is almost a mystical vision, producing in the one who attains it a state of true relationship with reality, a state of enlightenment or realization. Not all Hindus agreed in the nineteenth century or would agree today that this is the essence of Hindu belief. But this particular interpretation enabled many Hindus to present 'Hinduism' as a potential world religion of equal standing, for example, with the three great monotheisms, unhindered by the complications inherent in the study and presentation of the actual Hindu's experience of his religious heritage and its diverse origins.[22]

The most influential preacher of this 'new Hinduism', which is often called 'neo-Vedanta', was Vivekananda, who took his 'gospel' to the Parliament of Religions in Chicago in 1893. Vivekananda was the disciple of Ramakrishna, one of the most striking and saintly Hindu figures who in the turmoil of the nineteenth century, when Hindus were challenged by Christianity and Western ideas, rethought the value of the Hindu tradition and revitalized it in the changing environment. It seems that the disciple, and the Ramakrishna movement which he founded and which has become one of the main vehicles of 'neo-Vedantist' teaching, deliberately presented their master as an exponent of neo-Vedanta, and played down his sympathy with different strands in Hindu thinking.[23] What is certain now is that many educated Hindus accept this interpretation and emphasis as 'essential' Hinduism. Consequently even if 'Hinduism' in this sense was 'invented' only a century ago, it has become a highly significant element in religion as *now* experienced, particularly among the educated. It will therefore loom large in our later discussions of authority and spirituality, alongside the interweaving of Great and Little Traditions which have formed the bedrock of the Hindu religious experience.[24]

So far our discussion of the comparability of the contemporary Christian and Hindu religious experience in a time of change has focused on the problems of definition and demarcation of the areas of life involved in that experience. The rest of this chapter follows through some of the implications of the differences uncovered, particularly in the relationship of religion and society, and in ways of thinking about religious matters.

It is immediately obvious that the relationship of the two religions to society is quite different. In the Christian case there is and always has been *interaction* between religion and the social order in which Christians live: interaction at the level of ideas, institutions and customs. Often Christian beliefs have buttressed social and political institutions. Biblical passages advocating obedience to the temporal power propped European monarchs for centuries, a pattern of interaction which reached its most extreme in the doctrine of the Divine Right of Kings. The British coronation service still displays in elaborate symbolism monarchy as having a sacramental nature, and provides the most sacred setting possible for the homage to the new monarch of the peers of the realm. At a less august and intellectual level the popular nineteenth-century children's hymn proclaimed a similar message of divine sanction for the existing social order.

> The rich man in his castle,
> The poor man at his gate,
> God made them high or lowly,
> And order'd their estate.

The actual institutions of religion have been inextricably interwoven in the fabric of society, through landholding and investment, through the involvement of churchmen in politics, through the establishment of a state church, and often through lay patronage of ecclesiastical positions. Moreover, until this century it was in Britain virtually impossible to be named, married or disposed of after death without ecclesiastical formulae and the presence of an ecclesiastical functionary. But there is no necessary identification of Christianity and a particular social order. Christian beliefs can be and have been powerful in undermining established institutions and customs. The abolition of slavery is an obvious example; the contemporary radical movements in South America and their 'liberation theology' is another. Nor is it insignificant, if altogether more parochial, that in modern English hymn books the verse quoted above has been tactfully forgotten as unfitting in the more egalitarian later twentieth century! It is the presence of several different types of teaching about power and social relations in the writings of the varied authors of scripture, as well as the process of reinterpretation, which has enabled this changing interaction between Christianity and society.

In the Hindu case, however, there is not so much *interaction* between religion and society as *identity* between the two. A particular social order, built on caste, is the only way in which man's true nature and right relationship to reality can be expressed. That society is the one in which *dharma* becomes specific; in which the individual knows precisely what his religious duty is.

Scholars have disputed the origins of caste: but for centuries it has been central to the Hindu religious experience.[25] Caste society rests on a hierarchical system of social stratification, its component parts being separated from one another and ranked in descending order. The principle of ranking is not economic (as in a society divided by class), but ritual, and the ritual criteria are embedded in the concept of purity and pollution. Certain substances such as human and animal waste or dead bodies are considered polluting. Occasions of contact with such substances are consequently polluting, as are occupations connected with their handling. The highest in Hindu society have as little to do with such substances as possible, while the lowest are considered actually untouchable by the higher castes because, as refuse-collectors, leather workers, midwives and the like, they are permanently contaminated by persistent contact with them. Should higher caste people inadvertently or by such inevitable occasions as birth and death become polluted, they are temporarily cut off from social relations with their caste fellows and elaborate rituals are provided for purification and the re-integration of the unfortunate individual or family into the social order.

Accounts of caste have in the past tended to describe a fourfold division of Hindu society: priests (Brahmins), warriors (Kshattri-yas), traders (Vanias), and labourers (Sudras), with untouchables right outside caste society. However, this is literary description, and caste as experienced by Indians is far more complicated than this interpretation based on scriptural texts alone. There is no single, all-India 'caste system'. Each region has its own hierarchy of small caste groups ranked in ritual order. Always the Brahmins are at the top and the untouchables at the bottom; but the precise position of those in the middle is more fluid and on occasion open to dispute. Each of these small groups (*jatis*) is an enfolding and inescapable social community for its members. They enter their *jati* by birth and leave it only at death or by being out-caste, a very rare occurrence. It regulates their life-style, dress and diet, whom they mix with socially, and – crucially – whom they marry. Although not all caste members will follow the same occupation, the one which normally gives the caste its name, they will engage in jobs of equivalent ritual standing. Taken as a whole the caste system produces an efficient framework in which interdependent groups do all the jobs essential to the smooth functioning of an agrarian society. The system is maintained by early socialization, so that few Hindus until this century could conceive of life outside caste or outside their particular caste, except for the religious ascetic who renounced all wordly ties. External pressures also keep the individual in his social place, whether these are the informal constrictions and formal sanctions of his own *jati*, or the pressures even extending to violence exerted by higher castes, anxious to preserve their superior position. Indeed, for the Hindu the notion of individuality is very restricted. Each person only finds his meaning as part of the group: he can only work out his *dharma* as a member of a caste. Individual mobility is not only impossible: it would be impious and would condemn the person who attempted it to social isolation and life devoid of religious meaning.

As Christians and Hindus are linked to their social environments in such different ways, social change will have different effects on them. In the Christian case change in the social order will not of itself be a direct challenge to belief. It may well make belief and the practice of religion more difficult, by undermining the supportive community of believers. Mass migration to towns, for example, breaks up village life with its ready focus in the parish church and cuts migrants off from established patterns of religious observance. But it does not make religious belief impossible. However, for the Hindu, any radical change in caste ordering of society is an axe at the heart of the religious experience, and threatens to leave a man without a *dharma*. The difference in the implications of social change depends on that primary distinction between a religion with a credal core, and one whose essence is orthopraxis.

The nature and degree of social change experienced by the two countries with which we are concerned has also been markedly different. In Britain change in the fabric of society has been far more radical than in India, and the time scale during which major changes have occurred has been much greater. These began at the end of the eighteenth century as the accelerating forces of the world's first industrial revolution began to uproot the old social order based on rural communities, controlled by those who owned the land. Increasingly migration to towns and new economic opportunities eroded established patterns of social interaction and dominance. Improved communications encouraged physical mobility, and expanded people's horizons and the groups in which they interacted and perceived themselves. Changes in perception and the spread of new ideas were deeply influenced, too, by the massive expansion of education. The cracks in the old agrarian society, and the domination of public life by the landed, reached a climax in the twentieth century, under the pressures of economic change, the necessity of fighting two world wars, and the deliberate manipulation of governments dedicated to planning a more rational and egalitarian society. In Britain the twentieth century became the urban and suburban age.

A few stark facts reflect the depth of social change.[26] By 1961, with a population of over 51 million, Britain had the fourth highest density of population in the world (573 per square mile) and 80% of the population lived in towns. In the years after the 1914-18 war land sales and taxation broke up many of the great landed estates which had once given their owners social and political dominance; and gradually wealth became more evenly distributed. Social stratification and distinctions of wealth and status became infinitely more complex, as the number of salaried earners in a variety of new professions increased, fewer families could afford to keep servants, and decreasing numbers were involved in actual production. Boundaries between classes became blurred and personal mobility within the social order increasingly possible, as mass education reinforced the influence of new economic opportunities and deliberate social levelling via taxation. By the last half of the twentieth century there was almost complete adult literacy. In 1950 a Gallup Poll showed that reading books was far more widespread in Britain than in any other society in the world. 55% of the British sample claimed to be reading a book at the time of the poll, while two years earlier three out of four people in Britain were reading a national newspaper. The potential for the spread of new ideas is obvious from these statistics, a potential which was immeasurably expanded by the coming of radio between the wars and of television immediately after the Second World War. The fact that women were for the first time sharing in the expansion of education and swelling the ranks of the employed had implications for greater flexibility and change in the upbringing of the next generation, and presaged a weakening of family influences encouraging social stability.

By contrast social change in India has been far less radical; and it has occurred unevenly in geographical terms and at different levels of society.[27] The reasons for this are economic and political, as well as the natural conservatism of a social order so firmly

anchored in a dominant ideology which puts a high value on
stability. The British, who had dreamed in the early nineteenth
century of re-fashioning Indian society, were badly scared by the
1857 mutiny and the violent response of some Indians who felt
that society, and caste in particular, was under threat from their
imperial overlords. Consequently they were extremely reluctant to
tamper thereafter with Indian customs and the social order. It was
not until an independent government came to power in 1947 that
any conscious social engineering was undertaken through legislation and taxation. Only then, for example, was the practice of
untouchability prohibited, and untouchables were given extra help
to raise their economic and social status, even though the British
had heartily disapproved of the practice. Moreover, India's industrialization was very limited in proportion to the size of the subcontinent, and took the form of industrial enclaves in great cities
such as Calcutta and Bombay, which had a restricted effect in the
country's vast rural areas. Urban population has indeed increased
rapidly in the mid twentieth century (44.15 millions in 1941 to
109.1 millions in 1971); but so has India's total population. The
result is that only 20% of Indians lived in towns in 1971, a very
slight increase on the figure of 17% for 1951. The majority of
Indians still live in the countryside, and earn their livings in rural
occupations. The proportion of the male work force dependent on
agriculture and allied pursuits remained nearly 70% between 1951
and 1971; and in 1961 only just over 10% of working men were
employed in manufacturing industry. The pattern of women's employment shows a striking contrast to that found in Britain. Whereas in Britain the expansion of female employment was the result
of industrialization and particularly of better education fitting
women for a wider range of non-manual jobs, in India women
have traditionally been heavily employed in agriculture. This is still
the pattern, and though female education has led to a greater
employment of women in the professions, industrial development
has not given them expanded opportunities. Indeed, economic development appears to lead to a *decline* in the proportion of the
work force who are women, except among the educated.

Standards of education and levels of literacy are far lower in
India than in Britain. By 1971 nearly 40% of men and 19% of
women were literate. This masked a gross disparity in literacy
between town and country: roughly 34% of men and 13% of
women in the countryside were literate, compared with 61% of
men and 42% of women in towns. Despite the rising literacy rates
the growth in India's total population has meant that there are

more illiterates now than there were at independence. The difficulties of providing schools for India's millions, and even more of
ensuring attendance at school, are massive. In the 1970s about
82% of all primary school age children were enrolled, but in the
middle school stage only 35% of the 11-14 year olds were enrolled.
Girls are still far less likely to attend school than boys, although
their educational opportunities and achievements have increased
dramatically in the later part of this century. Partly because of
these educational standards it is less realistic to talk of 'mass
communication' in India than in Britain. In 1972 India's 11,926
newspapers had a circulation of 32 million – but this is among a
population of 548 million. Radio listening and ownership has
increased markedly since broadcasting was introduced into India
in 1927. It was estimated that in 1972 only 11.8% of families had
radios; but ownership and access are not identical, and in many
villages the men at least will cluster round the one or two available
transistors after work. Television is, however, transmitted only in
limited areas, and is prohibitively expensive for all but the
wealthiest.

Such blunt facts indicate the limited nature of change in Indian
society, in living patterns, employment, and the means of dissem-
inating ideas. Caste society has also inhibited change. It has *accommodated* change without being overturned by it, a process which
has been helped by the piecemeal nature of the challenges to it. In
contrast to Britain, there have been no massive forces working to
uproot the old order. At the bottom of the hierarchy, for example,
untouchable leather workers have taken to leather work in shoe
factories, still remaining within the system at approximately the
same ritual level. 'Clean' castes with traditions of literacy and
government service have flocked into education and the new professions to which education is the door, while traditional trading
castes have branched out into a wide range of modern banking,
commercial and industrial enterprises. The sheer logistics of urban
life do make it difficult to adhere to strict standards of ritual purity
and segregation, and the lure of secure work attracts people from
many castes into factory employment. But despite such loosening
of traditional ties and conventions, particularly in towns, caste
groups are still important social entities which dominate the lives
of their members and can take on new significance in politics and
in mutual self-help in a changing environment.

Moreover, the social order has a built-in safety valve. It permits
group mobility though not personal mobility. Consequently if a
particular *jati* finds its economic position improving, it can over

several decades or generations raise its ritual position by a process known as 'sanskritization'. This is a type of 'ritual keeping-up-with-the-Joneses'. It involves imitation of the life style of a locally prestigious caste (generally one with more Sanscritic customs), and a fictional justification for higher status, often through some myth about the *jati*'s more exalted ritual origins and its subsequent fall in status which is now to be made good. Such group mobility does not always succeed. Where it does, by using the standards of caste it confirms the total social order rather than challenging it.[28]

Another aspect of the relationship of religion and society is the impact of the political order upon the religious experience. Here again the cases of contemporary India and Britain are dissimilar. Britain has experienced no political revolution bringing to power a regime overtly hostile to religious belief and practice. The Church of England remains the established church while other major Christian denominations are given a recognized place in public life.[29] The main point at which political change has impinged on the religious experience is perhaps in the emergence of liberal and particularly socialist ideologies, with their emphasis on human values, and their commitment to human engineering of the economy, the environment and society. Such ideas and strategies are not necessarily inimical to Christian belief and practice; but there is often within them an implicit questioning of values and institutions previously upheld by the churches. The whole apparatus of the welfare state has, moreover, taken out of the control of religious individuals and bodies a wide range of education, medical and welfare services, thereby reducing the significance of religious institutions in public life.

In India the political experience of the twentieth-century campaign for independence has direct implications for Hindus in two main and conflicting ways. In the first place, specifically Hindu institutions and organizations became involved in the nationalist movement, while the 'Hindu-ness' of India became an integral part of the assertion of Indian national identity over against the British. In this process of assertion, by such different figures as Tilak, Gandhi and Golwalkar, there were elements of religious revivalism as well as re-interpretation of the Hindu heritage. But India was a plural society, with a significant Muslim minority. This confronted Hindu politicians with acute problems. How far should they equate Hindu identity with Indian-ness, in order to rouse enthusiasm and tap organizational support among Hindus? Or should they eschew such a propaganda platform and network and speak of a national identity which would incorporate religious minorities? The Indian

National Congress, the main focus of the nationalist movement, never solved this dilemma. Although most Muslims voted through the ballot box or with their feet for a separate Muslim homeland in Pakistan in 1947, India's governments are left with the legacy of the unresolved dilemma. The state's norms, as enshrined in the constitution and subsequent legislation, are non-sectarian, if not secular. But the pre-independence emphasis on Hindu characteristics and values as part of Indian nationality has left behind an embarrassing revivalist strain in Indian public life, as well as a less destructive but firm assumption among most Hindus that being a Hindu and an Indian are indivisible.

A final problem of comparison lies in the basic assumptions with which people approach the phenomenon of the religious experience: how they perceive it, and what they expect to find within it. Different ways of thinking *do* distinguish Hindus and Christians. They have developed in part from the nature of the religious reality experienced by the two groups as described earlier in this chapter. It is always difficult to fathom other people's basic assumptions, because they are so basic: they are taken for granted, and rarely discussed. Our comparison is made the more difficult in this area by the fact that educated Hindus will use English to describe their attitudes and experiences to the foreigner. But the reality referred to may be very different from that for which English speakers in Britain would use the word. This will be apparent in the discussion of 'spirituality' in Chapter 5. Here a note of some of the conceptual differences will indicate this area of difficulty in our comparison.

A major difference in the way Hindus and Christians think about religion has already been hinted at in the distinction made between a religion whose core is an experience enshrined in an orthodoxy, and one whose heart is orthopraxis. At the level of thought this means that for the Hindu there is no real distinction between the 'religious' and the 'secular'. Life cannot be compartmentalized in such a way, as *dharma* is worked out in the whole of life, physical, mental, emotional and social. The Christian distinction between the two reflects the actual experience of rapid change in Western Europe in the last two centuries. But its roots go far deeper than this, back into Jewish tradition from which Christianity emerged. Central to Jewish faith was the idea of a God standing in some sense outside his world, confronting it with his claims, as well as working within it. The stories of Noah and the flood, Jonah and the whale, reflect this attitude. The vision of a majestic and in some way external God underlies the Old Testament historians' attempt to trace the hand of God managing affairs through unlikely instru-

ments in the turbulent relations of the tribes of Israel and their
neighbours and in the impassioned appeals of the prophets to the
chosen people to come to their senses and realize what God was
trying to do with them. Here was the glimmering of and opening
for a distinction between the religious and the 'worldly'. The whole
world was not seen as in some mysterious way 'breathing' the
divine, partaking of and displaying it, as in the Hindu cosmic view
of ultimate reality pervading all existence. In the development of
the Christian tradition the emergence of Protestantism emphasized
this latent theme of a division between a religious and a secular
sphere, one where God could be found, and one where he could
not. In various ways Protestant thinking and practice confronted
the individual even more dramatically with an awesome deity – by
its starkness of worship, its eradication of older festivals deeply
rooted in folk life and in the soil, and its rejection of saints as
mediators between God and man. In Peter Berger's evocative
phrase, there occurred a real 'disenchantment of the world'.[30] The
repercussions of this 'disenchantment' have, as we shall see in
Chapter 5, prompted groping by some late twentieth-century
Christians for an authentic spirituality, to remedy aspects of deprivation and poverty in Western spiritual experience which owes
much to this legacy of compartmentalizing the 'religious' and the
'secular'.

Further distinctions between Hindu and Christian ways of thinking about the religious experience are implicit in this absence of a
shared concept of religious as opposed to secular. For the Christian
the response of the individual to the demands of the divine is of
primary importance. Each man and woman stands alone before
God, and the decisions he or she makes in response are crucial.
Salvation, seen as incorporation into the divine life offered through
Christ, in the present and the hereafter, is at heart an individual
matter. This religious individualism, to some degree inherent in the
Christian experience, despite ideas of a cosmic salvation rooted in
the New Testament, was carried to its extreme in Protestantism,
which emphasizes each believer's justification by faith rather than
by observable membership of a sacramental fellowship of believers.
In Hindu thinking the individual has far less religious status and
significance. Except for the 'renouncer' who breaks out of the
social order to become an ascetic, each person works out his
salvation, his liberation from the cycle of re-births and the opera-
tion of *karma*, in a social group. A solitary figure cannot do this,
as social relations are the stuff of *dharma*. Here clearly are different
understandings of the meaning of individuality and of salvation.

Here, too, is a different emphasis on the essential nature of ultimate reality. For the Christian, as for the Jew and Muslim, reality is a transcendent God. He works in and through his creation; but he is also apart from it. For the Hindu, reality is immanent: it underlies and breathes through all existence, and need not even be conceived of in terms of a deity.

The Hindu emphasis on the immanence rather than the transcendence of ultimate reality helps to explain why Hindus compared with Christians have so little trouble with the question of reason and faith as ways of grasping reality, and the anguish of possible conflict between them. For the Hindu there is no disturbing dichotomy between reason and faith. Truth is veiled by matter, and hidden within the manifold variety of existence. To 'know' truth a man must search for it with all the faculties of perception at his disposal; but primarily he must look within himself for truth, guided by experience rather than external teaching about objective facts. At the heart of reality lies total mystery, which can only be revered and adored by the rare person who approaches it in a state of inner enlightenment. It can never be 'known about', only experienced. The Upanishads and their style of teaching make this plain. They have a 'logic' totally alien to the Western mind trained in the post-Cartesian age with its heavy emphasis on the process of discursive reasoning as the proper means to knowledge. The Upanishads offer the disciple a series of intuitions, often odd, inconsequential, unclear and seemingly unconnected, for those used to 'the ponderous tread of conceptual thought'.[31] They aim to shatter ordinary categories of judgment and ways of knowing: to prod the disciple towards a new level and mode of perception, that of direct intuition or illumination.

By contrast in the West it is now assumed that the basic mode of understanding is the conceptual one, i.e. 'knowledge or belief that ...'. This assumption has become dominant since Descartes, but it has its roots in Greek thought. It is also of course a striking contrast with the emphasis of those who first experienced Christ and recorded their response to him in what is now scripture. For them the religious experience was not so much 'belief that ...' but 'belief in ...'. It was a matter of conviction at the roots of being, not just at the level of the rational mind: it led to and inevitably implied faith and obedience. It was in a sense being grasped by, rather than grasping, ultimate meaning. This is far nearer to the mode of perception central to the Hindu idea of knowing in religious matters. For early Christians there was no dichotomy between reason and faith; and it has only become a practical problem for ordinary people in the West with the recent expansion of education and the spread of literacy. What was once an intellectual's problem has become every man's problem. The religious experience in practice involves far more than man's rational response and capacity for cognition. It engages him at various levels of understanding and commitment. How does this square with the primacy placed on reason and the development of the conceptual faculty through modern education?[32] The implications of this will be explored in Chapters 4 and 5 both in the Christian context and in the Hindu experience, where recent exposure to Western style education and its assumption of the primacy of rationality has brought new problems and developments.

There can clearly be no easy comparison of changes in the religious experience and responses to change among Hindus and Christians, in the light of these problems of method, evidence and conceptualization, and the diversity of the two contexts in which changes are occurring. It will not be easy for a person from either tradition, or from outside either tradition, to understand what is happening inside a tradition he does not share. Nor will it be easy, as some people naively assume, for members of one tradition to appropriate the strategies for resolving problems caused by change, and to adopt the ways of coping with crises of religious identity, faith and practice, which may well be fruitful for those whose religious tradition and context is quite different.

However, the Hindu and Christian share at least three fundamentals which it was argued at the beginning of this chapter are common to all religions. Both traditions present total world views, intimations, if not explanations, of reality. Both have networks of authority to confirm men in these cosmic visions and webs of communication to transmit them, in the form of sacred texts and people. Both have patterns of behaviour, in religious cult and total life-style, deemed to be appropriate responses to these visions. The effects of change on these shared and fundamental aspects of religion will be the basis of our comparison.

Chapter Two

How Dead are the Gods?
The Hindu World

=

The next two chapters are a jigsaw. I want to fit together a picture of the contemporary Hindu world in India and the Christian experience in Britain in order to gauge the vitality of these two religious traditions as world views which still influence public and private behaviour. Observable facts of religious practice will be important evidence, as will people's reporting of their own beliefs or lack of them. But equally significant are the less tangible pieces of evidence, particularly those which show how people involved in the situation see their experience. We must therefore see how educated Hindus and Christians understand and interpret the significance of change for their religious tradition and the extent to which they feel any sense of crisis or of potential in maintaining their religious understanding of the world and religious practices in the changing environment. Their interpretation of their situation will be influenced by the degree to which the religious outlook conflicts with or is confirmed by the values and customs commonly accepted in society around them, and the standards implicit or explicit in the way the state and its structures of power function. Social and state norms will therefore be part of our total picture.

However, I do not intend any sweeping or simplistic comparisons with the past. There is not implicit in the picture of the present any simple assumption that earlier times were 'ages of faith', or that previous generations were 'more religious' than our contemporaries. Rarely are there accurate and comparable observations to make such comparisons possible in more than an impressionistic way. Moreover the realm of belief and religious practice, so subtle in its nuances, so often particular to the experience of the individual, can never be understood from the evidence of facts and figures alone. Hints of the reality of the religious experience must be drawn from a wide range of evidence, and filtered through sensitive imagination and understanding in the observer.

You cannot count Hindus as you can the number of Christians, by membership of a church or experience of a rite of initiation like baptism which is recorded by religious authorities. There is no Hindu equivalent of a church to which people can 'belong', and in the Indian census, for example, all who are born into Hindu castes are classified as Hindus unless they deliberately proclaim themselves as atheists or converts to another religion.[1] For our enquiry I have collected what evidence I could of the belief of the urban educated, particularly those who have completed secondary education and have received or are receiving college education. These are of course those who, as teachers, lawyers, doctors and politicians, now or in the future, influence most the public values of India's state and society.

But what does 'belief' mean in the Hindu world? As we have seen, no theological beliefs are *necessary* for a Hindu in the way they are for a Christian. In the Christian context the image of God and the doctrines associated with it, inherited from past generations of church teaching and folk religion, are sharply defined. Therefore it is possible that the sceptical twentieth-century Hindu has less difficulty in asserting his 'belief' in divinity and divine power than would his counterpart in Britain who found the image of a Father God meaningless, and the formulations of classical theology difficult to stomach. The very formlessness and flexibility of patterns of belief in the Hindu context keeps people within the ranks of those who say they 'believe', and decreases the number of those who feel obliged to call themselves agnostics or atheists.

In Pune, a large industrial city and educational centre in western India, the city's 610 Marathi-speaking Hindu college teachers were the subject of an enquiry into their religious attitudes a decade ago.[2] More than 70% of them were of the second, third or fourth Western educated generation of their family, therefore one might expect them to be unusually influenced by the prevailing forces of change. Of the 291 who replied, 200 (68.7%) classified themselves as believers, 48 (16.5%) as agnostics, and 43 (14.8%) as non-believers. Several years earlier, figures of belief among a sample of 100 male Hindu college teachers in Gujarat, further north, revealed that 89% believed in the existence of God.[3] An enquiry into the world of the Indian intellectual in the 1950s showed an even smaller number of educated Indians who said they were agnostic or atheist – a mere 10% of those questioned.[4] A younger generation of educated Indians in secondary schools and colleges in the late 1960s and early 1970s display a similar pattern. In a survey of Pune students, conducted in 1976, 293 Hindus replied. When asked if they believed in God or 'a superior power', 67.6% said that they did, while 11.2% classified themselves as agnostics, and 21.2% replied that they definitely did not believe; 300 students in the same city questioned in 1970-71 showed slightly higher 'belief' rating. 75.7% called themselves believers, 11.0% were uncertain whether they believed in God, while 11.7% were prepared to say that they did not. A much smaller sample of fairly affluent 16-22 year olds in Bombay in 1978 produced similar results, though in that case the girls' conservatism clearly bumped up the overall 'belief' rate – 90% of them compared with 60% of the boys called themselves 'believers'. Research among students in South India in the late 1960s confirms this picture – that a large majority of educated, urban Hindus across several generations still see themselves as believers, retaining a religious understanding of their world.[5]

But does this religious world view conform to the philosophical formulations and mythological insights of classical Hindu tradition? How real to the educated are the gods of the Great Tradition? Among 175 believers questioned in the South Indian town of Chirakkal only three spoke in the terminology of Advaita – the classical formulation of non-dualism, the essential unity of the phenomenal world and the divine. The rest thought in terms of one and many gods but placed particular emphasis on a general feeling of dependence on a superior power, describing it as a basic power, energy, *sakti*. Investigation in a far smaller South Indian town in 1969 revealed a similarly broad spectrum of gods and goddesses and spirits inhabiting people's religious world, but few people understood religion in Vedantic terms.[6]

Among the Pune lecturers all knew about the metaphysical foundations of Hinduism, but 80% said that these were too vague and difficult to be a suitable basis for personal religion, and that their own conception of God and religion did not embody such ideas. The idea of *karma*, to take one example, was obviously still alive for a sizeable group of believers; but over 40% rejected it or fluctuated in their attitude to it. A selective process of rejection was occurring in the religious world view of such people, as in the perception of one evidently devout and sensitive Hindu I met, who dismissed the concept of *maya* (the illusory nature of material things) as irrevelant for ordinary living. Of the 100 Gujarati college teachers questioned a little earlier, 79 believed in the survival of the soul after death, but only 59 believed that the soul passes through a cycle of births and deaths. In the South Indian student group most had some knowledge of the great Hindu scriptures, particularly the *Bhagavad Gita*, and the epics which recount the exploits of the gods and goddesses of the Great Tradition. 57% of them admitted to belief in *samsara* (the cycle of transmigration of the soul); 56% believed in *karma* operating within this life and carried over into the next life, while even more believed in it just as a force of causation in this life. But though these students appeared quite well informed about the classical religious tradition into which they had entered, a Bombay University professor in 1978 shared with me his deep distress about the ignorance of many of his students on these matters, and the fact that much in Hindu philosophy was not now understood or being presented to the younger generation. Ignorance of the traditions of Hinduism and the meaning of its symbols, combined with a regretful nostalgia, was a predominant theme in the responses of 50 educated women interviewed by Rama Mehta in the 1960s. For most of them, even the sizeable minority brought up in a traditional Hindu home, the concepts of *dharma*, *karma* and *moksha* were not living principles for guidance in actual life, and *maya* was clearly a dead letter, though the women knew what the concepts meant.[7]

Another way of assessing the vitality of the Hindu world view is to investigate the way Hindus have responded to modern scientific knowledge and technological change and the extent to which natural and social causation has in their eyes been taken out of the realm of gods. In the South Indian towns which have been studied, attitudes to the natural world have clearly been changing, though not in any simple or uniform way. Modern medical knowledge, for example, has eroded the power over men's minds of the Hindu goddesses whose actions have in the past been in part explanation and cure of disease. Deference to modern science is now evident in the reinterpretation of some old traditions – like growing the sacred basil plant, but now on the grounds that it is medicinal and sweet-smelling; or bathing in sacred rivers partly for religious reasons and partly for the water's allegedly beneficial chemical qualities. (In Chirakkal town, for example, only 11% of a sample of 187 still thought that bathing in the Ganges purified from sin and ensured salvation.) Pune students in 1970-1 clearly felt uneasy about manipulating the natural world, looked on the natural order with awe and veneration, and tended to feel that natural disasters were evidence of divine wrath. But they insisted that it was proper for men to manipulate their social environment through reform measures, economic planning and industrial and technological development. They were not all in agreement about the relationship of new knowledge and modes of thought to their religious tradition. When asked whether religion and rationality were inconsistent nearly 40% thought they were; nearly 30% said 'no'; and 30% did not know.[8] In the total group of Pune students questioned five years later (including the minority from non-Hindu backgrounds) a similar confusion was evident. To the question whether religious principles and scientific discoveries went together 47% responded that they did not, 39.5% felt that they did, while 13.5% did not know. Among their elders, the Pune college teachers, those who called themselves believers clearly did not feel any tension between scientific knowledge and method and religion. (Only 2.5% felt they were antagonistic, while 43.5% felt they were independent areas of knowledge and 51.5% saw them as harmonious, both being paths in a search for truth.) Nearly three-quarters of a group of Indian scientists from various universities questioned slightly later similarly perceived no conflict between religion and science, though this group did include a substantial number of Christians.[9]

Astrology is important here. It has played an important part in the Hindu's perception of his place in the universe and guided his attempts to cooperate with the favourable forces and avoid the evil powers surrounding him. It is common knowledge that astrology is still considered significant even among those committed to non-religious values or trained in rational, scientific enquiry. When the Communists came to power in Kerala in 1957 they ensured that their ministry was sworn in at an auspicious time, while in one meterological institution scientists avoid doing anything important at inauspicious times of day. Perhaps the most famous example of public deference to astrological advice was the moving of the actual moment of independence in 1947 from an inauspicious day: to the inconvenience of all concerned, who had to attend a midnight ceremony!

In their private lives many educated Hindus still maintain astrological practices, for social reasons as well as continuing belief in their efficacy. 60% of the South Indian student group studied affirmed belief in astrology and/or palmistry, and of this group 60% frequently consulted astrologers and palmists. Just over half the entire student group followed the weekly astrological forecasts in the newspapers, regularly or occasionally. However, of the total Pune group of students questioned in 1976 (including non Hindus) only 17.25% admitted that they would only take a decision after consulting a horoscope. Among the Pune college lecturers astrological practices were very common, though often more for social convention than genuine belief in them. Even among self-professed agnostic lecturers over 60% continued such practices, as did 86%

of believers. However, of the scientists questioned in various academic centres, a majority did perceive a contradiction between astrology and astronomy. Women might be expected to stick to the old habits more tenaciously. But there is scant proof of this in the particular case of astrology. Of 408 Hindu educated women interviewed in Pune nearly 32% said they believed in astrology, 35.8% did not, and 20.7% did not know. Of the 50 educated women interviewed earlier, 19 had had their children's horoscopes cast out of deference to the wishes of their in-laws, but they had no faith in them and did not act on them. Of 22 who had had a more traditional background in the group of 50 all had had their children's horoscopes cast, at least 14 of them without family pressure. Some of these 22 said they did not heed astrological forecasts, but all of them did in practice. Ingrained tradition dies hard, even though tinged now with some scepticism. As one of the women put it, 'I am not prepared to take the risk of going against advice. Too much is involved. Besides, what one does is quite innocuous and no harm can come of it even if good doesn't result. . . .'[10]

But how important do Hindus think their religious tradition is in their own lives? The South Indian student group interpreted the notion of *dharma* in various ways, but 85% said that the principles of *dharma* applied to their own lives. Pune students in 1976 were rather more sceptical when asked whether religious principles were essential to living a happy and good life, and to understanding the fundamental truths of human existence. Only just under 60% of the Hindus in the group said religion was essential in this way. But just over 60% of the 300 Pune students questioned in 1970-1 found religion necessary to life. When young adults in Bombay were asked directly whether religion had an important place in their lives, under half of them felt that it had.[11] In my discussions with adult Hindus I sensed apathy on religious matters, or at least a lack of conscious thinking about religion. Some felt that serious thought in this area could be reserved for later life. Many of the Pune lecturers who replied to their colleague's questions admitted that they had never before considered religion so seriously. (The absence of conscious thought does not necessarily mean apathy, of course. It may be the result of living in the framework of a pre-eminently social religion whose assumptions are taken so much for granted that they are not consciously considered.)

However, what people *say* about religion must be checked as far as possible against what they actually do. One obvious area to observe is prayer. The understanding of prayer, its purpose, as well as its modes, is very different in the Hindu and Christian religious experience. But both have a tradition of daily private prayer in the home. For the orthodox male of high caste there is an elaborate schema of morning purification and prayer, while in every orthodox home there would be a small domestic shrine, whose deities would be honoured daily with prayer and probably the offering of fresh flowers and incense.

Among the Pune lecturers, whether they professed to be 'believers' or not, the presence of a domestic shrine or idol in the home was very common. (97.5% of believers' homes, 89.6% of agnostics' homes, and 81.3% of atheists' homes.) In 119 of the homes of the 200 believers (54.5%), daily *puja* and prayers occurred, though in the majority of these cases it was the women of the household or an older man who actually performed the prayer. It is now very rare to find educated Hindu men of high caste performing the whole of the lengthy morning *puja*, and many have abbreviated it drastically where they have not abandoned it altogether.[12] The group of 100 Gujarati lecturers questioned reported that 60 of them prayed daily, 4 once a week, 9 occasionally, 4 rarely, 23 never. It will be remembered that only 11 of these did not believe in the existence of God: therefore some of the 'believers' must never pray. A similar pattern of prayer was recorded among the educated women surveyed in Pune. 70% of them offered daily or occasional prayer.

Among the younger age group there are also high levels of personal prayer. Of the Bombay adolescents questioned only 16.6% admitted to *never* praying (26.6% of the boys, however, compared with 6.6% of the girls). In the South Indian student sample 65% had images of deities in their dormitories; 66% reported praying, while 51.9% reported praying daily. Women students did not appear to have changed their prayer patterns on leaving home, but among higher caste male students 10% dropped from the ranks of those who prayed frequently to those who prayed rarely or never. Amongst the 300 college students surveyed in Pune, the majority of whom were Hindus, 84% prayed, while only 14% said that they never prayed. (Here 16% prayed morning and night, 6% prayed at night, while 11.6% prayed occasionally. Most did not specify how often they prayed.)

Prayer in the Hindu tradition is not only a personal affair, but part of the web of ritual which holds the family together and integrates it into Hindu society through a host of ceremonies which are both social and religious. Private prayer at home is the most personal of these, and is therefore some indicator of the depth of personal religion. But it cannot be stressed too strongly that statistics tell us little about the content of private prayer and its significance for the individual: figures are blunt instruments.

Before we look at evidence of more public rituals it is worth considering another aspect of the vitality of personal religion. How much 'religious' literature do Hindus read for their own edification? (This links with the question of scripture as authority, and with the extent to which Hindus are 'well-educated' in their religious heritage, mentioned earlier in this chapter.)

I have been unable to find much evidence on the reading of the student age group. But of the 204 South Indian students questioned only 37.2% said that they read no religious literature. 25.9% read the *Gita*, often daily; 10.2% mentioned works by the modern reinterpreters of Hindu tradition, Vivekananda and Gandhi; while only 2 mentioned the great Hindu texts of the Upanishads. Of the Pune college teachers who called themselves 'believers', 61% felt that religious literature was an important influence on them. Again the *Gita* was an important work for many of them, with the great epics, the *Ramayana* and the *Mahabharata*. Otherwise they read devotional books in the Maharashtrian 'saintly' tradition, and the biographies of saints, past and present. They, too, specifically mentioned Vivekananda as a source of inspiration. Among the 'believing' group only 23% did not read religious literature at all; 21% read regularly; while 56% read occasionally. It is also significant that only just over 30% of agnostics and atheists among the Pune lecturers *never* read religious works. The majority of those who did read said that they did so for intellectual pleasure, but a sizeable minority admitted that they did so to gain inner strength. Of the 100 Gujarati lecturers interviewed in 1965-6 32% never read sacred books – a figure close to that of the Pune agnostic/atheist group. 27% read such works daily, 23% occasionally, 1% once a week, and 17% rarely. More educated women appear to read religious books. Of the 408 educated Pune women questioned only 20% never read any at all, while over 45% said that they read them as a matter of faith. The smaller group of 50 educated women taken from a wider geographical span showed considerable variation. Those who read most were from traditional Hindu homes and had a good command of a vernacular language in which to read. The majority of the sample who were really fluent only in English read far less, though most of them had read the *Ramayana*, *Mahabharata* and *Gita* in English abridged versions. These findings confirmed my own impressions. First, the *Gita* is the main literary source from which educated Hindus derive strength and a sense of the relevance of their religious heritage for the twentieth century. But second, many educated Hindus are deeply ignorant about their great scriptures. (Some of the reasons for this ignorance will become clear when we consider contemporary religious education in Chapter 4.)

The main outward religious observances for Hindus are a vast web of ceremonies, feasting and fasting, which mark the turning-points in the life-cycles of individuals, the festivals of the Hindu year, and the birthdays of various deities. These may involve ceremonies at home presided over by a Brahmin in the case of the higher castes, and/or visits to shrines and temples. But there is no tradition of weekly or regular congregational worship at temples. My own impression from personal observation as well as from detailed surveys is that this enfolding ritual life is still part of the natural experience of most educated Hindus, whether they profess to 'believe' or not. The habits of the Pune lecturers make the point (see Table A, p. 54). The public calendar of India is studded with Hindu festival holidays, and everybody is caught up to some extent in such celebrations, much as people living in Britain are swept along by the tide of Christmas festivities, whatever their beliefs. Moreover, in the Indian home, even where one family member may find the ceremonies hollow, deference to older members or a wish to bring children up in a truly Indian culture keeps the celebrations going. For many, religious ceremonial at turning points in individual life such as marriage and puberty (marked by the sacred thread ceremony for the high caste boy) are still very important; and considerable numbers of educated people still fast and visit temples (see Table B, p. 55).

However, changes are occurring in this area of the Hindu religious experience. It seems that the main public festivals such as Diwali in the Autumn, and Holi, the Spring festival, tend to be celebrated more fully and in a civic and neighbourly setting, rather than in home and temple, or by specific castes. The media industry, the comparative leisure and affluence of India's educated have contributed to this change, as possibly has the Christian celebration of Christmas with its parties and gift-giving.[13] But there has also been a very marked trend to curtail or abandon some of the family rituals, largely because of the time involved in these, as well as the cost of lengthy and elaborate ceremonial. Almost all the Hindus I talked with confirmed this. One study found that among villagers celebrating festivals only 7% had abbreviated their observation, while among the urban elite 63% had curtailed the rites. Of a group of urban, educated women in Ahmedabad (Gujarat), nearly

half had had only a three-day Vedic wedding, whereas the parents
of all of them had had wedding celebrations lasting three to five
days. Many Hindu weddings are now down to one day only.[14]

The momentum to carry on the traditional ceremonies, even
among those for whom the religious meaning has never been
known or has drained away, comes from family, and the wider
social pressure of caste and kin. Moreover the web of interlocking
public and private rites and celebrations make up a total and often
very enjoyable social world. It is hard for anyone to opt out of
this. It causes distress to the rest of the family, particularly if older
members are resident: it cuts both individual and family off from
the past, from relatives and neighbours. It leaves a void just when
some external ritual is needed to mark times of grief, joy and
change in the life of an individual or a family. Only the most
fiercely agnostic or atheist willingly does this. Understandably voluntary and personal observations such as prayer decline first,
whereas rituals involving the whole family are the most resilient,
particularly where older members of the family live in the same
house or nearby, or when parents wish to preserve something of
India's cultural heritage for their children.[15] However, the religious
significance of much of the ritual is clearly minimal for many of
those who continue the outward forms of observance. Many participants in marriages, for example, know no Sanskrit, the language
in which the sacrament is performed, the words are rarely translated for them, and they have but the haziest understanding of the
symbolism. This may not perhaps affect the religious experience of
those still caught up in a world totally suffused by Hindu symbols,
who accept the power of the Sanskrit sounds themselves, but for
the educated it increasingly matters whether they consciously understand what is being done. It is not insignificant that of the
young adults questioned in Bombay in 1978 a large majority felt
that dogma and ritual held no meaning.[16]

The curtailment of *traditional* ritual and its lack of religious
meaning for many educated Hindus does not necessarily mean the
'decline' of religion or the 'secularization' of society or at least the
educated segment of it. Though the gods may have 'died' in this
ritual and symbolic framework, they clearly 'live' through other
religious modes. There have always been flourishing manifestations
of 'popular' religion in India, often barely connected with the
austere metaphysics or the grand pantheon of the Great Tradition.
In this century many older populist and local forms of religious
expression appear to be waning. In a real sense the coming of
printing, the expansion of literacy, and the growth of mass media,

including the colourful portrayal of Hindu deities cheaply available at any street bazaar, have helped to 'popularize' the Great Tradition.[17] But there are other manifestations of religion, popular among the educated, which are either new or are recently developed aspects of older traditions within the Hindu experience. These will concern us in Chapter 5, but brief mention of them here shows the variety, and often apparently contradictory trends, present in the contemporary Hindu world. Within the encompassing diversity of Hindu tradition and experience there has been the strand of *bhakti* or devotion to a deity, which has often been directed towards Krishna. For the Hindu devotee, love and service of the god, rather than painful performance of *dharma*, is the road to salvation. Moreover salvation is interpreted not as absorption into the Absolute, but nearness to the beloved deity while still separate from him. There are strong indications that the *bhakti* strand of Hindu experience is being re-worked and reinterpreted in the twentieth century. *Bhakti* cults are flourishing and drawing into their circle large numbers of those educated, urban Hindus for whom traditional rituals no longer mediate a true religious experience, nor provide a credible framework for a distinctively religious attitude to life. Studies from various towns in different parts of India show the development of strong *bhakti* cults with activities such as *bhajan* or devotional song-singing. Organized scripture readings are also widespread, both in public and at home.[18] The Indian film industry is producing more 'devotional' films. Devotion (along with crime!) is increasingly popular as a film subject, though history, mythology and legend is decreasing matter for film.[19] In the context of the *bhakti* cult there is often a powerful and attractive religious leader who helps those who follow him on the devotional path he maps out to adjust to urban life without abandoning religious commitment. Such *guru* figures will be considered in Chapter 4; but for some educated Hindus they do indeed help to make the gods live again. On an all-India scale and at a deeper intellectual level the Ramakrishna Mission serves a similar function of re-interpretation and guidance. It is remarkable how many of the educated point to Vivekananda and the Ramakrishna Mission as a powerful influence in their own religious experience. Religious pilgrimage, too, is still a significant part of the religious life of the educated. In the run-up to the 1980 General Election even political campaigning in Mysore was held up by the 'exodus' of party workers to Sabarimalai in Kerala. Better rail communications make pilgrimage easier than ever, and more trains now run directly to major pilgrimage centres.[20]

So far our evidence has been of the vitality of personal belief, and of certain outward religious practices. The family environment is in large measure responsible for the socialization of children into the Hindu religious heritage (as we shall see in Chapter 4): it is also crucial as the supportive structure for the maintenance of many rites and celebrations. However, the wider context is also important, in as much as the standards of society and the state support or erode the religious world view. In any society the resilience of social forms and values which buttress religion is central to the maintenance of religion as a living force and a real experience. Where changes occur in this wider context religious change becomes almost essential if religious authorities are to survive and the religious experience continue to be authentic. This is particularly true where religion has been deeply interwoven with a particular social setting, as in the Hindu case, where right action in the context of caste society has been a main mediator of the religious experience.

Much is occurring in contemporary India to modify, if not erode, traditional social institutions and values. Some of the most significant forces for change were noted in Chapter 1. The growth of towns and the increasing numbers of Indians living in large cities has a variety of implications for our study. The very fact of living and working close together with strangers of different castes and communities makes social separation difficult to maintain, although members of the same caste still tend to cluster together residentially and reinforce their identity. Urban life makes some traditional ritual observances impossible. For example, just the need for fresh water to wash the domestic images for worship, and for other aspects of *puja*, is an almost insuperable problem in Bombay, for thousands of flat-dwellers who have no wells. Tap water is a compromise, as the layout of the piping almost certainly means that it has been ritually polluted on its way to the householder, while at some times even tap water is not available because of water shortages and supply failures. In Bombay there are in fact several centres where orthodox Hindus can go to get their most important rituals properly performed (for example, Admar Math, Anderi; Pejawar Math, Santa Cruz; Navavridawana Math, Malund). New types of jobs in factories and offices not covered by the traditional caste ordering of occupations have increased occupational choice and mobility; and in general in urban settings the work place is now considered a ritually neutral environment, where purity and pollution regulations do not apply. In towns there are more opportunities for education, with all that that implies for the

spread of new ideas among children and adolescents at a crucial
stage in their development. Moreover, this occurs for those very
young people who are cut off by urban living from close contact
with large family networks which for older people, and still for
village-dwellers, are the main sources of cultural and religious
training. It would be a gross over-simplification to say that urban
Indians now tend to live in nuclear rather than joint families. A
majority of urban families are still 'joint', though there are regional
variations in the patterns of family life; and often urban families
retain financial and social links with family members though they
do not live under one roof and share one hearth. However, the
educated are the most mobile geographically, the most likely to
practise family planning; and also those who, living in cramped
urban flats, have less room for grandparents, aunts and uncles.[21]

Increasing opportunities for women's education, the growing
numbers of educated women and the trend towards their employment outside the home also cuts at the heart of the process whereby
children in earlier generations were introduced to their religious
and cultural inheritance. Women gain new ideas from their education, develop new ambitions, and cease to be the conservative
core of Hindu society as their mothers and grandmothers were.
One late nineteenth-century Indian social reformer said that it was
easier to move the government than one's grandmother! This could
not be said of contemporary educated women, who even if they
are not out at work, spend less time with their children in traditional patterns of child-rearing.[22] Education has advanced rapidly in
contemporary India, sweeping into the ranks of the literate not
only more of those with family and caste traditions of literacy, but
women and low caste groups who in the past have been educa-
tionally deprived. At once the door opens for such people to occupational and possibly geographical mobility – potent solvents of
the old society. Moreover, the values inculcated in India's educational system are not those of Hindu tradition; the curriculum is
close to that followed in Western countries, largely as a result of
British influence in education for well over a hundred years. To
take just one example: the idea that men can plan, change and
control society questions the idea of *dharma* within a role demarcated by religion. It suggests that ills such as poverty may be the
result of inefficient government rather than *karma*; and sickness
the consequence of infection instead of malign, supernatural
powers.[23]

Such forces of change are having subtle but strong and visible
effects on the norms of Indian society and particularly of the social

world of the educated Hindu. Society is still ordered on caste lines,
its calendar celebrates the Hindu deities, its strategies for marking
and coping with crises and turning-points in individual and family
life are still preponderately those of the Great Tradition. But for
many Hindus the assumptions of hierarchy and separation implicit
in caste, of the religious worth of the old social structure, have
gone; and the power of caste conventions and sanctions has declined. In the various student groups questioned this was clear. Of
the South Indian students 61% stated that they did not believe in
the traditional divisions of Indian society and the code of conduct
traditionally ascribed to each caste division. Understandably the
higher caste students were more in favour of caste distinctions and
function than were those from lower castes (though interestingly
it was the high caste *men* rather than women who were most
tenacious of the old beliefs). Of the Pune students questioned in
1976 a large majority (81.5%) said that in social life people should
act on principles of common humanity, without regard for rules
inculcated by religion and caste. Students questioned in the same
city in 1970-1 also tended to disapprove of the maintenance of
caste inequalities. In the homes of the 50 educated women studied
by Rama Mehta ideas of inferiority and superiority based on caste
were completely absent; and even among those brought up in more
orthodox homes there was no wish to maintain any rigid, hierarchical caste ordering of society. However, what people *say* (particularly when quizzed by an outsider presumed to favour less
traditional ideas!) is not a reliable guide to what they actually do.
As the South Indian students admitted, it was easier to be 'liberal'
about caste at university than at home, where a more traditional
setting exerted constraints on their behaviour.

Caste ties are obviously still strong in India, reinforced as they
are by the intra-caste linkages of close kinship through marriage.
The locally resident members of the caste provide a natural social
group, while further afield they help house students away from
home and act as house-hunting and job-finding networks in larger
towns. Marriages outside caste are still comparatively rare and
marriage is one of the bastions of the whole system. It is highly
significant that of the Pune students questioned in 1976 71% were
not prepared to marry whom they wished if this conflicted with
parental wishes based on religious and caste differences: only 17%
were prepared to fly in the face of tradition in this way. A majority
of the Pune students questioned in 1970-1 also felt that marriage
across caste and religious boundaries would be impossible for
them, though they thought they would not object to their children

entering such marriages. Of Rama Mehta's 50 educated women
only 11 had no objection to inter-caste marriages. Caste position
is still an important determinant of social esteem, though education, wealth and career prospects are increasingly important additional components of social standing among India's educated.
Moreover, caste networks are significant forces in politics, which
politicians ignore at their peril; although caste is only one factor
among several in creating political loyalties.

Although caste *ties* are still significant in the world of the educated, caste *sanctions* against those who offend against caste *dharma* are now virtually a dead letter. Caste councils which once
disciplined the errant have often fallen into decay, and caste condemnation of those who contravene the traditional codes is rare
and holds no terrors for our educated Hindus. This change can be
seen in the relaxation of the purity and pollution rules evident
throughout India, but particularly in towns among the highly educated. The sheer logistics of maintaining purity in an urban setting
and the spread of egalitarian ideas are partly responsible, but wider
opportunities for friendship in educational institutions also promote this relaxation. Of the Pune students questioned in 1970-1
a massive 94.5% said they forget rules of caste and religion with
friends, and eat what is offered to them. Among the South Indian
students 70% had personal friends who were not Hindus, and
90% said they did or would eat with non-Hindus: however, most
of these could or would do so only in public places, not at home.
This 'compartmentalization' is a common phenomenon, affecting
many professional people as well as students. The work place,
whether college, office or factory, may be ritually neutral and its
relationships unaffected by caste. But at home people who at work
appear caste-less and 'modern' slip back into more traditional
habits and attitudes, apparently without a sense of strain or
contradiction.[24]

Further evidence of the vitality of caste divisions is the fate of
the 'untouchables', those ritually degraded people whose offices
are essential to the functioning of Hindu society and the purity of
the higher castes. Although the status of untouchability has been
abolished by the constitution and subsequent legislation, many
people continue to treat the ex untouchables in the old way; and
the law is often a dead letter rather than a powerful weapon of
social reform. Violence against ex-untouchables is commonly reported, reaching the gravity of murder on occasion for such
'offences' against old patterns of avoidance as walking down a
village street inhabited by Brahmins. Cases of violence and insult

appear to be on the increase.[25] Such manifestations are more common in tight-knit village communities. The world of the educated is more tolerant. But it is also cushioned by the fact that comparatively few untouchables reach the ranks of the highly educated, so problems of relationship as among equals, and of competition, do not arise to the same extent.

An insight into the values accepted in the social world of educated Hindus comes in discussion on India as a secular state. By virtue of its post-independence constitution the Indian state claims to be secular: to have no affiliation to a particular religion, and to treat all its citizens equally, regardless of caste or creed. There is still some criticism of this by orthodox Hindus, who feel that this stance strikes at the heart of the Hindu religion, and undercuts public and private morality, whereas in traditional Hindu thought it is the duty of the state to establish the life of religion in the hearts of its subjects.[26] However, my own conversations and observations and the results of group studies suggest that most educated Hindus have no quarrel with the idea of India as a secular state. Most of the Pune student group in 1970-1 favoured it; and those Pune students questioned later in the same decade agreed by the large majority of 77.5% that the state should be neutral in matters of religion. But the common definition of 'the secular state' is different from that accepted in the West: this was noted in Chapter 1. To the Indian using this English term the secular state is not one which is divorced from religion or uninterested in religion. It is one which maintains an attitude of respectful and cordial impartiality to all religious traditions; which provides a framework in which all religions can flourish in mutual tolerance.[27]

This approval for official tolerance does not mean that educated Hindus have any wish to see the 'secularization' of Indian society on the lines which they think is occurring in Britain or America. (Whether their interpretation of what is occurring in Britain is accurate is of course another matter.) They do not reject India's cultural heritage, despite their unease with certain parts of it; nor are they happy when they see their children adopting some 'Western' attitudes and styles which they associate with vulgarity, immorality and irreligion. In educated Hindu reaction to the West there is much ambiguity: but the image of the West projected in films is not a little to blame for the hostility of many to what they see as Western standards and values.

Indian society could not be called 'secular' in the sense of 'uninfluenced by religion'. Its public and private spheres are still shot through with religious symbolism and custom. But it does seem that certain areas of life are no longer considered to be subject to religious authority. Areas of life are to some extent being differentiated, separated out into distinct spheres, each governed by its own priorities and standards – political, social, economic or religious, although this process of differentiation has not gone as far as in Britain. One reason is the slighter social change in India. Another is the strand in Christian thinking (mentioned in Chapter 1) which permits separation between 'religious' and 'secular' to a far greater extent than does Hindu tradition, which is mediated through the social order and practised in the social setting of caste.

It is sometimes said that, compared with those brought up in a Western tradition, Indians are more prepared to accept different values in different contexts without strain. Compartmentalization of the traditional sphere of home is one aspect of this, and observers have noted other areas of life where there appears contradiction to the outsider, but apparently not to those within the situation. Such general characteristics or attitudes are hard to prove. But if this is true it would be one reason why educated Hindus appear cheerfully to combine modern scientific knowledge, openness to social change, and concern for effective economic planning, with much that appears traditional and even irrational. The former does not spill over into the increasingly compartmentalized sphere of religion and cause a sense of crisis.[28]

Another force preserving Hindu tradition is the intermeshing of Indian culture, soaked as it is in the Great Tradition, with a powerful sense of Indian national identity. Not even Indians who consider themselves to be unbelievers or secular in their private lives would want to decry Hindu tradition and its considerable renaissance and re-interpretation at the hands of religious and political leaders in the last hundred years. To do so would appear contemptuous of India itself and of the 'Indian' spirit.[29]

A very powerful aspect of change in India which helps shape the environment in which Hindu religious experience retains or loses vitality can be found in the implicit and explicit assumptions on which the state of India has operated since 1947. Increasingly government personnel, regulations, laws and administrative structure impinge on the lives of ordinary people, in striking contrast with the colonial era when the British maintained a system of light and non-interventionist government, for reasons of financial economy as well as fear of meddling with a society they only partially understood. Now the state deliberately moulds India's society and economy, sets the standards and goals of public life, and attempts to create an overtly national community in place of the old India

with its regional diversity and diffuse authority structures. This
changes the public environment in which Hindu traditions and
values have to 'prove' themselves.[30]

There has been much argument over the extent to which the
Indian state is 'secular' in the sense of being separate from religion,
as church and state are separate in Western 'secular states'. Such
strict separation is virtually impossible where religion, because of
its relation to the social order and its lack of internal 'ecclesiastical'
government, cannot be relegated to a separate sphere and governed
by an autonomous 'church'. The Indian government finds itself
willy-nilly involved in legislation on social matters which infringes
on Hindu tradition. It is forced to deal with problems of Hindu
temple property and endowments just because there is no church
to which there can be delegation of such responsibility. The courts
attempt to define a separate sphere of an essential core of 'religion'
in which they do not interfere; but in practice this proves almost
impossible. The Western categories of religious and secular just
cannot contain the ambiguities and complexities of the Indian
situation. Consequently the norms of India's 'secular state' have a
strong influence on the vitality and acceptability of Hindu traditions and structures.[31]

For example, the traditional Hindu social order is built on the
concept of hierarchy and inequality: religious tradition demands
and sanctions inequality, between castes and between men and
women. The Indian state, however, treats its citizens as individuals,
valuing them equally for their essential humanity rather than dif-
ferentially on account of their ascriptive status, their religion or
their sex. The abolition of untouchability by law is one striking
aspect of this assumption of equality, as is the stream of post-
independence legislation designed to raise the status of women
nearer to an equality with that enjoyed by men. Caste as such has
not been abolished; this would be impossible just with the tools of
law or administrative action. But castes as such receive no constitutional protection, and one of the most strident slogans of successive governments has been to 'abolish casteism' in the new
nation's life. The value of each individual as an equal citizen is also
enshrined in the practice of total adult suffrage.

The state supports standards contrary to Hindu tradition by its
massive investment in modern education. As we have seen, implicit
in the educational system, as well as explicit in some parts of the
curriculum, are ideas of individual worth, equality of people and
races, the possibility of individual mobility in space and in society,
and the propriety and efficacy of human planning and reform. It

is not just a question of importing techniques and knowledge which do not touch the core of those who are exposed to them. These are not neutral values, but powerful assumptions which help mould the thought forms of pupils. Social manipulation and economic planning swung into top gear with a series of five-year plans after independence, designed to create a 'socialist pattern of society'. Secular mechanisms are publicized as the means to the solution of India's social and economic problems. At least in the state's eyes (whatever its official rejection of a secular or irreligious *society* as opposed to secular *state*) 'salvation' is proclaimed in secular terms without reference to any transcendental powers: the means are of human contrivance, not divine dispensation.[32]

Indian governments have also involved themselves in the reform of Hindu institutions. Temples and monasteries, with their enormous funds and potential for influence in public life, as well as for the misuse of funds donated by the faithful, have come under state scrutiny through the Hindu Religious Endowments Commission and are increasingly subjected to governmental regulation and supervision. The state cannot stand aside. Where there is no religious authority capable of initiating and controlling reform, it finds itself drawn in to regulate where practices offend against modern assumptions of propriety. In relation to traditions rather than institutions and organizations, it also feels constrained to step in and reform where no religious body exists to do so. Cases in point are personal and family law: bigamy has been forbidden, divorce permitted, laws passed regulating the age of marriage. By its involvement in reform the state in fact challenges parts of the Hindu tradition and sets its standards up against those of the older religious world view. Moreover its reforming activities have changed the locus of authority for social regulation in Indian society. Caste councils can no longer set the standards of behaviour of their members in these crucial spheres: Hindu *pandits* trained in the scriptures do not provide the only principles for solving problems of social behaviour. India's citizens must look to the one government and its democratically elected legislators for authority in such matters. These new legislators are not only deeply influenced by new standards, but are responsible to their voters who have a wide variety of interests and wishes. Unlike older sources of social authority and regulation, contemporary law-givers are not motivated primarily by a desire to understand and maintain tradition, nor are they proficient in traditional learning.

Whatever the theory of the separation of state and religion, enshrined in the phrase 'secular state', India's governments have not stood aside from religious matters. But neither have they tried to 'secularize' society and politics. For example, parties overtly based on caste and religious loyalty are permitted to function, though Hindu communalist parties were temporarily banned after Gandhi's assassination by Hindu fanatics in 1948. Moreover, prominent government figures and institutions are often visibly involved in activities which proclaim the Great Tradition. In part this reflects the inseparability of religion and India's cultural heritage: in preserving the latter, the government is involved in publicizing the former. *Bhajans* are broadcast on All-India Radio, which is a government monopoly. Government subsidies support the translation of Hindu scriptures and the performance of classical dancing, developed in South Indian temples as part of worship. Government officials are present at religious functions and visit Hindu teachers. Interestingly, many educated Indians do not see this as improper for officials of a 'secular state'. Of the Pune students questioned in 1976, 71.5% felt that the official presence of government representatives at religious ceremonies (of whatever denomination) was not contrary to the principle of India as a secular state.

What picture then emerges from the pieces of the jigsaw? The Hindu world is clearly not a static one. The Hindu religious experience must prove itself authentic in an environment which is changing at a pace and to a degree unsurpassed in India's recent history. Many of these changes and pressures on the old order are in subtle ways hostile to Hinduism as a religious tradition imbedded in a particular social situation. But Indian society could in no sense be called secular, and many of the outward manifestations of religion are still strong, both in public and private life.

It would probably be wrong to talk of a sense of religious crisis in contemporary India. This is partly because change has been slower and less widespread than in Britain, as we shall see; and partly because Hindus know that their traditions have in the past proved immensely flexible and capable of adaptation. Another reason is the nature of Hindu 'belief'. It is not as easy in the Hindu as in the Christian context to define people as 'believers' or 'unbelievers'. Most Indians call themselves Hindus because they are so by birth, culture and participation in Indian society. A stark, personal choice for faith is not demanded of them, and does not mark them out in the way that belief now does a Christian in Britain. Many educated Hindus are therefore little troubled by the religious implications of changes in Indian society; they may be apathetic and unthinking on religious matters. Or where they do perceive the impact of change on religious beliefs and practices, they are content to let others defend the traditions and modify them for modern consumption, being unwilling to appear 'un-Indian' by any overt criticism of the new reformers.

Among those who think more deeply and self-consciously about their religious inheritance there is, however, considerable appreciation that changes in attitudes are occurring as a result of contact with the West and that these new aspirations and values are often not in harmony with some aspects of Hindu teaching or practice. Many are apprehensive lest oppressive and inegalitarian social structures which have been the framework of the transmission of Hindu thought should damn Hinduism *in toto* in the eyes of the world and of their compatriots. Quite ordinary, educated people with whom I discussed such things, college students, housewives, doctors, broadcasters and university lecturers, who would not claim to be religious 'experts', are aware of the need for adaptation in social customs and structures at the very least, if Hindu traditions are to be viable in a changing India. Some Hindus take refuge in gloom at the prospect of change, particularly those who have been brought up in deeply traditional environments or earn their living through Sanskrit learning or ritual ministrations.[33] Others see the changes in India and the questions these raise for Hindu society as an invitation to be met creatively. The Ramakrishna Mission, for example, preaches the 'gospel' of Vedanta and engages in social service, determined to make the traditions relevant to urban and educated Hindus. Local institutions such as the Jnana Prabodhini in Pune work for a revival of Hinduism through religious instruction, social work and education, aware that religious practice must change if some of the core Hindu ideals are to hold their own in modern society, while parallel bodies produce new or remodelled rites to mark the turning-points in individual and family life – an intriguing equivalent of Christian liturgical reform!

There is also ample literary evidence of serious thought, even ferment, among writers deeply committed to Hindu traditions and insights yet determined that they should not hinder India's development in the modern world. They sift what they see as 'acceptable' and 'essential' elements in the older religious teachings and rework them for their contemporaries in India and abroad.[34] For internal consumption there is a flood of tracts from numerous ashrams and their leaders, which expound 'Hinduism for modern man'. As they deal with moral and spiritual problems confronting individuals they bear witness to and attempt to resolve some of the tensions inherent in the religious experience in a changing world. They demonstrate what our other evidence has suggested: that there is still much vitality and potential for a creative response to change in the Hindu vision of the meaning of man and his world, though the articulation and practical working out of that vision is changing. Some of the implications of this will concern us in Chapters 4 and 5, when our comparison turns to the two other fundamentals of the religious experience which our educated Hindus and Christians share – the networks of authority which confirm men in their cosmic vision and the webs of communication which transmit them; and the patterns of behaviour through which men respond to their vision.

Table A: Religious Observances of Pune Lecturers

Ritual	Believers	Agnostics	Atheists
Rituals in homes	90%	87.5%	81.3%
Deities' birthdays celebrated in homes	71%	37.5%	44.1%
Other festivals – e.g. Diwali	97%	93.5%	97.6%

Source: V. G. Pundlik, 'Religion in the Life of College Teachers'

Table B: Observance of Various Rites

Nature of Observance	(1) Pune Lecturers Believers	Agnostics	Atheists	(2) Urban Elite	(3) South Indian Students	(4) Hindus among Pune Students	(5) Pune educated Women	(6) Bombay Young Adults
Sacred Thread Ceremony	73%	41.7%	32.6%	51%	100% (of eligible males)	—	—	—
Fasts	55%	35.4%	18.6%	—	—	—	94.3%	—
Marriage (religious) actual or intended	79%	58.3%	48.8%	—	74%	—	—	—
Marriage (civil) actual or intended	2%	4.2%	25.6%	—	—	36.5%	—	—
Visits to temples/shrines, etc. **Daily	3.5%	0%	0%	Regularly 29%	* Regularly 47%	—	—	Sometimes 63.3%
Occasionally	66%	72.9%	23.3%	Irregularly 49%	Rarely/Never 50%			Often 21.6%
Never	7.5%	18.8%	62.8%					Never 11.6%

Sources:
Column (1) V. G. Pundlik, 'Religion in the Life Of College Teachers'.
Column (2) B. D. Varadachar, 'Socialisation and Social Change'. *Dimensions of Social Change in India*, ed. M. N. Srinivas, S. Seshaiah and V. S. Parthasarathy, p. 386.
Column (3) P. H. Ashby, *Modern Trends in Hinduism*, p. 54
Column (4) G. Poitevin, 'Quelle sécularisation? des dieux ou des hommes?' *Spiritus*, 64, XVII, p. 253.
Column (5) S. Kirtane, 'The Religious Practices of the Educated Women in Poona', cited in Pundlik, op. cit., Appendix I.
Column (6) Survey of religious and social attitudes of young adults, conducted by 3 Sophia College students, February 1978.

Notes: ** M. Zaveri found similar figures among 100 Gujarati Hindu men lecturers, cited in Pundlik, op. cit, Appendix I. When asked how often they visited places of worship, 4 replied daily, 12 replied once a week, 33 replied occasionally, 43 replied rarely, and 8 replied never.
  * These figures are for attendance while at University, not at home.

Chapter Three

How Dead are the Gods?
The Christian Experience

=

Educated Hindus who anxiously watch their children's fascination
with the West as it is filtered to them through books, magazines
and films are not alone in accepting stereotypes of Western societies. Many who live in the West also talk glibly of 'the decline
of religion', 'the permissive society', and 'secularization' – often
with little thought of what these shorthand phrases mean in the
actual lives of men and women. Their reasons for so doing are
diverse. Some are just ignorant. Others wish that such states and
processes *should* occur; or conversely, those who lead moral and
revivalist crusades wish to paint the contemporary scene as godless
and immoral. Yet others hope to profit from dramatic headlines
hinting at the exposure of decadence and scandal. Consequently
our examination of the Christian experience in contemporary Britain must start with observable facts and not from any overarching
theory or easy generalization.

In gathering the evidence from which to piece together a picture
of contemporary Christianity we are much better provided than in
the Hindu case. There are statistics for church membership and
religious practices collected over a considerable period of time
which have been interpreted with increasing skill and sophistication. These tell us about Britain as a whole, particular regions, and
specified social and age groups. For this enquiry I have not only
relied on published evidence. Because the main focus of this book
is on educated Christians, and on the comparability of their experience with that of educated Hindus, I conducted two surveys in
my own University of Manchester to parallel as closely as possible
the two unpublished surveys by Indians in Pune and Bombay
amongst university lecturers and educated adolescents repsectively.
My questionnaire to lecturers went to 183, from departments in
the Faculties of Arts, Science and Law, to include as wide a span
of academic disciplines as possible. 81 responded; three returned

the forms but declined to fill them in: this was a response rate of
just over 44%. My questionnaire to students went to the 263 in
the Department of History, covering all three years of the various
history honours courses. 106 replied – a response rate of just over
40%. Because these two samples are small I cannot claim that the
figures which emerge from the enquiry are representative of people
involved in higher education throughout Britain. However, they
are of value when set against the statistics for the whole country;
and particularly so in the context of our cross-cultural comparison
because they are a sample so similar to that worked on in India.

We now turn to the evidence. As in the Hindu case we must
look at outward practices, the inner belief and piety which makes
sense of and vitalizes the outward forms, and the strength of
religious institutions. But here the churches will be our focus rather
than the social framework, because they, rather than social institutions, are the main mediators of the Christian religious experience. As in our study of India we must also assess the extent to
which current social and state norms confirm or weaken the Christian world view and patterns of religious observation.

In Chapter 1 we noted that it was historically improbable, and
certainly not proven statistically or otherwise, that earlier centuries
were 'ages of faith', or that the ancestors of twentieth-century
Britons were uniformly 'religious' in their attitudes and habits. We
do, however, have some firm nineteenth-century evidence to use as
a starting-point from which to trace patterns of religious change,
particularly the 1851 Religious Census. On one chosen Sunday
36% of the population attended church. But religious observance
varied markedly from area to area, and between social groups.
Large towns were lamentably 'irreligious' in terms of church-going
compared with small towns and country areas. In the slums there
was alienation from all the churches. Among the middle classes
church-going boomed, and among the lower middle classes, those
in positions of social deference such as servants, and the decreasing
rural population, church-going also remained the normal habit.[1]

Statistics apparently indicating change since the mid-nineteenth
century do have to be treated with care and taken in their social
context. Church-going patterns mirror such demographic factors
as the age of the population and the degree to which it has been
uprooted from village society, as much as loss of belief. Moreover,
different churches use different criteria for membership while religious observances, such as attendance at communion, do not have
the same significance for all denominations. With these warnings

in mind we can observe the religious scene in twentieth-century Britain which is the context for the Christian experience.

In the early 1960s the largest religious grouping in Britain was of those who accepted the label 'C of E' – about 60% of the population. The other 40% were Free Church (10%), Church of Scotland (10%), Roman Catholic (10%), small sects including Muslims and Hindus (4%). Only 5% would not accept *any* religious label. However, acceptance of a label tells us little about commitment to a church or the reality of an individual's religious experience. (For example, in 1958 only 23% of confirmed Anglicans made their Easter communion. Large numbers of those who call themselves Catholic are also inactive: in 1962 only about 40% of Roman Catholics attended Mass weekly.) The main trend, however, has been one of decline in active church membership. This decline has been erratic rather than chronologically steady. It has affected rural areas least, and is not uniform across the denominations. The proportion of Catholics in the population has increased because of Irish and Continental immigration, high fertility and church policy towards mixed marriages, as well as conversions. The Free Churches have continuously lost members in this century, while the Church of England has also lost adherents, though least in rural dioceses such as Hereford, Carlisle and Gloucester.[2]

We now narrow our focus to the more highly educated in Britain. A survey of third-year students at Oxford, Cambridge and Bangor, published in 1967, revealed 28% who considered themselves to be convinced and practising members of Christian churches. Of these 16% belonged to the Church of England and the Church in Wales.[3] Just over a decade later, of the students questioned at Manchester University only 26.4% admitted to *no* religious label. 51.3% of the Manchester lecturers questioned at the same time declined a denominational or religious identity. (Among both groups the largest denomination was the Church of England, followed by the Roman Catholics.) The large difference in the number of non-affiliated in the two groups is striking, because the more predictable pattern, judging by other studies, would be for church allegiance to drop off among the 18-30-year-old age group, whereas in this case the younger generation are markedly more church-orientated than their teachers. Far larger samples would be needed, however, to test whether this is a national phenomenon of a minor religious boom among students or an oddity produced by other factors such as the type of students who are admitted to read history at Manchester University. Further evidence of religious affiliation is the number of students and lecturers who are baptized and confirmed.

Amongst students belonging to churches where baptism and confirmation are separate rites 64.1% had been baptized and confirmed, and 35.9% baptized only. Among lecturers in similar
churches 78.6% had received both rites, while only 21.4% had
been baptized and not confirmed. On this evidence 'institutional
drop-out' between babyhood and adolescence has clearly increased
in the last two generations.

Church membership figures are not the best guide to the place
of Christian faith and the churches in people's lives. There may
well be 'members' for whom belonging is a formal label to be hung
out at the end of a hospital bed, while others may admit to belief
in God but have no ecclesiastical affiliation. Evidence of actual
church-*going* is a slightly more reliable guide to the real significance
of religion for people, though even these statistics mask a wide
range of commitment, apathy, boredom and scepticism. In the mid-
1960s, throughout the whole United Kingdom, 15% of the population attended church each Sunday, 20% were present on every
other Sunday, 25% once a month, 40% every three months, and
45% once a year. 20% turned up for special occasions such as
marriages, while about 35% never entered church for worship. In
England this represents a decline to about 15% from 25% attending church weekly in 1900. The most recent figures for Sunday
church-going in the mid-1970s were gathered for a BBC television
Anno Domini programme by the Opinion Research Centre, and
showed that 14% of the population attended once a week, 21%
once a month, and 47% once a year or at least they wished it to
be thought that they did![4]

Turning again to the more educated, several studies indicate the
church-going habits of selected groups. In the mid-1960s a sixth-
form survey of 4,000 children at 25 schools revealed that 57%
attended church once a week, 12% once a month, and 31% less
regularly. Over a decade later a 1978 survey of 959 school children
of 14-18 years from different types of schools produced a markedly
different result. 33% reported that they never attended church; but
13% attended weekly, 8% once a month, and 44% just occasionally (3% did not reply). Obviously parents' habits and pressures
have a major influence on the extent to which school children go
to church, and it is difficult to compare these two results because
we do not know if the parental backgrounds were similar, and
because the 1978 sample was so much smaller. When students
more removed from the home environment have been questioned,
their practices more closely conform to the national pattern across
the whole population. Among a group of students questioned in

the mid-1960s 32% attended almost every week or fairly frequently, 20% attended sometimes, and 48% very rarely or never.[5] The church-going habits of Manchester students and lecturers in 1978 are listed in Table C (p. 86). They, too, indicate rather more than 30% attending regularly.

Even more interesting is the cross-tabulation of belief and worship among the two Manchester groups, set out in Table E (p. 87). This shows that of those who claim to be believers in God, between 50% and 60% attended church regularly, while a significant proportion (between a quarter and a half) of agnostics attend church sometimes. Only the atheists appear to have abandoned church almost completely, apart from invited, social occasions. Belief and church-going are evidently not identical. The fact that so many still believe in God but do not express and receive support for that belief through the external forms with which the churches have traditionally ministered to their flocks is highly significant. We shall return to this in Chapter 5, in our consideration of the dilemma of finding an authentic contemporary spirituality. It will be even more marked in the following section on the evidence of personal attitudes and private practices compared with the bald statistics for public observation. But before looking at the inner world of the contemporary Christian experience it is worth reviewing some further evidence of the public vitality of Christianity in twentieth-century Britain.

One of the major functions of religion in all societies has been to help men make sense of inevitable changes and crises in human existence, and to mark these occasions with rites which can in some measure make them endurable and meaningful. It is still very rare, though possible, to die in Britain and avoid the ministrations of a Christian minister over one's remains. The major turning-points always marked by religious ritual in previous generations on which there is now real choice are marriage and birth. Marriages in the Anglican Church, for example, have fallen from 907 per 1,000 in 1844, to 698 in 1899, 496 in 1957 and 474 in 1962. By 1962, of every 1,000 marriages 296 were according to civil ceremonies, but in 1978 it was reported that the number of civil marriages had for the first time overtopped the number solemnized in churches. The older pattern of religious marriage was reflected plainly in the survey of Manchester lecturers; among the married over 80% had been married with a religious ceremony. The baptism figures among students compared with lecturers quoted earlier follow the declining trend in society as a whole.[6] Considerably fewer parents are choosing to affiliate their babies to churches through this rite, and are declining to mark the naming of their children with the traditional religious ceremonial.

The churches are manifestly no longer the guardians of *rites de passage* considered essential for the smooth functioning of British society, except in the case of death. They still cater for many who are not regular church-goers; and this suggests that no other institution is fulfilling quite the same function. But there are many for whom the churches' ministrations have lost not only religious meaning but social significance even at these crises of personal and family life. This is in striking contrast to the Indian evidence that social life is still inextricably interwoven with Hindu rites and ceremonies, and that even self-confessed agnostics and atheists find it hard to disentangle themselves from traditional obligations and patterns of observance.

Although traditional outward observations of the Christian faith appear to be on the wane in Britain, there are ways in which modern technological developments are permitting new patterns of participation in religious activities. On the one hand industrialization and the growth of town life has uprooted people from the routine of village living of which church-going was an integral part, while family cars often take parents and children away from church and Sunday school in search of relaxation and pleasure. But on the other hand radio and television project Christianity at least potentially into virtually all Britain's homes. Here are media for communicating the faith more widespread and effective than earlier generations of preachers and evangelists could have dared to hope for. The churches have recognized this, and the broadcasting authorities cooperate with them in providing air time for religious programmes. (That BBC and ITV and local radio do so indicates not only that they feel it is their duty in some measure to support Christianity but also that it is in their interests, as there are audiences for such programmes.)

In 1978 BBC Radio regularly broadcast four and a half to five hours of religious programmes each week, taking Radios 1, 2 and 4 together. In the same year it put out between forty-four and a half and forty-five hours of special religious programmes; and this figure did not include those planned for Christmas. Live coverage of ceremonies in Rome in the 'year of the three Popes' would also have bumped up these figures. People do not have to listen, of course. But there is evidence that many do, even if it is only because they leave their sets switched on for background company and amusement. The People's Service on Sundays on Radio 2 has an average audience of one and a half million, while half a million listen to the Sunday morning worship on Radio 4. The weekday breakfast spot, 'Thought for the Day', attracts one and a half million listeners. BBC television and ITV also carry religious programmes on Sundays, special occasions and specifically religious festivals. On Sundays about 24% of the adult population watch BBC's religious programmes and 18% watch ITV's equivalents. The most popular programme is BBC's 'Songs of Praise', which attracts about 35% of the population each Sunday evening. About 45% of adults watch or listen to Sunday broadcast services.[7]

It is of course impossible to measure the seriousness with which listeners and viewers approach such services, their effects on personal faith and life; or to judge whether vicarious hymn singing is a religious experience or an armchair exercise in nostalgia. However, there is in television and radio not only the potential for a new form of religious participation without having to attend a church or public occasion; there is also opportunity for serious religious enquiry which would be beyond the resources of local churches and the capacities of most ministers. In 1977 BBC television screened a documentary, 'Who was Jesus?', led by a Cambridge theologian. This programme searched for the Jesus behind the gospel stories, making available in the process to viewers the results of modern biblical scholarship and the insights of contemporary theology. Radio 3 in 1978 broadcast the Bampton Lectures on 'Creation and the World of Science'. Radio 4 presented studies of C. S. Lewis, William Barclay, Pope John Paul I, and the controversial Anglican Bishop Hugh Montefiore, to name only a few twentieth-century Christian thinkers and leaders; it also broadcast enquiries into the churches in Latin America, Eastern Europe, Italy, South Africa and England. BBC radio and television ran a parallel and complementary series on the world's great religions, entitled 'The Long Search' and 'The Long Search Continues'. The quantity as well as the quality of such religious broadcasting must be set against the evidence of the churches' institutional decline. The potential of the mass media, including the vast market for paperback theology and works of devotion, is part of the context of the contemporary Christian experience in Britain.

But what goes on in the inner, private lives of individuals who make up the faceless statistics for public observance? In Britain there are still residual social pressures on people to remain within range of the churches, for white weddings and Christmas midnight services, for example. But these pressures are not nearly so great or continuous as those constraining Indians to keep up the exterior of Hindu custom. Therefore we must delve more deeply into the

inner, more hidden world of the individual, if we are to assess the
vitality of the Christian experience. What do people say they believe, and what religious actions do they perform in private when
convention need not be regarded and 'what the neighbours say' is
irrelevant?

Our material has already shown that far more people believe in
God than attend church; and that although church-going has
slumped in the last hundred years there has not been any equivalent
decline in belief. Surveys of the British population in the 20 years
after the Second World War indicated that about 80% believed in
God, half of these envisaging God in personal terms, the other half
using the name to denote some force or spirit controlling life. The
percentage who believe in a personal God seems to have dropped
in the last decade. By the mid 1970s only 29% of those polled for
the *Anno Domini* programme mentioned earlier said that they
believed in a personal God. Studies of adolescents in their last years
at school revealed that between 66% and 75% definitely believed
in God in the early 1960s. By contrast, the 1978 survey of just
under 1,000 school children in their final years of school discovered
that 26% definitely believed in God, 26% believed at times, 36%
thought they believed but were not sure, while only 12% said they
definitely did not believe. Patterns of belief among university students and lecturers are rather different from those of the whole
population. Far more of these groups label themselves as agnostics
or atheists, and the percentages of those who believe are far lower
than those of their Indian counterparts. Table E (p. 87) sets this
out in detail.[8]

Of course declaration of 'belief in God' does not imply acceptance of traditional Christian theological formulations on a wide
range of issues such as the person of Jesus, the after-life, sin and
salvation. As in the case of our educated Hindus we must enquire
a little further into the theological sophistication of belief and the
hold on men's minds of the Christian 'Great Tradition'. From
recent surveys of the population at large it appears that about 45%
believe in life after death: in fact a quarter of these professed to
believe in reincarnation, which is a Hindu rather than a Christian
belief, while 21% visualized the after life in scriptural terms of hell
and heaven. 64% professed to believe that Jesus is the Son of God,
while 66% are more or less sure that he can save from sin. The
Devil is evidently not so credible: only 18% believe in him. 25%
believe that the miracles reported in the Bible actually happened,
and 10% believe in the literal truth of the Bible.[9]

A study of students in the 1960s showed individuals picking and choosing elements of belief which they could accept, and even the practising church members among them not feeling bound to accept a total belief package of orthodox theological formulations. Only 1 in 3 of the students who were practising Christians believed in hell, while 12% of them were sceptical about an after-life at all. Students were also very selective about accepting as historically true the Bible record of events. 88% of the total believed that Jesus was actually crucified (100% of church members); 25% believed in Jesus' ascension (65% among church members); and 19% believed that Jesus was born of a virgin (51% of church members). Deep ignorance of the Bible also emerged from this enquiry. One orthodox Christian student, hoping to be ordained, had never heard of Jericho![10] Scripture questions on children's quiz programmes such as 'Top of the Form' underline the haziness of many intelligent young people about the source book of Christianity. Among Manchester students questioned in 1978, 58.5% said that theological statements had meaning for them. This did not imply belief in such statements, however. More interesting is the fact that only just over 70% of 'believers' found theological statements meaningful: 30% did not. (Of the major Christian denominations, Roman Catholic students clung most firmly to the validity of theological formulations. 84.2% found such statements meaningful, compared with 47.5% of those who labelled themselves C of E.)

The importance of the religious experience in the life of the individual is very difficult to assess. There is limited statistical evidence of how people actually rate the significance of their religion. The 1978 schools survey of late teenagers shows 6% of the total rating religion as 'very important' in their everyday life. 32% replied 'fairly important', 40% 'not very important', and 22% 'not at all important'.[11] Of the Manchester students questioned the same year 39.6% said that religion had an important place in their lives, and 57.5% replied that it did not. In contrast the Bombay adolescents (asked the same question in the same year) were evenly split at just under 50% each way. Predictably in both cases more girls felt that religion was important to them (48% of Manchester girl students compared with 34% of men students; just over 63% of girls in the Bombay sample compared with just over 33% of boys). The boys' responses in the two cities, separated by over 7,000 miles and centuries of religious tradition, were virtually identical. Among the Manchester students who gave themselves a denominational label, 52.5% of Anglicans admitted that religion did *not* have an important place in their lives, while only 15.8% of Roman Catholics made the same admission. Other denominations were too sparsely represented in the sample to allow for comparison.

Among the Manchester lecturers who replied that they adhered to a religion (51.9% of the total), 83.8% said that they considered religion to be an important element in their lives. This suggests that for those who have reached adulthood and professional stability and still accept a religious label religion is far more than convention or a casual affiliation to a church. This is confirmed by the lecturers' replies to the question whether they adhered to their religion for social reasons alone. Among those to whom the question applied, a minute 5.3% said that social reasons alone kept them within a religious affiliation. This contrasts markedly with the Pune lecturers, for whom social pressures to conform to Hindu custom and continue with religious rituals were far stronger.

What people actually *do* about religion in private is a better indicator of the inner vitality of the Christian experience. As in the contrast between figures for belief and church-going, the evidence suggests the continuing strength of a religious vision, or at least a hankering after religious experience, which may well have no correlation with adherence to or attendance at a particular church. In the total adult population about 44% claim to pray daily, while 58% teach their children to pray. Among the smaller, highly educated groups studied fewer appear to pray daily, but a substantial proportion pray, even though erratically. Among the students Rees questioned in the mid-1960s only 48% claimed *never* to pray, while 34% prayed sometimes, and 18% regularly.[12] Manchester evidence for patterns of prayer among students and lecturers is collected in Table F (p. 88). It shows that prayer is not confined to those who claim definitely to believe in God; and, furthermore, that a sizeable minority of believers pray rarely or not at all. Only Roman Catholics and Anglicans were large enough denominational groups to compare for the frequency of prayer. Among both staff and students a higher percentage of Anglicans never pray (16.7% of Anglican students and 10% of Anglican lecturers compared with 10.5% and 0% among their Catholic counterparts). A markedly higher percentage of Roman Catholics pray daily (42.1% of Catholic students and 57.1% of Catholic staff compared with 23.8% and 30% of their C of E counterparts). These figures also show that though the student group was more 'religious' in terms of belief than the lecturers, once lecturers had committed themselves to faith they tended to pursue and sustain that faith more wholeheartedly, to judge from their practice of private prayer.

Because the Pune evidence showed the enormous importance of

family worship and rituals to Hindu lecturers, I thought it was
worth enquiring into the strength of Christianity as a *family* experience among the comparable group in England. Among those
Manchester lecturers who actually live in a family and answered
the question, just over 20% observed some family religious rite.
Family prayers and grace before meals were the most frequent.
Almost all those who do observe such rites as a family are
'believers'; but it is significant that well under half (40.7%) of
'believers' do *not* try to make Christianity a family experience
through such means. However, well over half (63.2%) of 'believers'
made sure that their children received religious instruction at home,
and even more saw that one of the parents took them to church
(73.7%). 69.6% of 'believers' had also arranged or intended to
arrange that their children should receive a religious rite of initiation. This evidence contrasts strongly with the pattern among Hindu lecturers, for whom *family* religious observance was a strong
social framework from which it was hard to escape despite personal
beliefs. For the Christians it seemed to be far more an expression
of personal faith, and even for the 'believer' no automatic pattern.

A final indicator of the private significance of Christian faith in
contemporary Britain is the extent to which people read religious
books. Like prayer, private reading shows where individuals put
value, vision and longing. Bible reading is far less common in the
whole population than private prayer. Only about 11% read the
Bible regularly at home. In the 1978 sample of older school children
73% owned a Bible, and 80% a New Testament, but only 4% had
read the Bible on their own the day they filled in the questionnaire,
9% had read it that week, and 14% in the previous month.[13]
Among the students questioned in Manchester the same year the
figure for Bible owning was very similar, though nearly 86% of
'believing' students owned a Bible. However, even among
'believers', Bible reading was more often than not an infrequent
expression of faith. (12.5% only read it daily, 18.8% often, 39.1%
occasionally. A significant 29.7% of believing students *never* read
it. 28.6% of Anglicans and 36.8% of Catholics admitted to *never*
reading the Bible.) Among the Manchester lecturers who called
themselves 'believers' a rather higher proportion never read the
Bible – 38.7%.

The fairly low incidence of regular Bible reading tells us much
about the value contemporary educated Christians put on a source
of spiritual nourishment which has been traditionally recom-
mended as almost essential for the mature Christian, particularly
in the various Protestant traditions. However, for educated Christ-

ians in university settings other religious reading is also an important clue to whether religious and intellectual enquiry and development are occurring in step, or whether 'believers' are prepared to retain an understanding of religion probably inherited from their families. Rees concluded from his student survey in the 1960s that reading had a minor influence on young people's religious attitudes.[14] In the 1978 Manchester survey only 43.4% of students read religious books other than scripture, and just over 30% had actually bought such a book in the previous three years. Among 'believers' 54% read non-scriptural religious books, and 38.1% had bought such books in the previous three years. It is intriguing that although Catholic students appear to read the Bible somewhat infrequently they seem to read and buy other religious books more enthusiastically, and to outstrip their Anglican colleagues in this respect!

Among lecturers 55.6% felt that reading had had a major influence in shaping their attitude to religion, though this included non-religious and anti-religious books. 17.3% said they read religious books (including scripture) regularly, 39.5% occasionally, 43.2% never. Among 'believers' 56.8% felt that reading had been significant in their religious development, and only 13.5% said that they *never* read religious books. Nearly 65% of them had bought religious books in the previous five years. (Of those 'believers' who hazarded a guess at quantity, the majority had bought between two and six.) Among the books read and bought by them, theological works predominated, apart from scriptural texts. Of the 'believers' who responded to this question over 83% read theological books and 75% had actually bought such books in the past five years. Clearly among the 'believers' the majority are not prepared to 'compartmentalize' their faith but submit it to scrutiny and intellectual discipline much as they would their academic subject. This confirms the earlier evidence that 'belief' among the lecturers is not only a more significant commitment than among students, but also a greater personal commitment than 'belief' among Hindu lecturers in Pune.

We must now set these pieces of evidence about the religious beliefs and practices of educated Christians in the context of modern Britain. As we saw in the Indian case, the contemporary environment can affect the vitality and strength of a religious tradition at various levels. Every religious tradition has core assumptions, if not well articulated beliefs, specifically religious institutions which channel and propagate belief, and a supportive community of believers and sympathizers, without which those who believe will feel insecure and isolated. The social situation in which a religious tradition is set affects these three levels, and if that situation changes, so may the tradition find itself renewed or severely attacked. At the intellectual level forces may be at work which make the core beliefs of a religion increasingly untenable unless they are adjusted to meet criticism and new forms of knowledge (though it should be stressed that intellectual change affects only the educated in any society until it is generalized for the bulk of the population. Often material factors are far more important in moulding people's religious attitudes than what occurs specifically in the world of thought[15]). The structure of a society, its distribution of power among different social groups, and its demographic patterns are crucial in buttressing or eroding religious institutions and patterns of observance. More subjective but still significant, are a society's ethos and assumptions, which emerge both from its structure and its dominant ideas, whether these are barely questioned assumptions at the level of folk ideology or the articulate arguments and philosophies of the educated.

Social and demographic change has occurred in Britain in the last hundred years on an unprecedented scale. Chapter 1 stressed the great contrast with the Indian situation, where change has been less rapid and widespread. Social change in Britain has hammered the churches as credible and relevant institutions. The complexity of the interaction between the churches and a changing society is still being unravelled by sociologists of religion: what follows is only a brief sketch of some of the main trends and problems, as the setting for the experience of educated Christians, particularly for readers unfamiliar with the works of professional sociologists.[16]

The most radical shift in British society was caused by a rapid expansion of population, and the migration of vast numbers of people to towns and their commuting suburbs. This occurred while the established church at least kept its ecclesiastical framework of parishes designed to serve an agrarian society. This meant that far more town-dwellers were put in the care of one parish priest working from a single parish church than any man could possibly cope with. The Paul Report of the early 1960s painted a bleak picture of gross disparity between the work loads of the rural and urban clergy, showing that where population was densest the clergy were most strained, beset by difficulties, and had least pastoral 'success'. In the later twentieth century declining numbers further aggravated the problem.[17]

However, the transformation of an agrarian country into a densely populated, industrial society did more than just stretch the old religious institutions to the point of pastoral inefficiency and breakdown in communication. It shattered old communities and bonds between people, and eroded relationships of deference which had supported religious institutions: it undermined older patterns of behaviour, often including the habit of church-going. The transformation occurred in two stages; and in each stage change had a differential impact on different social groups. The industrial revolution of the nineteenth century, associated with heavy industry, produced Britain's large and often desolate industrial towns; it uprooted many people for ever from the secure relationships and habits of village life. A result of this social movement was a lowering of the level of outward religious practice, mainly among urban workers, and mass alienation from the churches in the squalor of the new slums. But although there was alienation from organized religion among the working class, there was rarely among them a committed atheism or secularism: generalized approval of Christianity and religion went hand in hand with a disregard for if not overt hostility towards the churches, while among the educated and socially dominant there was little change in outward religious observance.[18]

It was the second industrial revolution of the twentieth century, born of a new electronics technology, which really shattered the old society and began to create a new one which was infinitely more complex in its division of labour, social gradations and interrelationships. New work opportunities for both sexes combined with the provision of mass education created a society in which spatial and status mobility became far easier and for some groups essential. Some of the older bonds which had survived the industrial change of the previous century such as personal and domestic service, the small firm and family business, the stable close-knit family, were swept away, their disappearance hastened by the experience and aftermath of two world wars. Among the working class, social, cultural and spatial mobility *might* involve the mobile in adopting life styles which incorporated church-going. More often change atomized society at this level, wrenching individuals out of well-worn grooves, and surrounding them with the material blandishments of an increasingly consumer orientated economy. In this environment of competitive consumption older structures of discipline, including the churches, had little appeal or apparent social relevance.

Britain's young people were deeply affected by the fragmentation of society, the spread of education and their dramatically improved earning power. The growing desire to 'do one's own thing' led many to reject the roles cast for them by their parents' generation. One casualty of this change was the network of ancilliary organizations for youth provided by the churches. Sunday schools lost out, so did church youth clubs, boys' brigades and the like. This was far more a rejection of the cultural styles projected by these organizations than a rejection of religious belief or the possibility of belief. (Figures for belief among young people quoted earlier in this chapter support this interpretation.) However, this decline in participation weakened structures which had recruited adult church members in previous generations. The participation of young women in education, their entry into a better paid job market, and their exposure to siren calls for glamour and independence and the rejection of older female stereotypes from the advertising media of the consumer society, is probably of particular significance in the breakdown of older patterns of religious observance, as women have through the home generally been the main non-professional 'transmitters' of religious belief and practice.

Yet another group of people shot by their education and expertise into a perpetual cycle of physical mobility and upward social and professional aspiration are the educated, professional élite of managers, executives, teachers and the like. Detailed research is needed into the effects of their consumer-dominated milieu and geographical mobility in pursuit of their careers on allegiance to churches and religious observation. But it seems likely that in many cases these forces would weaken commitment to a church, not least because they remove such people from close-knit communities where kinship and friendships of long standing buttress church participation in communities of social interaction and pleasure as well as faith.

Contributing to these changes in society was of course a revolution in the technology not only of work but of leisure. The car and the television, though they could carry their owners in person or vicariously to places of worship, more often carried them to the seaside and the country on Sundays, or to the escape-land of the film and the Sunday serial. (It is a sign of the changing pattern of Sundays that the Catholic obligation to attend Sunday Mass can now be fulfilled on Saturday evening. Some churches have felt constrained to alter the times of their evening services to fit in with television programmes, and the decline of evensong in the Anglican tradition in part reflects the competition of television and church-going as leisure-time activity.)

However, religion and industrial society are not necessarily in-

compatible. In India people drawn into the industrial sectors have
adapted their beliefs and religious practices to suit their changed
situation. In America, the industrialized consumer society *par ex-
cellence*, where the gadgetry of leisure has reached exotic propor-
tions, religion has boomed; not just in its more orthodox forms,
but in a wide range of novel and often bizarre movements which
draw on Christian and non-Christian traditions as well as the
insights of modern psychology. In twentieth-century Britain many
have rejected the old patterns of religious association and observance, not belief itself. There are many signs that varieties of religious beliefs flourish – new and old, orthodox and distinctly
strange. Secular, rational man is a sociologist's construct, not an
individual whom you are likely to meet. Quite apart from the
numbers who still profess Christian belief or some form of deism,
there are remarkable phenomena of renewal and revivalism such
as the charismatic movement of the later twentieth century. This
will be discussed more fully in Chapters 4 and 5. In the context of
this chapter what is significant is the fact that that many of those
involved are highly educated, members of the middle class and
professional élite – some of those most affected by spatial and
social mobility. Moreover, there is a vast range of folk 'theology',
mythology and superstition which is immensely powerful. An investigation into this murky sphere of English character revealed
that 1 in 6 of the population believe in ghosts; 1 in 3 in the war-
time services carried some form of tangible, protective magic; nearly half the population has consulted a fortune teller, and nearly 2
men and over 3 women in every 10 follow astrological advice. 4
out of 5 read weekly horoscopes, though for half of these it is just
fun. In the 1978 survey of older school children only 10% *never*
read their horoscopes, but only 9% admitted to believing them,
while 26% definitely did not. 50% believed in UFOs and 41%
believed in ghosts or spirits. Among the children who were definitely connected with a church markedly fewer read and believed
their horoscopes; fewer believed in UFOs, but more (45%) believed
in ghosts.[19]
      Although social change and mass education does not appear to
have eroded the capacity for belief in the non-material, there are
other significant ways, over and above the effects of geographical
and status mobility, in which change has lessened the social significance of the churches and their clerical professionals. This century has seen a vast acceleration of social differentiation and
segmentation – the separating out of different compartments of life
– with the result that institutions and organizations are accepted

as competent and relevant in particular spheres only, while individuals perform various roles which can be distinguished from each other and often held apart in daily life. Jim Smith, for example, can see himself as a family man, a professional engineer, a trade unionist, a church member, and a wild flower enthusiast in his spare time. He wears different hats on different occasions, and adapts his behaviour to the context of his life in which he is operating. The enthusiasm for wild flowers is out of place in a trade union meeting, while his engineering expertise is left outside the church door. Similarly, institutions and organizations are not seen as omnicompetent, but equipped to cope only with particular areas of life. Welfare is the job of the social services, education is the task for schools, and health the business of the National Health Service. The family and the churches, for example, which once had competence in all these fields, now find their areas of competence and relevance reduced. To take a particular instance, it is almost impossible for a parent to teach a child at home, even if he or she is a trained teacher. Government has spread its oversight, provision and regulation into areas once the preserve of the private citizen and voluntary body. In the case of the churches, non-religious agencies have taken over the wide range of welfare roles which once they performed.

At the same time, the growth of professionalism and expertise within clearly demarcated disciplines and skills has increased the distinction between the different roles individuals perform at different times. This has had serious repercussions on the parson's role in society. No longer are clerics society's 'wise men' in matters both material and supra-material. Others are as well or better educated; others have more professional knowledge and skill and are called on to solve the predicaments of life which once were thought to be within the parson's competence. These trends, like geographical and status movements in the population, do not necessarily erode belief, but they do reduce the area of society and of personal life in which Christian institutions and professionals are perceived as significant.[20]

Intellectual currents are also part of the social situation of any religious tradition. Change at this level tends to affect the highly-educated minority first and most powerfully: 'popular religion' is far less influenced by new developments in thought and philosophy which can shake the world of those who gain their living, stimulus and pleasure through the exercise of intellectual skill. However, as our concern is the educated in Britain and India it is proper to indicate changes in thinking in this century which may affect the tenability of religious belief. In India the major intellectual changes occurred through contact with the West and particularly its educational influence. In Britain the sources of new philosophies and knowledge were far nearer home, in Britain or on the Continent, arising out of Europe's intellectual tradition and its social and political experience. Owen Chadwick's study, *The Secularization of the European Mind in the Nineteenth Century*, has shown how far advanced were changes in the world of thought and in the adaptive responses of religious formulations by the beginning of this century. Liberalism with its insistence on religious tolerance, the rationalist inheritance of the Enlightenment, scientific experiment and discovery, the influence of Marx, and the application of historical scholarship to the biblical record of the life of Jesus were powerful solvents of old religious formulations and certainties. Belief increasingly became a personal choice, to be reached at least by those for whom such trends mattered, through a painful weighing of new types of evidence about and interpretation of the fundamental nature of man, and the impact on him of*society and natural environment. Socially agnosticism and in some circles atheism became respectable; while religious affiliation and loyalty to a particular state or party were increasingly separated.

In this century trends have continued or emerged, philosophies and areas of knowledge have developed, which mean that religious belief is for many in part a real intellectual problem, and that Christianity's assertions about the nature of man have become highly questionable.[21] The works of Freud have had a revolutionary impact on the understanding of the individual and his inner development, including the tangled roots of his religious awareness in murky psychological depths which many 'religious' people would prefer to forget in preference for a simple gospel of sin and redemption. The popularization of Freud and the distortion of his discoveries in that process have been used by many as a stick to beat in themselves and others belief in God, or at least the image of God they inherited. So too had the rapid dissemination of Marxist ideas and the spread of other anti-religious ideologies and sceptical philosophies such as existentialism through the media and the educational system, all helping to create an intellectual environment where agnosticism at least is not only socially and intellectually respectable but expected. This is at the level of thought the equivalent of the erosion by structural change within society of the communities which supported Christian observance and allegiance: 'believers', at least in educated circles, have become a cognitive minority.[22] The great pioneers of the sociology of religion, Weber and Durkheim, examined the function of religion in society, respectively seeing religion as part of man's search for meaning in the face of the great problems of existence such as suffering, and as an aspect of the necessary human activity of community building. While both stressed the importance of a vital religious tradition for the well-being of any society, their analysis of the *function* of religion has tended to take many of their readers into the realm of scepticism about any religion as a gospel-bearing truth.

The contemporary intellectual scene is powerfully moulded, too, by the achievements of science. In popular estimation it is scientific discovery which has done most to erode the intellectual credibility of Christianity. There is perhaps as much of a myth about the conflict of science and religion as there is about the secularization of Western society, or the spirituality of the East. Certainly there was acrid controversy in the nineteenth century, which in fact predated Darwin's writings on the origins of man, but of which Darwin became the symbol.[23] But by our century the cruder aspects of this conflict were out of the way, and Christian teaching and biblical scholarship had responded to the challenge. Fewer Christians remained who could not hold in harmony the ideas of a Creator and the processes of evolution, or who thought that the Bible could be used as a scientific text-book rather than read as men's groping through image and parable towards the mystery of existence.

In assessing the impact of modern science on the environment in which Christianity has to maintain its intellectual credibility, it is useful to distinguish between scientific knowledge and the scientific method. The *content* of scientific knowledge does not threaten religious teaching as some nineteenth-century thinkers believed it did. Science is now so specialized that it is one if not several intellectual compartments, and its specialists do not claim that they can answer more than a limited range of questions from their limited evidence. They do not masquerade as the providers of answers to problems of the fundamental meaning of life. The disciplines of science produce their own intellectual humility. Moreover it is notable that the 1970s have seen the beginning of much anguished re-thinking about the direction in which scientific discovery is taking humanity (particularly when it is harnessed to the modern technology of warfare and the exploitation of the environment) and a deep unease and scepticism about the inevitability of human 'progress' on the strength of scientific knowledge alone.

Reflective of this non-combative relationship between scientific

knowledge and religious belief were the responses of the Manchester lecturers when asked the same question about that relationship as had been put to their Hindu counterparts in Pune. 24.7%
felt that science and religious belief were independent areas of
knowledge with no implications for each other, 40.7% felt that
they were harmonious in the sense of being different paths to an
understanding of reality, and only 14.8% felt that they were necessarily antagonistic. (17.3% felt that no one of these statements
described the relationship adequately.) Only a tiny minority of
'believers' (2.7% compared with 2.2% in the Hindu sample) felt
any tension between scientific knowledge and their faith; though
more of the British agnostics and atheists felt that such knowledge
and belief were necessarily antagonistic.

However, the *methods* associated with science profoundly affect
the environment of thought in which Christianity must sink or
swim intellectually. The observation and measurement of phenomena, the painstaking collection of evidence, and the creation of
hypotheses and models on such empirical bases are now accepted
and unquestioned parts of the contemporary British intellectual
inheritance. This has certainly not obliterated irrationality and
superstition from British culture; but it has emphasized and given
primary importance to the material and observable, and to the
processes of rational enquiry and decision-making. The areas in
which divine power is seen as causative are consequently dimin-
ished: floods, accidents, disease are explicable in terms which make
God and religion unnecessary. (This of course does not make such
calamities easier to bear, and much of the older world view is
expressed in the anguished reaction to personal tragedy still prevalent even among non-believers in such formulations as 'Why did
it have to happen to *me*?') People now assume that they can and
should manipulate the human body and psyche, their natural and
social environment, while technological achievement and the expansion of state power have given them the wherewithal to do this.

Here we enter the realm of less conscious reflection, of the
assumptions prevalent in contemporary society and its behavioural
conventions. I therefore thought it worth asking my students
whether they felt that they were reaching adulthood in a secular
society. There was evidently some confusion among them on this
issue. 20% hedged their bets and did not answer with a straight
'yes' or 'no'. 55.7% felt that British society was definitely secular,
while another 14.2% thought that it was predominantly so. The
'believers' were particularly marked in their assessment of British

society as clearly secular (66.1% compared with 35% of agnostics and 57.9% of atheists).

Britain is certainly a religiously tolerant society. No distinctions are made or discrimination exercised in society at large because of a person's religious beliefs or lack of them. The beliefs of the many migrants into the country have been absorbed into the social scene with little difficulty, from the Catholicism of the Irish and Poles to the Hindu, Sikh and Muslim beliefs of migrants from India, Pakistan, Bangla Desh and Uganda. These jostle with the colourful and exuberant Christianity of the West Indian churches in Britain's big cities. Such toleration of pluralism is the wish of the vast majority, at least of Britain's educated. (Where bitterness and prejudice against minorities does occur it is rarely caused by religious differences or expressed in religious terms.) Among Manchester University staff and students around 90% felt that there should be toleration for all religions in Britain. There was little difference in the attitudes of the different generations, or between those who do and do not personally believe. Moreover, there is almost universal support for the provision of religious education in schools. The Manchester surveys confirmed this. Large majorities of staff and students favoured it, and there was considerable support, even from agnostics and atheists. However, when the lecturers' sample were asked whether this should be according to the tenets of a particular religion or should be an introduction to major religious ideas drawn from a number of religions, a majority of those who answered this question thought that *both* types of education should be given, though a massive 90.2% favoured the 'comparative religion' approach. Even 'believers' clearly wished for far more than a particular religion to be expounded in schools; but understandably agnostics and atheists were firmest in this wish. Amongst the older school children surveyed in 1978 only 13% felt that religious education of any kind in schools should be stopped. Of the different types of religious education suggested to them as possible there was most support (43%) for the teaching of all major religions.[24]

Acceptance of religious pluralism, agnosticism and atheism goes hand in hand with general acknowledgment that religion is a personal matter. This assumption is sometimes rather inelegantly known as 'the privatization of religion'. Each individual now has to make a choice about religious faith. There can be no automatic inheritance of belief, given the scepticism of the general environment, and there is no automatic support for a choice of faith from a community structure. Society supports this state of affairs, this sceptical fluidity, in a way which would have seemed incredible to people in Britain a century ago and even more recently. Now society's norm is that what men and women do about their religious choices is their personal affair, and is not to be criticized, provided it does not lead to positive harm either to the individual concerned or to other people. (This proviso in popular thought is evident in the crash helmet controversy, in which Sikhs argued that their turbans were effective protection against motor cycle accidents and that it was contrary to their faith to remove them.)

Although in Britain religious belief is now essentially a private matter, a residual Christianity, or at least standards deeply marked by Christian teaching, still has major significance in the unspoken assumptions of contemporary British society. Christian festivals are almost universally observed and given recognition in the public calendar. (Though many Christians would argue that the essential message of Christmas has been swamped by office parties, tinsel and an adulation of the family, while Easter is little more than a time for garishly painted eggs, calorific gifts and a chance for a clothes-buying spree.) Christian rites and the presence of Christian ministers are still required for many of society's communal occasions, quite apart from their continued if attenuated guardianship of the *rites de passage* of individual and family. The Coronation is the supreme example. But the hundreds of Remembrance Day services, the annually televised Festival of Remembrance, or the singing of 'Jerusalem' by the Women's Institute, bear witness to the vitality of a deeply-rooted folk Christianity in British society. Most British people appear to have no other institutions or sets of symbols to enable them to cope meaningfully with such important occasions and experiences, either as individuals or as a community. Such very generalized Christianity has been made possible in Britain because Christianity has not been associated with a specific ecclesiastical package, as was the case in many continental Catholic countries. Patterns of widespread dissent and their relationship to politics in Britain have helped to save Britain from the sort of militant atheism and anti-clericalism which emerged in Europe in situations where political conservatism and Catholicism buttressed each other.[25]

What have in the past been seen as 'Christian standards' still significantly affect society's attitude to what is acceptable public morality. Despite a permissiveness about personal (particularly sexual) morality which has developed rapidly in the last two decades, there is considerable disquiet about 'immorality', 'deviance' and 'corruption' among public figures. This often comes close to a hypocritical acceptance of double standards – one for 'them' in public life which doesn't hold for 'us ordinary mortals' – particularly in sexual matters. But on a wide variety of non-sexual moral issues there is still genuine acceptance of norms which had their origins and justification in the Christian view of man. The public revulsion at violence (except as entertainment); the hostile reaction to strikers in the welfare services, such as the ambulance and hospital workers and grave-diggers, whose actions hit the old, poor, weak, sick and distressed in the unrest of January-February 1979, bears witness to this. Moreover, in many circles within British society there is still a highly moral seriousness, not only among the remaining Evangelicals but also among people who have abandoned Christian believing. The dissenting legacy in the lower echelons of the middle class, perpetuated in the Labour Party, is not a little responsible for this: but it is evident, too, among the intelligentsia in the ambience of humanism and radical politics.[26]

However much British society still draws on the remains of Christian moral capital for its platitudes if not its practical inspiration, the churches and their spokesmen are not at the heart of social life. Nor are their pronouncements received as from those having peculiar authority in matters of private and public morality. This was highlighted in the general disregard for the Archbishop of Canterbury's Call to the Nation of October 1975, even among practising Christians. In the matter of social norms as well as in the structures of society there has been a 'massive shift' of the churches 'from the centre to the periphery of affairs'.[27] The churches still have a large clientele in their members and those who belong to their ancilliary organizations; far larger than the adherents of any other voluntary association. But as a setter of standards organized Christianity has now to compete in an open market, greatly expanded by mass education and the media. It has no privileged position in society at large, and its teachings are often replaced or eroded by the materialism of a newly affluent, consumer society, and by utilitarian principles of conduct in which there is no place for older religious notions of divine power, providence and retribution.

Finally, the attitudes and structure of the state itself are significant aspects of the environment in which the contemporary Christian experience occurs. As on the question whether Britain is a secular *society*, I investigated among my students and colleagues their perception of the nature of the *state* in which they live. Only a minority felt that Britain is a secular state in the sense of not publicly supporting one religion, though the minority was much larger in the student group. Among the students there was little variation in their estimation according to whether they 'believed', or were agnostics or atheists. But among lecturers most agnostics and atheists were convinced that the British state is not secular. This may reflect the fact that as older people, lecturers have more factual knowledge about church-state relations, or because they remember a time when church figures and organizations were far more influential in public life. Lecturers were also asked whether Britain *should* be a secular state. 63% felt that it should be; but this majority was composed of a far larger proportion of agnostics and atheists than 'believers', of whom only just under half felt that the British state should be secular.

In fact Britain is not a secular state in the sense that it has no connection with a specific religion. There is an established church whose leaders sit in the House of Lords, whose professionals have often a marked role in civic life and ceremonial, and of which the sovereign is the head. The Coronation service is the most dramatic sign of the connection between the Anglican Church and the British state. The connection is two-way. Not only do Anglican clergy have an 'established role' in public life. The state intervenes in Anglican affairs, through Crown and Prime Minister influencing higher clerical appointments, and through Parliament adjudicating on Anglican arrangements for church worship and government. In the 1970s, however, the Church of England acquired a considerable degree of consultation and freedom in these matters. But though the state is tied by law and tradition to the Anglican Church, it is a tolerant state. There are no longer religious tests for admission to public office; Christian ministers of other denominations are often associated with Anglicans in public ceremonial. Members of all religious traditions and of none are equal citizens.

Although the constitutional framework of public life is not secular, the operations and assumptions of the state do in fact undermine the power of Christian institutions and beliefs in a number of ways. As we have already noted, the state has vastly increased its power and competence in public and private life in the last hundred years. It regulates the actions of men in spheres which a century ago would have been considered private; it provides for the welfare of its citizens in such matters as physical and mental health, recreation, housing and education, which were previously left to private charity and self-help. Consequently it bites far deeper into the pockets of its citizens through the taxation system; and this in turn gives it a further implement for the remodelling of society. *Laissez-faire* has vanished, even in the thinking of the Conservative party, banished by changes in political theory and social awareness, and the pragmatism which had to respond to the tensions engendered and the devastations wreaked by two world wars in British society. As governments have become more interventionist, more expert and more powerful, so they have absorbed many of the functions the churches once performed. But as significant as the expansion of state intervention are the assumptions and principles on which this is based.

In the first place, the very notion of planning, of engineering society and the environment, presupposes a man-centred outlook on life. It is humanist in the proper sense of the word. It places reliance on the power of rational thought and human endeavour to change the human situation. Belief that this should be so replaces belief in a divinely-ordained social and political order, and the primacy of divine providence. Human planning and engineering on this scale discounts the possibility of a God active in the universe, at least in ways traditionally understood. God has ceased to be practical politics. But what are the principles which *guide* state intervention? Very often these are fully acceptable to believing Christians and are deeply influenced by centuries of Christian thinking, or at least some strands within the Christian tradition. The multiplicity within the Christian tradition, as in the Hindu tradition, is a store-cupboard to draw from in a time of change; and this has proved a vital resource for those who retain belief as they adapt to the changing situation, as will become clearer in Chapter 5. For example, basic health, education and housing are humanitarian concerns with which no Christian can quarrel when the state takes them in hand and puts its vast resources behind them. Even the principle of redistributing wealth via taxation can be supported by aspects of Christian teaching, particularly compassion for the poor, and the equality of all men as children of God.

However, there are points of conflict between traditional Christian standards and standards which are increasingly accepted by the state, mainly through changes in the law. The potential for discord was well demonstrated in the controversies which have erupted in Britain since the late 1950s on the relationship of law and morals, particularly on such sensitive questions as homosexuality and abortion. In both cases the law has been changed in the last two decades to permit actions contrary to traditional Christian teaching. In the one instance homosexual acts in private between consenting adult men has been permitted; while in the other, abor-

tion has become legal on certain medical and social grounds. These
problems have arisen not so much because the state has made a
deliberate decision not to follow Christian teaching *per se*, but
because the mechanisms of law are sensitive to public opinion.
Members of Parliament who make the law are not only members
of the public in their own right, reflecting a wide range of religious
and moral attitudes: for their electoral survival they also have to
note the wishes of their constituents. Moreover, the enforcement
of the law becomes increasingly difficult if that law is out of step
with public opinion and does not have the acquiescence of the
majority of the community. On both these issues by the 1960s
there was a growing disjuncture between publicly accepted standards of morality and the law. Consequently the law became increasingly unenforceable, and led to compound problems such as
the possibility of blackmail in the case of homosexuals, and back-
street abortions. Changes in the law thus represented state acceptance of changing social norms. Neither change occurred without
real public conflict. Among lawyers the homosexual issue in particular precipitated a fundamental debate on the degree to which
British law should reflect Christian principles. The position now is
that the law does not automatically uphold traditional teaching,
particularly in moral matters. Some areas of life are now seen by
the law to be the private concern of the individual, unless his
actions harm other citizens. The growing plurality of British society
and the shifts in public opinion have forced the state's norms as
displayed in its laws to become more secular.[28]

This examination of contemporary Britain has indicated the
changes which influence most markedly the vitality of the Christian
vision of the meaning of man and his world. From the mosaic of
evidence emerges a picture of a society which is not peopled with
some new breed of 'secular man'. Some commentators, often from
within the safety of academic citadels, have proclaimed with joy
the emergence of this sociological phenomenon, their faith in it
buttressed by the community and sub-culture in which they operate. Some churchmen and theologians, reacting against unaccept-
able roles in which they are cast, and distressed by the ambivalence
of their position in a time of rapid change, have accepted this new
sociological gospel somewhat uncritically. However, the evidence
of contemporary society, though it shows rapid and disorientating
change, does not prove that most people are secular in the sense
of being totally out of touch with religious institutions, uninfluenced by religious traditions, or devoid of a sense of awe, fear and

aspiration at the mysterious and unknown in the human experience, which lies at the heart of religious awareness.

The figures for 'belief in God', private prayer and support for religious education, in society at large and among the highly educated, demonstrate the persistence of religious belief and aspiration. But it is equally plain that these figures do not tally with figures for church going. What has occurred is the freeing of much belief from ecclesiastical attachment, and in many cases the liberation of the religious experience from frameworks guarded and dominated by the churches. Far from *enabling* religious experience, the churches now appear to be a positive barrier and hindrance to such experience. Students were not found to be 'secular'; but many were indeed 'unchurched'. As one observer reported

> Religion is far from being dead: it is still a vital force in many university students. The need for religion, the need to believe, is practically universal. However, religion is moving away fast from its organized and institutionalized forms ... into personal channels. Religion is being more and more personalized, and is more and more conceived as a personal experience. Dogmas and beliefs are shed, or modified ... The ethical and social side of religion is more and more stressed, and Jesus is more frequently regarded as a great teacher or great prophet than a Divine Being. The value of prayer is almost universally acknowledged. The keynote of religious beliefs ... is a groping and searching for religious values.[29]

A Nottingham University investigation into religious experience in contemporary Britain in the 1970s discovered a similar picture. One third of the population claim to have had some sort of religious experience in their lives, but half of these, in the words of *New Society*, 'wouldn't touch the church with a barge-pole'.[30]

'Extra-ecclesial', free-floating religious aspiration and expression is found in a wide variety of places, using many idioms, and drawing on many traditions. Some of it is still basically Christian, though tenuously connected with the churches rather than being anchored in the main stream of orthodox Protestant and Catholic traditions and their ecclesiastical structures. The charismatic movement is an obvious example. So is the intense interest in techniques of meditation which often drive Christians outside the churches in search of guides on this path; and the experimentation with new forms of Christian community as the churches prove an arid desert for exploration of the mysterious, wherein little understanding and support is given to the explorer.

Other manifestations of hankering after and exploration of the
mysterious and numinous occur outside the Christian tradition as
well as beyond the boundaries of its structures. At a high level of
insight and intellectual sophistication people from a variety of
disciplines brood and write on the spiritual deprivation of contemporary society, the dangers of this for the individual, the community and the natural environment, and the need for an
experience of the transcendent. Jung was a seminal figure in the
diagnosis and re-evaluation of twentieth-century society and culture. Writers of the later part of the century engaged in similar or
parallel assessments have included T. Roszak, R. D. Laing, E. F.
Schumacher, Philip Toynbee and even the abrasive journalist, Ber-
nard Levin. Less articulate and reflective, but more dramatic and
visual in its rejection of society's values and structures, was the
underground, the counter-culture of youth which erupted first in
America and then in Britain in the early 1970s. In its American
manifestation this included the 'Jesus Movement', adapting images
and elements in the Christian tradition. In Britain there was no
exact parallel in this: a variant of the 'Jesus Movement' was en-
gineered by tough-minded moral reformers and Evangelicals. But
much of the message of the genuine British underground was concerned with a quest for personal vision and experience of the
transcendent, through a new life-style liberated from the cramping
conventions and morals of society at large, where experiment with
sexual freedom and drug-taking were seen as possible routes to
wholeness and authenticity for individuals and communities. Acceptance of the apparently irrational, of the hunch that wholeness
and peace come through contact with forces and an essential order
beyond the visible and tangible, are also visible in contemporary
interest in the *I-Ching* and Tarot Cards; and the development of
self-awareness, encounter and growth groups.

Religious aspiration also erupts in new structures and organizations, though these sometimes prove temporary. New organizations reached their most exotic in America; but to a lesser extent
they have become part of the highly fluid and variegated religious
culture of contemporary Britain. Often they draw their inspiration
from Eastern religions: they stress community, changes in life style,
and personal experience, through techniques of meditation. Hare
Krishna devotees and the Divine Light Mission are among them.
Transcendental Meditation has appealed beyond the student age-
group and is taken seriously by professional and business people.
It is not insignificant that in 1977-8 BBC radio and television
devoted considerable time to analysis both of such new movements

and techniques of meditation, and to scientific examination of the claims advanced for the beneficial effects of meditation.[31] However, the spread of such organizations and movements in Britain is limited, fashions change; and by 1978 there was little evidence that these trends had percolated through to schools or that older school-children seriously considered them a possible religious option.[32]

Such evidence of the vitality of religious belief, practice, and vague aspiration outside the religious tradition and structures most readily accessible in Britain is not surprising if we remember the nature of religion as a universal phenomenon. It is the groping of man towards a vision of himself and his environment which gives meaning to immediate reality, to the unseen future, to the inheritance of the past; which enables him to deal with experiences beyond the material, whether they are of delight or dread. If it is part of being human to search for meaning, to experience mystery and awe, to be haunted by a sense that what is tangible and visible is not the total sum of reality, then it is natural that in any society there should be signs of such activity. However, change in society, in the intellectual environment, in culture and politics, can have a radical effect on particular religions, their institutions and intellectual formulations, without eradicating the religious as a potent element in the lives of the individual and the community. Change in Britain has not eradicated religion. But it has modified profoundly the context in which Christianity as the particular religion previously dominant now functions. As our evidence has shown, Christian institutions, Christian practice and Christian formulations about God and man now have a changed and changing place within society; not least in the milieu of the educated, who have been among the most exposed to the winds of change.

In comparison with educated Hindus in India educated Christians in Britain see their situation with a far greater and more urgent disquiet, almost amounting to a sense of crisis. Few fail to see the changed position of the churches and of Christian beliefs in Britain now, compared even with half a century ago. All are aware that in retaining faith they have become part of a cognitive minority, adherents of a vision of reality not shared by most of those with whom they live and work, no longer buttressed by society's assumptions and conventions. Furthermore, most perceive and accept that there is a new religious pluralism in their country.

Another dimension of their self-perception is the disquiet of many about the churches and their relationship to them. This is, as it were, the domestic dimension of the Christian dilemma, though it is closely connected to the more external forces of change in society. Questions of authority and the guidance the churches can and do give in a time of rapid change are burning ones; they cause believers as much concern, distress and also hope of renewal as does the position of the churches and of Christians in the contemporary world.[33]

Late twentieth-century Christians live in an environment which inevitably causes immense strain in those who, rather than abandoning faith or quitting the churches, remain within or loosely attached to them. It demands adaptation and reformulation of beliefs as well as practices. But change need not only be a threat. The contemporary Christian lives in a world which is religiously far more open and exciting than that of his grandparents and remoter ancestors. His world is more alive with possibilities for renewal than perhaps that of his Hindu counterpart in India, where social and intellectual changes have not wreaked such havoc with older assumptions, social communities and religious structures. How educated Christians respond to the fluctuations and fluidity of their religious environment, what they make of both the pain and the possibilities, is the concern of the subsequent chapters, as we compare the religious experience of our two groups so widely separated by distance and culture.

Table C: Church Attendance among University Staff and Students

Frequency of visits to places of public worship	Students	Lecturers
Often (i.e. monthly or more often)	33.0%	30.9%
Sometimes	31.1%	24.7%
Invited/social occasions only (e.g. weddings)	33.0%	39.5%
Never	2.8%	3.7%

Source: Manchester Surveys, 1978

Table D: Belief At Manchester University Compared with Indian Evidence

Belief Position	Students	(Bombay Adolescents)	Lecturers	(Pune Lecturers)
Believer in God	60.4%	(75%)	45.7%	(68.7%)
Agnostic	19.8%	(16.6%)	35.8%	(16.5%)
Atheist	19.8%	(5.0%)	18.5%	(14.8%)

Sources: Manchester Surveys, 1978; Survey of 60 young adults in Bombay, 1978, conducted by Sophia College students; V. G. Pundlik, 'Religion In the Life of College Teachers'

Table E: Belief and Church Attendance

Belief Position	Category	Attendance at place of public worship			
		Often (Monthly or more)	Sometimes	Invited/Social	Never
Believer	Student	54%	31.3%	12.5%	1.6%
	Lecturer	62.2%	24.3%	13.5%	0%
Agnostic	Student	0%	47.6%	47.6%	4.8%
	Lecturer	6.9%	31.0%	55.2%	6.9%
Atheist	Student	0%	14.3%	81.0%	4.8%
	Lecturer	0%	14.3%	78.6%	7.1%

Source: Manchester Surveys, 1978

Table F: Prayer Patterns among University Staff and Students

Frequency of Prayer	Students				Staff			
	Total	'Believing'	Agnostic	Atheist	Total	'Believing'	Agnostic	Atheist
Daily	22.6%	35.9%	4.8%	0%	16.0%	32.4%	3.4%	0%
Regularly but not daily	16.0%	26.6%	0%	0%	13.6%	29.7%	0%	0%
Occasionally	24.5%	28.1%	38.1%	0%	16.0%	21.6%	17.2%	0%
Never	35.8%	9.4%	57.1%	100%	53.1%	16.2%	79.3%	100%

Source: Manchester Surveys, 1978

Chapter Four

Gurus and Gospels:
Religious Authority and Communication
in a Changing World

=

One aspect of the religious experience common to all religious traditions is the exercise of internal authority and the need to communicate the tradition. Each religious tradition, having originated with a vision of ultimate reality and its implications for men and their world, tends to build up a network of authority and communication to protect and spread that vision. In times of change this area is always one of controversy and stress. To those who are not professional theologians 'the problem of authority' sounds dry as dust, and often marginal to the actual business of getting on with believing and its consequences in the ordinary world. It is little wonder that when people come together in discussion, whether from different Christian denominations or from different religious backgrounds, this is the area where they tend to run into the sand. In fact the problems are real and pressing – when seen in terms of flesh and blood rather than in doctrines isolated for intellectual debate and acceptance.

Here the historian can help. He does not deal just in theory and doctrine, but tries to understand and communicate something of the heat and dust, the blood and tears of actual living. He also has the perspective of time. So on this topic a historian properly asks what is and has been the purpose and role of authority in the religious experience, and in different religious traditions. Why is this an issue which causes controversy and stress in a changing world? And what is going on in different religious traditions which may illuminate a common problem? The historical understanding of religion as a social phenomenon also illuminates the close connection between authority and the communication of religious vision. Religious transmission and education in a broad sense is part of the problem of religious authority in a changing world; though when theologians debate authority they rarely connect the two.

When change occurs in society authority becomes an issue for any group which collaborates for a common purpose, whether it be a family, a school, a voluntary body, or on a wider scale a state. Questions of authority rouse particularly bitter controversy not just because they probe the central purpose on which a group collaborates. They also touch the depths of individual personalities, because so many people rely on external authority structures to give them security and meaning, and any change in the nature and exercise of authority challenges their precarious sense of personal identity. Those who cooperate in a shared religious tradition are not immune to these problems; indeed they are the more vulnerable to them because the issues with which religion deals are central rather than peripheral to man. When old certainties are eroded by change and new issues emerge, decisions have to be made in the religious context about the appropriate response of the believer. The nature and significance of change must be interpreted for him in the light of the tradition's perception of ultimate meaning. Somehow in a changing world the vision of truth at the heart of the religious tradition must be recaptured, re-seen in the new context, if that tradition is to live. How does this problem manifest itself in the world of our two educated groups: and are there in the Hindu and Christian traditions sources of authority which respond *creatively* to change, or do they merely serve to desiccate the tradition and constrict those who have inherited it?

Here a word of warning is important in our comparative enterprise. To understand the nature of religious authority, to grasp the power of the sanctions behind it, in any tradition requires an effort of sympathy and imagination from anyone not born within or converted to it. Physical sanctions, or deprivation of religious ministrations, are fairly easy to see and describe; but their psychological meaning for the believer, and the inner compulsion he feels to submit to authority, is far from easy for the outsider to comprehend. The power of the priest in traditional Catholicism with his sacramental ministry as the doorway to grace, in his own person the mediator between God and man, is outside the experience of the Hindu, to whom the social performances and sanctions of caste society are crucial. Probably neither the Hindu nor the Catholic would easily understand the peculiar power to command conformity which is generated within evangelical Protestantism by the need to use the right language and to have the right conversion experience to 'prove' that one has been truly saved and is not in danger of backsliding.

       *   *   *

One way of looking at this problem of religious authority and communication in a changing world is to visualize two concentric rings or circles. The inner ring is the realm of religious authority and communication as normally, and perhaps too narrowly, understood. It is composed, first, of the *sources* on which a religion is based; and second, of the means by which those sources are protected and interpreted, and their message communicated to succeeding generations. As we saw in Chapter 1, the function of authority is to provide the credentials of a religious vision and to guard and transmit it. Part of the guardian role has been to draw the boundaries between those who are thought to have grasped it and the outsiders who have not, and to confirm the insiders in their world view by teaching and varieties of actual control. Another facet of 'guardianship' is development and reinterpretation of the vision as the external environment changes. It is in a sense historically impossible to talk of 'orthodoxy', even in a religious tradition as soundly based in creeds as Christianity. Christian beliefs have continuously been changing in emphasis and expression; a marked feature of Christianity has been 'its mutability and the speed with which innovations come to be vested with religious solemnity to such an extent that anyone who questions them find[s] *himself* regarded as the dangerous innovator and heretic'.[1]

The precise nature of authority will vary from religion to religion, depending on its origins and its central vision. Most religions have certain foundation texts, scriptures which contain the core understanding of truth. By extension authority will be vested in those who have special access to or knowledge and understanding of the scriptures, by virtue of birth or training. There will be other authority bearers, those with particular powers of insight or action which keep them close to the core of a religious tradition and enable them to mediate it. Such specialists come in various shapes and sizes. Some may be untrained, illiterate but spirit-filled wise men and women of the local community; some, holy men accepted as guides because of years of self-discipline and immersion in the religious tradition; some prophets and preachers, fired with zeal and/or learning; yet others priests, formally endued with sacramental powers by birth, or a rite of separation and hallowing. There may well be institutions and communities which support and integrate the functions of these authority-bearers and themselves are accredited with religious authority and entrusted with the task of communication. In each religion the particular blend will vary, and differing importance will be attached to different sources and types of authority. But the blend will form a

living tradition on which believers draw for inspiration, guidance
and control, however little they may distinguish in their own minds
between its components.

The second, outer ring, is the encompassing social community
in which a religion functions. This can act as another part of the
total framework of authority and communication – but only when
its norms and standards, its conventions and life-styles, buttress
the world view of the religious tradition; when it accredits religious
specialists as messengers of meaning vital for the wellbeing of the
whole community; and in essence accepts the cognitive structure
of the religious tradition. More tangibly, the encompassing society
can prop religious authorities by tolerating their exercise of sanctions against those who ignore or disobey them. In some cases they
do not merely tolerate but actually aid their exercise of sanctions.
The wider society is therefore a major part of the problem of
religious authority in a time of change. In the Hindu milieu this is
particularly clear because the institutions and communities which
bear religious authority coincide with the wider social community
through the mechanism of caste. But even in the Christian context
the wider society is important, though there is not this exact coincidence. (In some Protestant societies the ethic of plain living,
high thinking and worldly success generated forms of social control
which buttressed formal church authorities and were often far
more formidable in compelling conformity than the exercise and
theory of ecclesiastical and sacerdotal authority. To fall foul of the
Scottish Kirk and its local lay elders must have been an unpleasant
social as well as religious experience!) Clearly, if there is change in
this 'outer ring' it will have repercussions on the 'inner ring'. If the
wider society's norms and institutions change, then the more formal religious authorities may find themselves in an exposed and
questionable position. Furthermore, the transmission of religion,
particularly education of the young in its world view and practices,
will be easier and more effective if the encompassing community
shares the process. There will be logistical trouble if religious education is left to specifically religious functionaries. But more fundamental problems of education will develop if society in effect
fights against a religious tradition, and is seen to do so by the
young.

Before we turn to our comparative material it seems worth
underlining an obvious point: that is, that the two circles are far
more distinct in the Christian than in the Hindu setting. In the
Christian tradition religious authority has always been narrowly
bestowed; entrusted to a body distinct from society at large, and

to the small group of its functionaries. In Hindu tradition religious authority is vested in a far wider range of people: it is more diffused as more people and groups have specifically religious functions to perform. In Hindu society the boundaries of the 'inner' and 'outer' rings overlap. But even when the two rings are distinct, as in the Christian setting, their interaction is vital. What happens in state and society closely affects the authority of churches, their functionaries and Christian scriptures.[2]

If we look first at the 'outer ring' in contemporary Britain, the evidence presented in the previous chapter points to a stark truth. Despite the residual Christian influence in social norms, despite the presence of a genial civic Christianity, the encompassing community in which educated Christians now live has ceased to buttress Christian believing. It certainly does not willingly receive, or help to spread, the Christian gospel as true or essential to the wellbeing of society and state. It judges Christianity as an optional extra for the enthusiast, a private diversion like bird-watching.

There are several aspects of this erosion of the 'outer ring'. One, primarily intellectual, is particularly significant for the educated. This is the process of differentiation, specialization and growing expertise: areas of life are separated out, governed by their own standards and conventions, and dominated by their own group of specialists. Science, economics, psychology, medicine, sociology – all are seen to answer questions in specific fields: and those fields are consequently withdrawn from the competence of the religious tradition and its specialists. The area in which Christian faith is an accredited authority has contracted, in the minds of those who retain belief as well as those who have abandoned it. Fewer believers would now feel that the Bible can explain natural phenomena. In political, economic and professional life, as in the scientific, the churches make no attempt to exert a special authority. They act as one of a number of pressure groups having a particular viewpoint: where they do attempt to guide their members it is in terms of general principles which members must work out in their own situations rather than in specific prescriptions for action. For example, in March 1979 the churches in Britain urged their members to use their votes in the forthcoming European, General and Local elections: none dared to suggest how those votes should be cast. (In continental Europe where there are specifically Christian or denominational political parties, the situation is rather different.) The intellectual shift is manifest in and underscored by the social and economic trends towards large corporate structures in business, government and politics; these are run on rational principles of efficiency and are beyond the institutional influence of the churches.

This trend relegates religious authority to a specifically 'religious' sphere. It suggests that religious authorities are trustworthy in as much as they know about ultimate meaning (in the Christian context about God and his dealings with the world of men), just as in the same way a plumber is a trustworthy authority on the subject of drains. If one feels no need to consider drains one can ignore the plumber: if one is happy to dismiss questions of ultimate meaning one can forget the churches and their spokesmen. Casting the religious authority figure in the role of yet another 'specialist' among many flies in the face of what religious authority is all about. It is not authoritative because it 'has all the answers' about ultimate reality, as a mechanic would have all the answers about the reality of a car's engine. Religious authority is credible because it points to a vision of reality, because it maps and guards the road to it by which men have travelled in the past so that men may try to do so in the present. It is significant because it can enable men to perceive truth, because it can help to liberate their vision; not because it 'has truth' in a neat doctrinal package like a car maintenance manual. The present trend in understanding all authority is closely linked to the legacy of Greek thought, which has dominated the European mind for over a thousand years. This stresses the importance of rational enquiry and cognition, giving primacy to 'knowledge about' things, rather than intuition and modes of knowledge which draw on other faculties besides the rational. This legacy has moulded Christian thought about the nature of faith, and shaped theology. In a real sense it has helped to desiccate the Christian tradition, as well as contributing to the contemporary differentiation of distinct areas of life. If such differentiation is accepted, it makes a nonsense of religion as a perception of reality which includes the whole of life. The tension this generates is clear, and we shall return to its manifestations and possible resolution in the next chapter.

In contemporary Britain the erosion of the 'outer ring' of religious authority and communication is the result of social as well as intellectual forces. We have seen how the processes of industrialization and urbanization, the expansion of population, and the increase in geographical and social mobility, have over two centuries destroyed the old hierarchical society in which Christian belief was an integral and formative part of accepted standards and values, Christian rites were part of social convention, and Christian institutions and functionaries had an influential place in public and private life. This is no longer so. Churches have been pushed to the periphery of public life. Observance of Christian worship has declined. Belief is increasingly a private matter, and does little to mould the public ethos. This is not meant to imply that there was ever an 'age of faith'. We do not know whether the Christian faith was more real to many more people in the past. We can only measure outward expression and conformity. What is clear is that the encompassing community once buttressed the Christian tradition, but no longer does so, or only to a very limited extent.

It is not surprising that one result of this change has been turmoil over religious education. It is still a compulsory part of the school curriculum. But there have been radical changes in what actually constitutes religious education, particularly in the last twenty years. In many schools old-style scripture has been discarded, to make way for 'exploration'. One reason is that many teachers of religion are no longer believing Christians. Decreasing home support for scripture is another, quite apart from genuine educational trends encouraging self-expression and personal discovery. Society at large no longer assists in transmitting Christian faith as firmly as it once did in its formal educational provision any more than it does in its conventions and assumptions. But it still wishes its young to receive some knowledge about religion.

My Manchester surveys illustrate these trends. Over two-thirds of staff felt that there should be religious education in state schools, but nearly all of these favoured the 'comparative religion' approach. A slightly lower percentage of students favoured RE in schools. Predictably, almost all students had received some religious education, over 80% of them at school. Just under a half had received some at home, and a slightly lower figure had received some at church or at Sunday school. But a more significant figure was that only one third thought that school had actually *influenced* their religious beliefs. Parents were the strongest source of religious influence. Just under half the student sample said so, the influence being most marked for 'believing' students[3] (see Table G, p. 120). When asked directly about their religious position compared with that of their parents, only 29.2% replied that their beliefs differed from their parents', and 26.4% said that their practices differed from those of their parents. Among lecturers there was far less correlation between attitudes of parents and children — predictably, considering that university staff, being one or two generations older than students, no longer lived in close contact with parents, and since the older ones would have had parents educated at the

turn of the century, when Christian practice was more widespread
and personal choice in religious matters less axiomatic. 40.7%
reported that their beliefs were different from their parents', but
only 35.8% said that their religious practices were different. When
they were asked about the major influences shaping their religious
attitudes, their replies were remarkably similar to those of the
student generation, though the older people had been more influenced by church, Sunday school and university, and particularly
by reading[4] (see Table H, p. 120).

It is the home which really counts in communication of faith (or
lack of it). Consequently, as fewer parents profess belief and attend
church religious communication will become less effective. Formal
religious education in schools is even less likely in the future to
communicate anything more than a superficial knowledge about
Christian stories and beliefs. It is also noteworthy that despite the
availability of the new mass media for communicating Chistianity,
none of the staff or students in the Manchester samples noted that
these had been a significant source of religious instruction or influence for them. The encompassing community in Britain has virtually opted out of the process of transmitting the Christian faith.
Christian 'specialists' are thus left with a massive problem: isolated
as communicators of a message, the country's homes do not also
spread in word or deed.

Indian evidence suggests that the 'outer ring' is in rather better
repair in the Hindu context. To a far greater extent than his
educated Christian counterpart in Britain the educated Hindu still
lives in a society which supports his religious tradition. The process
of differentiation has not gone so far so fast. Religious authorities
are still accepted as legitimate in a wide area of private and social
life, in some instances indeed which Christians would deem entirely
inappropriate. Examples I have encountered or heard of include
educated families who consult a family *guru* in a court case; people
hedging their bets in illness and consulting palmists and mediums
alongside more scientific medical practitioners;[5] continued deference to astrologers' advice even by government departments and
prominent politicians. But increasingly politics, business and the
professions are areas of life differentiated and governed by their
own norms.

One aspect of this limited differentiation is a conscious attempt
to buttress traditional religious authority over a wide area by
invoking modern scientific knowledge. It is not uncommon for
educated Hindus to justify traditional belief and practice on scientific grounds, or to 'find' new discoveries in the Hindu scriptures.

(Aeroplanes and the atomic bomb are a case in point, while in 1978 a Pune organization claimed that the Vedas had grappled with the contemporary problem of pollution and suggested remedies.[6]) Yet another facet of this determination to make religious authority 'respectable' in the modern world is to claim that Hinduism is a 'scientific' religion. Those who preach the gospel of Vedanta, the 'invented Hinduism' of the educated, are the loudest in this claim. Radhakrishnan wrote in 1946 that the Indian religious tradition 'approaches the problem of religion, not in a dogmatic but in a scientific spirit'; and half a century earlier Vivekananda had lectured on Advaita Vedanta as 'The Scientific Religion'. A prominent leader in the Ramakrishna Mission told me in 1978 that Hinduism was a scientific religion because it rested on the empirical method, in that the believer based his belief on his own experience and on that of such experts as Ramakrishna and Vivekananda, much as one would trust the authority of an atomic scientist on his subject.[7]

But the most marked contrast between the worlds of our two groups is that India has not experienced massive social and economic change, uprooting old social frameworks and challenging the values they uphold. Hindu society remains intact. This is crucial for the Hindu religious inheritance, because it is that society, rather than distinct religious institutions or specialists, which mediates religious values and experience, and secures compliance with the tradition's dictates. However, as we have seen, notable change is beginning in the world of the urban educated. Town life may cut off a family from its caste fellows, and so diminish the strength of the caste as an enfolding community and take the power from its sanctions. Observance of ritual becomes difficult and at times impossible, while education brings new ideas, many of which conflict with traditional values and ways of understanding the influence of non-material forces in men's lives.

Change is not only beginning to erode the strength and competence of religious authority. It is also crucially affecting the transmission of Hindu tradition. In Hindu society there has been little formal religious instruction, partly because for most Hindus there is no rite of entry into adult religious status or full membership of the religious group which demands prior instruction, as in the Christian case of baptism and confirmation. The experience of the high caste male in preparation for the sacred thread ceremony is the one exception here. The theory of the high caste boy then going to live with a *guru* for education has rarely been enacted; and the Vedic schools which taught Sanskrit were for Brahmin

boys only, in particular those who were destined by their families
to act as priests rather than follow some other profession. Most
people received their religious instruction in the most informal
ways, imbibing it almost unconsciously within their families,
through family ritual, as mothers and grandmothers retold the old
myths and venerated the family deities, and by seeing it enacted by
travelling story-tellers, singers and dramatic players. In the twentieth century books and pamphlets have tended to replace these
oral transmitters of the religious tradition. But, as we have seen,
religious literature may be published but many do not read it.

The Pune college teachers confirmed the importance of family
influence in their own religious experience and of the 'believers'
83% traced the origins of their belief to their family either solely
or partly. 25% of them specifically mentioned their grandparents
in this context. In this generation the strength of traditional family
education was obviously still strong; and of those who had wholly
abandoned belief the vast majority did *not* trace this to their upbringing. Most of the South Indian students questioned said that
they had had no formal instruction in the Hindu scriptures, at least
until their late 'teens. The Bombay adolescents questioned said that
home was the main source of their religious education and a considerable number of them had received none even there, though
this sample included a few non-Hindus.

From these group studies and my own observations it is evident
that the traditional modes of religious education are failing to
influence the growing generations of the late twentieth century. No
longer do children of the educated automatically imbibe the religious experience with its myths and symbols. They tend to live in
geographically mobile families which are fairly small, if not nuclear, where the mother may work to combat soaring inflation and
school bills, and where both parents are less 'observant' than the
grandparents' generation because of disinclination and the pressure
of time. Nor do they find any substitute for this in school or
college. Outside Christian convent schools there is little religious
education, though children learn the Hindu myths in reading books
and through essay and recital competitions. My Hindu friends were
surprised but highly intrigued by the idea of formal church or
Sunday school training. Many are also alarmed that in educated
families the transmission of their tradition's stories, beliefs and
implicit assumptions in the old, informal way is at risk.

It is significant that some Hindu groups, such as the Chinmaya
Mission in Pune, are beginning to provide special religious teaching
for children. Another development in the last decade has been the

growth of children's religious books, particularly the production of comic strip versions of the great myths. These are available in English – obviously intended for those children most exposed to change.[8] (One parent did suggest to me, however, that his children preferred Tarzan and that the gods and goddesses meant no more to children when presented in this fashion than these other colourful but improbable heroes and heroines of children's stories!)

A majority of the Pune college lecturers favoured providing optional moral and social-cultural education in schools, though their emphasis was on imparting knowledge of India's religious tradition and leaders rather than any instruction in traditional religion. Among the Bombay adolescents a large majority also considered it was important to give children some basic religious instruction, though they were not asked to specify the place. If new modes of religious teaching are not created as social change accelerates, then it seems highly likely, as some of those I talked with feared, that without even the basic provision for religious education which survives in Britain, the Hindu tradition might become a social husk for the coming generation, its living kernel lost.

We now turn to the 'inner ring'; and ask how changes in the 'outer ring' impinge on the obvious sources of religious authority in the lives of our two groups. In this area there are no comparable statistics, although there are some figures for Manchester University staff and student attitudes to religious authority. There are also studies of Anglican parsons in Britain and Brahmin priests in Tamil Nadu, conveniently for the purpose of our comparison from roughly the same time in the early 1960s.

Our first comparison concerns the authority of scriptural texts in the two traditions. Scripture is an important source of authority in any religion where it embodies the original vision of truth from which that religion grew. But scripture's place is very different in the two traditions which concern us. That difference stems from the different Hindu and Christian understanding of creation, revelation and saving knowledge. Christian belief sees creation as the work of a God who reveals himself uniquely in the created order and in human history. Man is saved through divine action in time: consequently knowledge leading to salvation must be rooted in an understanding of the significance of God's dealings with men in time. Here scripture, in the forms of myths, poetry, prophecy, history and teaching, bears witness to and interprets man's experience of God in the concrete and specific, as well as in the timeless apprehension of the visionary. For the Hindu creation is a repeated process of destruction and creation: Brahma recreating what Shiva destroys. The created order is not fundamentally significant as the stuff of divine disclosure: it is, rather, a 'veiling' of reality. Man's world and history is not definitive, but rests on ultimate mystery, whose play it is. Temporal history is not the decisive arena in which that mystery is disclosed. Hindu incarnations point to a reality beyond time and for their significance need not actually have occurred *in* time,[9] whereas for the Christian, incarnation was a specific historical event and *by so being* points to reality beyond time.

Consequently for the Hindu 'saving knowledge' does not depend on awareness of historical events; it is liberation from false awareness into a dawning of reality which comes from possession, almost invasion, by truth: awareness of truth at the deepest level of one's being. Scripture assists in this illumination, enlightenment: but is not a total record or guarantee of revelation. For the Christian, scripture is crucial because it witnesses to divine self-disclosure in time, particularly in the person of Jesus. Knowledge about that self-disclosure is a precondition for accepting the salvation it offers, and then for opening oneself to a continuing process of revelation and redemption.

Implicit in this differing attitude to the nature and power of scripture is that in strong contrast to the Western, Christian tradition, Hindu teachers have not stressed the faculty of reason as a primary means of knowing God and receiving divine revelation. Knowledge comes though a training and purification of the whole person, an inward awareness and search for the immanent rather than transcendent divinity; for the ultimate reality which is mystery. In reaching this awareness of mystery reason has only a limited part to play. The whole method of Upanishadic teaching underscores this. The Upanishads are designed *not* to lead the disciple by logical steps and historical demonstration to a belief in God, but to batter his normal modes of thought by shock, disjuncture and disorientation, to prepare him for a dawning of awareness beyond rational thought. Similarly the stress by Hindu teachers on silence is to still the mind so that it becomes aware at a depth undisturbed by the ordinary and rational ways of cognition. In such meditation the Veda can 'speak' to the disciple in a way that is very different from the descriptive and discursive teaching associated with biblical teaching and study.[10]

In the contemporary Christian context there is a major crisis in the believer's relationship to and understanding of scripture. We have already noted how few believing Christians actually read the

Bible regularly. Therefore it is not surprising that scripture does
not seem to have a central, authoritative place in the religious life
of educated believers. Of my Manchester samples nearly 68% of
believing staff accepted scripture as a source of authority; but only
about 52% of believing students did so.

These figures are the tip of the iceberg in the crisis of the authority of scripture among educated Christians. It was made possible by mass literacy in the last century which for the first time
opened the Bible directly to Christians, at least in Protestant traditions. The Bible came to be seen as straight history, a handy
reference book for accurate information about creation, Jewish
history and the life of Jesus. Equally uncritically it was used as the
directly inspired word of God into which the faithful could dip at
random for instant comfort and guidance. The Bible became the
'victim' of mass education, used in new ways impossible when it
was a closed book to so many, or mediated through specialists
who often interpreted it in figural and symbolic terms. But biblical
criticism spreading from Germany shattered cosy assumptions and
displayed with all the skills of secular historical scholarship just
what Christian scripture is – a collection of different types of
source material which witness in different ways to man's growing
awareness of God over centuries. Revelation is here; but mediated
through different authors writing for specific readers in particular
historical contexts which influenced their understanding of divine
action. The implications of this for the nature of scriptural authority dawned on scholars first. But as they began to filter through
to educated Christians, so debate became more generalized and
bitter. It was one issue, for example, in the *Honest to God* controversy of the early 1960s, or the more recent wrangle over the two
paperbacks, *The Myth of God Incarnate* and *The Truth of God
Incarnate*.

Fundamentalism is still a living force in the later twentieth century, even in academic circles; and many students seem attracted
by the security and simplicity of faith it offers. But the agonizing
process of understanding anew the nature of scripture continues
for those who feel they have no choice but to accept the findings
of historical scholarship if they are to retain their intellectual integrity. Such Christians have increasingly been forced to ask what
the revelation of God may be for their own time, rather than
resting content with concepts and formulations fitting for men of
the Mediterranean world nearly two thousand years ago. As a
prominent Anglican historian and theologian put it: 'A theology
can be built on the Bible thus understood, but the old appeal to

the authority of the Bible cannot be sustained among those who are intellectually free.'[11] This throws believers firmly back into the situation of the first Christians. They must now 'experience Christ' in their own terms and context, then live and write a gospel of the late twentieth century.

A further dimension of the crisis which does not hit the headlines is that many, even among educated Christians, are unaware of the implications of modern scholarship. The laity are exhorted to read their Bibles; new translations flow from the presses; revised liturgies bombard congregations with more numerous readings of scripture than ever before. But rarely are lay Christians seriously helped to understand what scripture can and cannot tell them. For the educated this carries the risk of a gross disjuncture between their religious experience and the skill and integrity with which they expect to operate in their professional lives. If Christian scholars and ministers could in parochial and pastoral as well as academic contexts help educated Christians see the Bible not as a text book but as evidence of human and halting glimpses of a vision of God, they would begin to release them from the constricting Greek legacy which emphasizes the intellectual nature of knowledge at the expense of other ways of knowing, which are as vital in the religious experience: for example, the way of the mystic, or more commonly the way of relationship experienced with God individually and corporately in a believing community which reflects intelligently on the myths and mysteries present in its scriptures.[12] A renewed understanding of the nature of scripture and its authority might open more Christians to a continuing process of revelation, and awareness of the potential for religious understanding at different levels of human personality. Here Christians may have much to learn from Hindus and their use of and expectations from their scriptures.

The Christian crisis over scriptural authority was precipitated by modern critical scholarship. This has not occurred in the Hindu world, nor is there comparable controversy over scriptural authority. There has been little development or application of new critical skills and most pandits stick to traditional forms of scholarship and teaching – learning by heart, studying commentaries, stressing the power of the actual Sanskrit words in rituals. Even if there was scholarly turmoil its repercussions would not be so penetrating as in the Christian experience; for Hindu scriptures are not authoritative because of their historical authenticity but, as we have seen, because of their power to open men to illumination.

However, it would be wrong to suggest that there is not questioning and change in educated Hindu attitudes to scripture. In the last hundred years many sensitive Hindus have become concerned about the linkage between customs and social forms they can no longer accept and their religious inheritance; particularly the apparent sanction portions of scripture give to a social order which has become increasingly distasteful to those educated who have been influenced by the West. As one mid-nineteenth-century Indian Christian put the dilemma of his Hindu compatriots, 'Nowadays most young educated people think that the Hindu religion should be reformed. But if this is done, then it will appear that this religion is man-made ...'.[13]

Many have argued that society can be changed without abandoning religion; that scripture does not necessarily sanction customs now considered archaic or worse; and that scripture might indeed sanction change. From Brahmo and Arya Samajes through to Gandhi and his wish to transform Indian society and on to our own day, these have been crucial questions for thoughtful, educated Hindus. No simple answers are possible. Many, I judge, just ignore such issues at the intellectual level, and respond pragmatically, doing what seems right or feasible. Those who consciously grapple with change without discarding reference to scripture try to distinguish between a so-called pure or original tradition and later accretions; and to judge scripture by reason and conscience.

This is a fundamental challenge to orthodox scholarship and evaluation of different kinds of scriptural authority, whether the pandits recognize this and respond or not. Although they are increasingly aware of intellectual pressure from sceptical Hindus who demand standards based on empiricism, and from the discoveries and tools of scientific and historical study, most do not have the skills to enter into debate at anything but the most superficial level. For example, when in the 1970s it was publicly suggested that the Mahabharat War did not take place, the pandits were merely concerned to affirm that it did; they had no concept of the religious value of myth itself. Taking what in the Christian tradition would be called a fundamentalist position, they are in general incapable of handling Hindu myths and reinterpreting their riches in ways which convey glimpses of fundamental meaning to their educated contemporaries.[14]

An additional problem is the marked decline in Sanskrit learning in modern India. Because of the government's educational policy Sanskrit now has to compete with English and the regional languages in the school languages timetable slot. Most schoolchildren and students opt for English. Many college Sanskrit depart-

ments are now being closed down, while traditional Sanskrit
schools are declining in numbers, their lay patrons sometimes di-
verting their funds into support for modern, 'secular' education.
Less and less can a pandit support himself on Sanskrit learning
alone, through teaching and conducting and advising on rituals
needing specialist knowledge; and many pandits consequently are
not training their sons in their own traditional skills. (One head of
a Sanskrit Department in a Bombay college told me that he was in
middle life doing an MA in philosophy in order to equip himself
for a continuing academic career as his original discipline declined.)
As Sanskrit declines so the number of professional scholars decreases; so too does knowledge of Sanskrit among the educated,
and in consequence knowledge among the laity of any but those
portions of scripture which are translated into the vernaculars or
English.

A very marked aspect of the contemporary world of educated
Hindus is widespread lay ignorance of the Hindu scriptural heritage, an ignorance more profound than that prevailing in the Christian context in relation to the Bible. Most people still know many
of the stories of Hindu mythology made popular through translation, dance and drama, devotional pictures, the film industry, and
family story-telling. It is still worth while for politicians to invoke
and quote scripture. (In the 1977 election campaign after which
Mrs Gandhi and her 'Emergency' were evicted, the Janata alliance
stressed the fact that it, like Krishna, was born in jail.) Apart from
knowing the great stories, some educated Hindus can quote man-
tras and longer scriptural verses, but often with little knowledge of
their origins or context. Few possess or read any of the scriptures
other than the *Gita*; and that in a translation into English or a
regional language. College teachers commented to me on the ignorance of many of their Hindu students about their scriptures, though
there are virtually no statistics with which to quantify the degree
of ignorance.[15]

However, a singular development is occurring among educated
Hindus which implies major change in the approach to scripture
and understanding of its authority. I have called this 'the invention
of *Hinduism*'. As we saw in Chapter 1, the multiplicity of beliefs
and practices in the Indian religious inheritance has forced some
educated Hindus to re-think what they mean by religion, particularly since they have been confronted with the missionary expansion of other religions bearing definable, portable creeds. The
resultant trend has been a definition of the Hindu inheritance as
'Hinduism', equivalent to the world's monotheisms, its core and

creed being the Vedanta strand in Hindu tradition. Although Vi-vekananda was the most dramatic exponent of this 'invented Hinduism', thousands of educated Hindus have assisted in simpli-fying and standardizing their tradition into a shareable religious package. The process is founded on scriptural eclecticism, and blurs the old distinction of *sruti* and *smrti* in acceptance of scripture as authoritative.

M. K. Gandhi was one of the most prominent figures in the twentieth-century 'reformation' of Hindu tradition. His treatment of scripture was not only idiosyncratic but reflective of much of the confusion on these issues among educated Hindus. His priority was a regeneration of Indian society and political life through regeneration of individual Indians. This demanded their conversion in religious matters from dogmatic assertion or blind adherence to custom, their turning towards an individual search for ultimate truth, while treating the consciences of others with utmost sensi-tivity and non-violence. Essential aspects of this 'change of heart' (as he called it) were tolerance between India's religious com-munities, and the abolition of untouchability. When he returned from South Africa in 1915 to live permanently in India he made his attitude to the Hindu heritage plain when speaking about un-touchability. 'If it was proved to me that [untouchability] is an essential part of Hinduism, I for one would declare myself an open rebel against Hinduism itself.'[16]

Gandhi took scripture seriously, but not in the manner of ortho-dox pandits. He believed that the Vedas, other Hindu scriptures and the holy books of other faiths such as the Bible had authority as being divinely inspired, though not in every word. However, for him interpretation of scripture had to agree with reason and moral sense: therefore only the purified and realized man could truly interpret it. It was not surprising that in his own life Gandhi relied fundamentally on the authority of what he called his 'inner voice', and that even the wide range of scripture he held to be authoritative was so only in a secondary sense. As he admitted, 'I never cite scripture unless I have subjected it to the test of personal experience'.[17] In fact his capacity to cite scripture was limited because, as he freely admitted, he had not received a pandit's training or studied the scriptures in great range or depth. His whole approach to scripture was antipathetical to traditional scholarship. For him the greatest of the Hindu scriptures was the *Bhagavad Gita*, though this was a late scriptural book, *smriti* not *sruti*, and not part of Vedic scripture except in the loose description of all Hindu scripture as Veda which became common from the end of the nineteenth century. Gandhi's glorification of the *Gita* went totally against the orthodox view of scriptural authority; so did the teaching he extracted from it. He preached on the basis of this book what he wanted to be accepted as the core of the reformation of Hindu tradition and society in which he was engaged, even if this meant reading into the text values such as chastity and the dignity of physical work which were not originally there.

Gandhi's use of the *Gita* undoubtedly popularized it among educated Hindus, as has its exposition in very different ways by other reformers and scholars such as Tilak and Sri Aurobindo. It has become virtually a 'gospel' for educated Hindus. Indeed Gandhi viewed it and the Sermon on the Mount in a very similar light. This development in the status of the *Gita*, and contemporary Hindu eclecticism in approaching scripture, are most remarkable shifts in educated Hindu understanding of scriptural authority. But eclecticism side-steps real intellectual problems about the authority of scripture. And if there is to be a Hindu 'gospel' then its historical sources and their authority will have to be reassessed, and the significance of religious myth reinterpreted for the Hindu of the later twentieth century.

Study and interpretation of scripture is part of the work of religious 'specialists' in most traditions. We must now look at the authority of such people and the formal institutions of religion, for their status is also changing in the worlds of our two groups. The nature of that change is complex; but certain major trends stand out.

Some figures will remind us of the contemporary position of the churches and their ministers in Britain. The Manchester surveys showed that few 'believing' lecturers or students accepted living religious leaders as authoritative, and only just over half of each group felt that the church was a source of religious authority for them. It is in the declining status of the churches and their functionaries, even in *believers*' lives, that we see most clearly the effects of change in the 'outer ring' on the 'inner ring' of religious authority. The jigsaw of evidence pieced together in the previous chapter showed how social, economic and intellectual changes have worked together to push the churches to the periphery of life in Britain. The parson is no longer the omnicompetent wise man and social worker of the local community, but a relatively poor member of the educated class in a profession with declining prestige and many recruitment problems. Acute economic pressure, a declining social role, and diminishing congregations have led to much heart-searching among ministers about their role and authority. A significant number have left the parochial ministry to teach, serve particular institutions and professions, or to become ecclesiastical administrators and journalists.[18]

The sense of crisis among those whom the sociologists call 'the professional guardians of the sacred' has deeply affected the laity. They in turn defer to them in a much restricted area of life; and indeed often wonder whether even in the realm of religion ministers wield or should wield particular authority in teaching, preaching and sacramental action. The expansion of education among lay Christians, contemporary questioning of all authorities, and the modern stress on personal liberty and experience, are further ways in which changes in the 'outer ring' erode authority of the 'inner ring' of specifically religious institutions and specialists. Radical questioning is accepted even in the hierarchies of the most autocratic churches; and the exercise of ecclesiastical discipline against those who question or defy church authority is rare. Where it has recently occurred, as in the cases of the continental theologians, Küng and Schillebeeckx, it has not taken the form of excommunication and – significantly – it has raised public outcry, not just among believing Christians. What is at issue in this crisis of ecclesiastical and clerical authority is not just particular doctrines and their interpretation. It is the whole notion of the sacred, of the nature of the church as its guardian, and of its ministers as authoritative because of their particular knowledge of and relationship to the sacred. It takes contemporary Christians back again to the fundamental question of the different ways of knowing in the religious experience with which they are already confronted by the re-evaluation of the nature and authority of scripture.

There are positive and creative aspects of this crisis. They often deepen the crisis – at least initially. But they suggest that some of the churches and their specialists are responding courageously to change and are helping educated Christians to do so. Theologians wrestling with the problem of authority are one example; of particular note is the work of Hans Küng, which is now widely available in English translation and in paperback, and much read by Christians of many denominations. Many professionals without theological training but with their own technical expertise and standing are also questioning the whole understanding of ecclesiastical authority. The Catholic layman and psychiatrist, Jack Dominian, has been a significant contributor to the discussion. In the Anglican church, too, though the question of the church's authority has been much less pressing, some of the most outspoken

have been lay people or clerics with a base of operations outside
the regular career structure of the church.[19]

Such widespread discussion among educated Christians, both
clerical and lay, is renewing contemporary understanding of the
nature of the church. Fewer would now see it as the ark of salvation
in which men must take refuge; its image is increasingly that of a
community of pilgrims, in search of the City of God. In such a
church 'specialists' would not wield authority because they have a
'hot line' to God, whether through learning or sacramental power.
Their role would be a servant's one, in a diversity of ways assisting
and enabling the community to pursue its pilgrimage.

This shift in understanding authority is by no means complete.
As it occurs it produces chaos and liberation – clearest in Britain
among educated Roman Catholics after Vatican II, but evident in
other denominations, too. Anglicans have talked much of the role
of the laity in theology, in worship, in evangelism as well as in
church government and the stewardship of financial resources. But
what the churches will actually *do* to enact this new insight, in
particular how they will alter clergy training, whether they will
ordain women, what role they give to the laity, remains to be
worked out painfully. In the Church of England, for example, lay
participation in church life has undoubtedly increased in the last
two decades. But in worship, teaching, theological enquiry and
pastoral care the position has hardly changed. In these fields the
clergy are still dominant; and often the laity who cry out in protest
are isolated voices. A member of the House of Laity in the General
Assembly from 1960 to 1970 put the point pungently and publicly
in *The Times* in 1977:

> Yet the Church of England seems curiously loth to make full
> use of the very real resources of manpower which remain to it.
> Much is said of the ministry of the laity and of its value; but
> the laity are still kept very much in the shadow; useful (and
> indeed obligatory) on committees and conferences, welcome as
> providing a change of voice in the less important services, de-
> sirable as guardians of a parish's finances. But in what must be
> supposed to be the prime duties of the church, the bringing of
> souls to Christ, the bringing of help to those who are 'any ways
> afflicted or distressed' in these aspects of ministry the laity are
> left on the fringe of things.[20]

Even from traditions which have used the word 'minister' of their
religious specialists and have stressed the laity as the heart of the
community of faith, entrusted with 'the priesthood of all believers',

there come protests about clerical dominance. A prominent United Reformed minister publicly implored Christian bureaucrats to remember that they are there, not to build their own empires as an 'ecclesiastical buffer-state between God's kingdom and the real world', but to serve those who try to serve God in that world. Clerical self-abnegation would then restore 'spiritual authority and responsibility to where they properly belong, in the whole congregation of the faithful'.[21] But the extent to which clergy actually function as enablers of the community's pilgrimage, what help they give the laity at present in responding to change and working out the contemporary implications of faith, what success they have as communicators, seems to depend not on churches' policies and programmes but on individual aptitude and insight.

Yet a further dimension of the Christian dilemma over authority is the new understanding of the contemporary action of the living Spirit of God. It is implicit in the ecumenical movement; and explicit in the charismatic movement, seen by those involved as renewal by direct indwelling of the Holy Spirit. Within Evangelical Christianity in particular there has always been a stress on the personal encounter of the believer with the Lord, and the crucial nature of the individual response to this situation. But that strain of intense personal perception was moulded, channelled and controlled by religious formulae and the conventions of the churches: their members were often pillars of British society, unlikely to let enthusiasm overstep the bounds of social decorum. The emergence of charismatic renewal in both Protestant and Catholic churches in the last twenty years has been far more widely spread across denominational boundaries than older Evangelicalism. Socially it has been influential particularly among the educated and professional – just that group whose religious experience in a time of change is our concern. In the charismatic movement direct personal experience of the Spirit, and the variety of accompanying 'gifts' (including speaking with tongues), is valued more highly than intellectual knowledge. Moreover, the Spirit's teaching by personal intuition or prophecy within the charismatic group is esteemed above the traditional theological formulations of the various churches or the biblical text and the authority of the inspired prophet or interpreter above that of the conventional minister or priest. It is a religious empiricism based on the conviction that God is vibrant power, acting through the Spirit here and now, regardless sometimes of old concepts and institutions, though often reinterpreting and infusing them with new life rather than shattering them.[22]

The ecumenical movement also rests ultimately on a theology of authority vested in the transforming power of the Spirit, rather than in an exclusive book or institution. Its roots are genuine religious repentance and hope, though at an institutional level it also makes sense as a rational approach to a declining religious market and to scarce resources. The implications for religious authority are still being worked out, particularly in relations between the Roman Catholic Church and those churches which have emphasized the primacy of biblical rather than ecclesiastical authority. But both contemporary movements demand radical re-thinking of older assumptions of a restricted group of specialists having peculiar access to the sacred; they demand serious consideration of the nature of authority which flows from outpouring of the Spirit, regardless of denomination, training, ordination, sex or age.

Has this turmoil any parallel in the religious world of educated Hindus? If so, its signs will be different because of the absence of any central Hindu authority structure and the diffusion of religious function and authority. As we saw in Chapter 2, it was the social framework which in the past enforced compliance with religious norms and prescriptions. Therefore it is on that framework as well as a loosely connected web of religious specialists that we must focus to see whether in the Hindu context there is any equivalent to the crisis of institutionalized religious authority which has occurred among Christians.

Religious life for most Hindus has flowed through the channels of domestic ritual and the public celebration of festivals ordered within the framework of caste. Caste councils exercised authority to promote the *dharma* of each caste's members. They were composed of the caste's elders, who made decisions on religious matters where these related to personal and group relationships rather than ritual (which was the preserve of the priests and pandits). Sanctions ranged from fines to various shades of social boycott, culminating in total outcasting; they were enforced by the council and the whole caste. Whatever is still the case in India's villages, among the urban educated, castes now exercise very little discipline. As social networks they still have considerable vitality and significance. But the deviant have less to fear from social ostracism. Caste councils are often defunct and outcasting is almost as dead a letter as is excommunication in Britain. Either it does not happen, or its effects are marginal for people whose mobility and qualifications have freed them from the constraints of rural interdependence.

In the Hindu as in the Christian world the educated now credit religious specialists with less authority (though that authority is

often of a different kind from that exercised in the Christian context). The authority of the Sanskrit pandit rests on his knowledge
of the language and content of scripture: traditionally pandits have
taught Sanskrit and expounded scripture to the twice-born, and
have advised on tricky matters of ritual. Now they lament because
there is less demand for their services. Few educated Hindus wish
to learn Sanskrit or have their children educated in traditional
style, quite apart from the decline of Sanskrit in schools and colleges. Moreover, the educated tend to be less scrupulous about the
correct performance of ritual. On disputed points they will manipulate pandits, consulting several until they receive advice which
suits their life-style and social timetable. Some pandits consciously
use their skills to sanction modernization, giving rulings which
take into account both texts and pressures of their educated clients'
lives.[23] But far more opt out, seeing change as the source of decline
and betrayal rather than an occasion for renewing and reinterpreting tradition.

Brahmins trained in Vedic ritual who traditionally acted as family priests are also important religious professionals. By assisting
the family at festivals and for life-cycle rites they helped to act out
the traditions and their religious assumptions. Brahmin priests'
authority was thus as ritual specialists, rather than men endowed
with teaching authority as in Christian tradition. It depended both
on Brahminical birth and on technical training necessary for accurate performance of ritual. Such men, too, have found their
position in Indian society changing. Many reformist sects de-
nounced Brahmins and all authority based on caste. (One of the
most extreme examples was the Arya Samaj, whose members castigated Brahmins as alleged mediators between God and man, using
the condemnation, 'pope', which they had learned from Protestant
missionaries![24]) But most educated Hindus increasingly devalue
their role, though many retain a somewhat uneasy residual rever-
ence for them and their authority. Many still feel guilty if they
refuse to give the charity traditionally due to Brahmins; and even
among the educated women studied by Rama Mehta some still
feared a Brahmin's curse and made such comments as, 'I have
courage to contradict almost anyone but the priests'.[25] However,
the verbal and published evidence I have obtained indicates a steady
decline in the status of priests in Hindu society. Priests recognize
this, and lament their degradation into ritual technicians to be
hired when necessary, and even fired at will. Fewer educated, urban
families have hereditary family priests. Away from their ancestral
homes they choose priests for specific rites or a longer relationship

on grounds of reputation and competence: *performance* is the criterion and old relationships of respect are eroded.

In this century observation of some rituals has declined, others are being curtailed, while sometimes several once separate rites are amalgamated. So priests experience not only decreasing social relevance, but also economic stress similar to that suffered by their Christian counterparts in Britain. Their hardship is increased as offerings for the performance of ritual are commuted from kind to cash in a time of severe inflation. Some receive less than the lowest paid government servant, while even the most prosperous probably earn less than a college teacher, who is among the poorer paid of the Indian professional elite. It is small wonder that just as there are problems of recruitment to the Christian ministry in Britain, so in India there is a shift of Brahmins from the practice of the priestly profession. Many priests also do other work; and even more are not training their sons in the skills necessary for priestly performance. Just as parsons in Britain tend to be older men, so in India fewer younger Brahmins actually work as priests. Of fifty family priests studied in South India, only four had children who were carrying on in their profession; and none was under thirty years old.[26]

Here is a situation where many religious specialists will not use change creatively, and where there is no central authority to control response to change. The vacuum has permitted new sources of authority in the educated Hindu's religious experience. Government is one: for independent India's governments, unhampered by colonial rulers' fears of stirring up unrest, have intervened through legislation in a range of matters in which religious tradition is deeply involved, from family customs to control of temple funds. Another new source of authority lies in the various bodies which are helping Hindus cope with change without abandoning their religious inheritance. The Arya Samaj has done this for some. But now the Ramakrishna Mission appears to be particularly influential among educated Hindus, exerting influence throughout India and abroad. A more local example from western India is Jnana Prabodhini, an educational institution in Pune, which is deeply influenced by Vivekananda's teaching. Since its foundation in 1962 it has aimed to combine a revival of Hindu tradition with scientific training and economic development, endeavouring to influence and train an elite group of young people to regenerate the Hindu nation. In the realm of ritual, moreover, reforming bodies like the Dharma Nirnaya Mandal have been re-writing old rituals such as the Thread Ceremony and the Vedic marriage rites, to make them more relevant to contemporary life, and have provided vernacular translations beside the Sanskrit texts to prevent the almost total ignorance of what was occurring which was common among many of the participants.[27] The authority vacuum has also opened the way to the interpreters of 'invented Hinduism', and given the prophets of modernized Vendanta scope for establishing a new 'orthodoxy' without persecution or criticism. These new authorities range from English-speaking saints and sadhus, particularly those in increasingly popular or notable ashrams, to politicians, lay devotees and patrons, to teachers of Indian philosophy in English. Few of these have the traditional authority of the ritual specialist or the pandit, though a small number of pandits have lent their learning and authority to the process.[28]

Not only are 'new' authorities emerging in the Hindu religious world. Some older, more traditional institutions and leaders have expanded their horizons and are helping Hindus adapt to changing circumstances without abandoning belief and practice. Among these have been the spiritual heads of some castes and sects based in *maths*, their headquarters where the faithful will come perhaps once a year, to profit from their learning, wisdom and sanctity in lectures and private audiences. Such men are apart from and above the ritual specialists and pandits as spiritual authorities and advise the faithful not so much on doctrine, as on putting belief into daily practice. Swami Shankaracharya, head of a *math* near Conjeeveram in South India, is a prime example. Not only has he attempted to boost Vedic study and recitation and to foster a sense of identity among priests, he also guides the laity in areas of change; for example, sanctioning marriages which tradition once forbade (as between Shaivites and Vaishnavites), and encouraging them, when their work prevents lengthy, traditional forms of prayer, to pray briefly and then do their work in sincerity and a sense of service to their fellows as a form of prayer.[29]

When the Shankaracharya gives such spiritual advice he is acting as a *guru*. We must consider the authority of the *guru* figure among educated Hindus, partly because so many assertions and judgments have been made in this area, not least by European observers. *Guru* means teacher, but the word is now most commonly used to denote a teacher of and initiator into a spiritual way or discipline. The disciple (*chela*) defers to him because of his knowledge of reality, his own self-realization and illumination, demonstrated not only in his teaching but in his peaceable and ascetic life-style. (Some *gurus* and their disciples will claim that the *chela* must surrender totally to his *guru*, regarding him as God while he is on the path towards his own realization.)

We have no way of knowing whether more or fewer educated Hindus have a significant relationship with a spiritual teacher than other Hindus, or in comparison with the past. There are no statistics; and contemporary estimates of trends vary wildly. But it seems likely that the real *guru-chela* relationship was always rare, and still is. Most educated Hindus have been, and still are, content to pursue the goal of *moksha* through the path of *karma* and *dharma*, ordinary work done in the context of one's caste duty. A *guru* is only helpful or necessary to those following the way of knowledge or of devotion, where choice of action, guidance between various courses, and discrimination between truth and delusion in subjective experiences is important. People found their *gurus* in various ways. Some set out to find a man reputed for sanctity and this crucial power of discrimination or discernment, others inherited *gurus* through family connections, while for some sects and castes there were hereditary *gurus* like Sri Shankaracharya. Some of the latter are still important in the life of educated Hindus: but the link between an educated Hindu family and a *guru* is now rare. *Gurus* sought by personal choice are, however, significant as sources of religious authority.

Those who claim *guru* status today often deliberately appeal to Western visitors who have little knowledge of Hindu tradition and few criteria by which to judge their claims and teaching. The more exotic and heterodox *gurus* who have attracted foreign devotees and finance include the youthful Guru Maharaj Ji of the Divine Light Mission, whose jet-set life style has largely undermined his popularity and credibility; Maharishi Mahesh Yogi, the Beatles' *guru* and founder of the Transcendental Meditation movement; and the Pune-based Rajneesh, whose eclecticism, oratory and charisma draw hundreds of young foreigners and some Indians – to the distaste of many ordinary, educated Hindus who feel that he has gone outside the bounds of Hindu tradition, and is debasing their religious heritage.

There have also been some notable *gurus* whose credentials are unimpeachable, and who spread their influence widely by publishing as well as by welcoming enquirers into their ashrams. Among those who stay within the classical Hindu tradition of the *guru* and preach Advaita Vedanta are Swami Sivananda Saraswati (1887-1963) and his disciple who then became a spiritual master in his own right, Swami Chinmayananda. The former founded the Sivananda ashram at holy Rhisikesh in the Himalayas, and five years

later in 1937 inaugurated the Divine Life Society which now has
about 300 branches throughout the world, and is involved in
preaching, publishing and medical work. The ashram draws many
foreigners and south Indian devotees. Chinmayananda's Chinmaya
Mission is growing faster than Divine Life; it also is world-wide
and has about a hundred Indian branches. Other contemporary
gurus include Sathya Sai Baba, whose miraculous powers as well
as his preaching of *bhakti* have attracted thousands. Established in
an ashram at Puttaparthi, he claims the status of *avatar* or incarnation, which Sivananda and Chinmayananda have not. In western
India outstanding spiritual masters are Swami Muktanananda Paramahansa and Sri Dattabal Desai. Yet others remain local, hidden
figures, but just as powerfully part of the tradition of the realized
man whose life demonstrates the immanence of the divine, and
who is accredited with religious authority as a result.

The significance of such men, known or hidden, lies partly in
the influence they have in the lives of their followers, those whom
they enable to understand Hindu traditions afresh in a changing
India. But more important is the fact that even in the twentieth
century the *guru* is a witness, to disciple and non-disciple alike,
that self-realization is possible, that the experience of divinity
which scriptures and sages have taught is a living reality. The saint
in the Hindu world is quite unlike the saint of Christian understanding. Whereas all Christians are 'called to be saints', to live a
life in communion with God, often in quite mundane circumstances, in Hindu thought sainthood is supra-normal. It is achieved
only by hard discipline, and is the goal and the actual end of the
few. But those few confirm and embody a major theme within
Hindu religious experience, that of interiority, and the immanence
of the divine. *Gurus* are a continuing channel of divine revelation
and inspiration in a tradition which needs this constant infusion,
lacking as it does the doctrine of decisive revelation present in
Christianity. The 'authority' of the *guru* is thus important in the
contemporary Hindu experience, not just for these few who accept
his guidance. To millions of others he is authoritative not as an
agent of control but as a living witness to the possibility of the
experience of realization of the divine in each self, an experience
which they may never achieve but which validates their religious
world view.[30]

Educated Hindus and Christians face different situations of change,
bearing different legacies of religious authority. But our evidence
suggests that for neither group is there an authority in their ex-

perience which they unquestioningly accept, or which unreservedly helps them interpret change and respond to it in the context of their religious inheritance.

One result among both groups is a novel or increased stress on personal experience as the ultimate religious authority. In Hindu tradition individual experience has been valued, though there is unresolved tension between this and life within rigidly ordered society. Cults devoted to Krishna, and the expectation of individual realization of divine immanence, remind us of the past vitality of this aspect of tradition. It is an aspect which seems to be increasingly stressed among the educated. In our earlier sketch of 'the Hindu world' we saw how *bhakti* or devotional cults thrive in urban areas. For their adherents personal experience is the touchstone of religious reality. Although it occurs within a community of shared faith and emotion, the community is one to which devotees choose to belong, their bonds being ones of shared devotion, not of birth and caste. Their religious way is not the path of works prescribed by *dharma*, but music, dance, recitation and worship to bring alive their experience of such manifestations of divinity as Lord Krishna. In the more intellectually orientated 'invented Hinduism' stress is laid on the advaitic experience; and contemporary *gurus'* tracts designed for the educated also underline personal experience as the ultimate goal and authority in the religious life. Gandhi, too, played up the importance of each individual when he insisted that religion was beyond creed or convention, but rather the individual's search for truth in which the final authority was what he himself experienced as 'the inner voice'.[31]

Among educated Hindus there is now, far more than ever in the past, in a real sense a 'market place situation' in religious matters. It is not the blatant choice, the either/or of total conversion offered by the challenge of Islam or Christianity as in earlier centuries. Rather, it is a more subtle and pervasive situation of choice in which most educated Hindus live, because older, external religious authorities are weakening. To meet this prospect, the possibility of discarding or disregarding old religious authorities, the emphasis on an ancient strand of the Hindu tradition, that of personal experience as the fundamental authority, is both appealing and creative.[32]

The educated Christian lives in a social and intellectual environment which, to a far greater extent than that of the educated Hindu, values individual autonomy, testing of authority against experience, and has made a cult of 'doing one's own thing'. Developments in the specifically religious context reinforce this. Theologians rarely make dogmatic assertions now. Their hesitation and even confusion; the stress by some on God as the ground of being; and renewed emphasis on Christ as a presence to be experienced now; all this is filtering through to the educated laity. Discussion of the nature and role of religious myth which was once confined to the academic theologian's study is now far more public and popular. All this contributes to the disintegration of older, easy patterns of faith, of unquestioning acceptance of credal and moral packages from the hands of religious 'professionals'. Charismatic renewal reinforces this trend towards religious empiricism, and highlights the individual's experience of indwelling by the Spirit. I found it significant that nearly 60% of my Manchester sample of believing staff accepted personal experience as a source of religious authority. Just over 30% of students did so, the lower figure explicable because of their shorter experience of life. Another important finding of the Manchester surveys was that a large majority of believing staff and over half the believing students felt the figure of Christ to be authoritative for them. But since many did not associate this with scripture, some sort of contemporary Christ-experience was evidently in their minds when they replied.

The contemporary stress on experience as a key authority in religious matters reflects a wider intellectual and social ferment. The demand that authorities should be tested out by personal experience has deep roots in the empirical tradition of philosophy in Europe. It is part of one of the vast problems which have haunted European philosophy since the seventeenth century, namely 'How do we *know*?', 'On what authority is knowledge based?' In matters of religion Kant was a particularly seminal thinker, insisting that religion and morality could have no basis outside the experience of man: only in man himself and his experience of the human situation could notions of reality and divinity be grounded. Philosophical arguments and concerns have moved on since Kant. Old attempts to 'prove' the existence of God have been largely abandoned, and religious 'knowledge' is seen to be more intuitive and subjective than other sorts of knowledge grounded in objective evidence, but is considered none the less real for that. The residue of this intellectual turmoil contributes to the cultural and educational environment of the educated in Britain, which Christians share. It is reinforced by the wide range of social change and dislocation we have already noted. Consequently one of the hall marks of contemporary British life is the demand for personal experience and expression, and a revulsion against established authorities and structures, whether in religion, politics, family life, education or the arts.[33]

Far more than in India, the educated in Britain live in a religious market situation. The old religious monopoly when Christianity was a 'given' in the total social and intellectual order has collapsed. Fewer now inherit a Christian faith, and even those who do, have to reinterpret it for their own situation. Furthermore, their reinterpretation often has to be hammered out in comparative isolation; certainly without the support or constraint of the old communities which were the social buttresses of belief, and often without much guidance from religious 'professionals'. Christian belief, in its many contemporary variations, is now not the churches' sole preserve; nor is it within their control. As belief has become more a private option, an issue with which the individual has to wrestle, so the burden of choice is the greater, as is the emphasis on individual experience. As individual experience becomes a crucial authority in religion, so increasingly the religious life is seen as one of movement, from experience to experience, as the individual matures and moves in age, place and status. The spiritual journey is increasingly felt to be the authentic mode of religious experience for this age; a mode in which searching and doubt rather than dogma and acceptance of authority are dominant.

But to say that personal experience is the final arbiter in religion is a glib response to contemporary doubts about religious authority. Experience is a significant touchstone, but it is not more than a stopping-point in the spiritual journey of individuals and of whole religious traditions. It raises questions which people and traditions cannot side-step if they are to retain integrity. Religious experience is always to some extent conditioned by the past and by expectations, however unpredictable it may seem at the time. What are the resources for religious experience and its expression? How do you judge the authenticity of individual experience, and does this matter anyway? Moreover, even if a spiritual free-for-all was possible or desirable, the like-minded would certainly cluster to share and reinforce their experiences, in the process working out some sources of authority.

Our comparative enquiry into the nature of authority in the religious world of our two groups has been firmly based on observable evidence. But its historical dimension should provide a clearer understanding of a problem felt to be a real and urgent one by both educated Hindus and Christians. But there is no easy resolution of the dilemmas of religious authority in a time of change within our two traditions. The first necessity is therefore for believers to understand their situation; why they have a problem and why it takes that particular form. Here the image of inner and outer rings may help. Secondly, there can be no simple answers by borrowing from other traditions. Religious authority is formed through time, as much by the social and political context of a religion as by the nature of the vision at the heart of that religion. Christians cannot, for example, say, 'Let's have *gurus*' without discovering the function of a *guru* in Hindu tradition and society, and whether such a figure might have a role in Christian experience. Hindus cannot treat the *Gita* as a gospel like a New Testament gospel because it is not the same sort of source material and is vulnerable to critical scholarship if used in this way.

However, a historian's comparative perspective suggests that a way forward for the believer and the believing community is to perceive more clearly the essential *task* of religious authority. That is, not to preserve itself and enforce adherence because it 'has the truth', the knowledge vital for man's right response to ultimate reality. Religious truth is not a neat package which can be withheld or dispensed at will. Authority exists to enable, to liberate vision of ultimate meaning. But such vision is never entire or static. Consequently religious authority can only perform its proper role if it marshals the resources of the past (both its wealth and its warnings of pitfalls) and if at the same time it creates a framework in which believers can together confront the central issues which their world raises. If religious authority fails to facilitate pilgrimage towards truth for each generation it will not only lose credibility; it will turn its back on its very *raison d'être*.

Table G: Sources of Religious Education and Influence among Students

Belief Category	Source of Education			Source of Influence								
	Home	School	University	Church	Sunday School	Other	Parents	Religious Leader (living)	School	University	Church	Personal Experience
Believer	57.1%	74.6%	9.5%	58.7%	46.0%	1.6%	60.7%	14.8%	32.8%	8.2%	54.1%	34.4%
Agnostic	40.0%	90.0%	0%	20.0%	40.0%	0%	41.2%	17.6%	58.8%	0%	23.5%	23.5%
Atheist	19.0%	95.2%	0%	28.6%	33.3%	4.8%	70.0%	20.0%	40.0%	0%	20.0%	10.0%

Source: Manchester Student Survey, 1978

Table H: Sources of Religious Influence on University Lecturers

Belief Category	Parents	School	University	Church	Sunday School	Reading	Particular Religious Leader	Personal Experience
Believer	64.9%	29.7%	13.5%	59.5%	24.3%	56.8%	8.1%	32.4%
Agnostic	40.7%	40.7%	11.1%	33.3%	7.4%	51.9%	7.4%	25.9%
Atheist	42.9%	28.6%	7.1%	28.6%	21.4%	71.4%	7.1%	14.3%

Source: Manchester Lecturers' Survey, 1978

Chapter Five

A Spirituality for the Twentieth Century?

=

The enabling of a religious vision of, and response to, the world in which men actually find themselves lies also at the heart of this final part of our enquiry into the religious experience of educated Hindus and Christians. We have understood religion to mean a perception of the nature of reality, a way of understanding the meaning of man and his world. Whatever the differences between religious traditions, each one has developed appropriate ways for men to express its understanding of meaning, and respond to the vision central to it. These ways include specific acts of public and private worship, and rituals acknowledging and interpreting reality at turning-points in the lives of men and groups. But response to the central vision consists not just of what could narrowly be called 'religious acts', but also of an attitude to life – practically and more generally expressed in a life style, with appropriate patterns of public and private behaviour. It is a whole web of interconnections which people in the tradition construct between their beliefs and their total life environment in thought and action. It is this totality of response to the central perception of meaning which I call 'spirituality'. I do not use the word in the sense that it has sometimes been used (particularly in continental Europe) – of a particular religious school or discipline, with its overtones of peculiar spiritual athleticism, esoteric knowledge, or a group of the specially pious. We are talking here about the total orientation, style and inner feeling of a religious tradition.

This is one reason why this part of our comparison is peculiarly difficult, and why the most fruitful approach may be to ask rather than pretend to answer questions. In a real sense no one can ever *compare* spiritualities because one person can only know truly the spirituality in which he is immersed. Religious traditions have to be lived from the inside.[1] So the questions I ask inevitably spring from my own experience and study as an educated Christian in

Britain. I start from what *I* discern as areas and sources of disquiet and decay, as well as of strength and renewal in contemporary Christian spirituality in Britain. I then try to see whether educated Hindus grapple with similar issues, and whether our separate experiences of making sense of our traditions in the late-twentieth-century world have anything to say to each other.

The immediacy of the issue of a contemporary spirituality is another difficulty for us. It actually confronts those of us who have not abandoned our religious traditions: those of us for whom the gods are not dead, though we may feel we perceive divinity with eyes more darkened than those who handed on our traditions to us. We are so personally involved that it is hard to stand aside temporarily to analyse and compare our situations; even for those of us who are trained to be analytical, even clinical, about men and their societies. It is even hard to organize this comparison. So many of the problems involved interact on each other that it is virtually impossible to separate them for tidy discussion! But then one would expect this when probing the religious experience, if religion is about the whole of life and not just one compartment of it. Life is not tidy but generally rather messy. It has few clear lines of demarcation and its boundaries are often blurred.

Although this is in many ways the most difficult and diffuse of our three main areas of comparison it is arguably the most important. The problem of a truly twentieth-century spirituality is the issue before which educated Hindus and Christians actually stand. On their response depends the way they as individuals and their religious traditions travel in the future. It is also the area in which are focussed many of the questions our evidence has already raised. For example, this is where educated believers must in practice face the theoretical question of the nature of religious knowledge: is it essentially a question of rational cognition, of accumulating 'knowledge about . . .', or does it involve deeper levels of awareness? Or again, what are the implications of our evidence that many young people find no meaning in the ritual and theological formulations of their traditions? In my Manchester sample just over half the students felt that religious ritual and theological statements meant anything to them; just under one third of believing students admitted that they found both ritual and theology meaningless. In the Bombay adolescent group (of whom 75% called themselves believers) 70% felt that dogma and ritual had no meaning. As we have already seen, the British evidence indicates that faith and religious experience has for many become detached from church-going – a fact Christians themselves admit.[2]

A historical approach helps in understanding the areas of growth and tension in any spirituality at a particular point in time. Spirituality is transmitted and mediated partly by specifically religious institutions, specialists and written sources; by believing parents, teachers and friends through personal influence. But where a religious tradition has dominated a social structure and style, or actually moulded it, social conventions and assumptions carry the same message. (This ties in with our image of the inner and outer rings of religious authority and communication.) These various carriers contribute to a living tradition on which people draw for religious insight and expression, though often they may be only vaguely aware of its different agencies. But what happens when some of these carriers or mediators of spirituality are undermined; when the tradition in effect ceases to hang together, to make sense as a living whole? For this is what can happen in a time of marked social and intellectual change. The result is often the end of a situation of religious monopoly in that particular society. In its place comes increasing religious choice, as we have seen in the case of Britain, and to a lesser extent in the Indian world of the educated Hindu. This may threaten old religious authorities and weaken former mediators of a spirituality. But the other side of the coin is great potential for growth. This is true for whole religious traditions and their structures; if they find ways of re-interpreting and communicating their messages appropriate for the changed situation; if they actually see that they must in a sense 'woo the market'. For individuals, too, choice means potential: the opportunity of deeper faith, a spirituality more fitted to the real world, as well as the possibility of declining belief, uneasy observance of irrelevant religious rituals or their abandonment.

Some observers call this situation one of 'religious privatization' – an ugly jargon word, but one we must consider briefly. Among the educated, in Britain and to some extent in India, *belief* has become a matter of private choice, an area of life which state and society recognize as one for individual decision. But those who do not reject belief have to draw on some common pool of experience and expression for their vision of reality, for the ideas in which they clothe it, for the symbols and styles in which they express it. This is true for every individual, however uncomfortable he may feel within his inherited tradition and critical of it; however freely he draws on resources from other traditions made accessible by modern communications and this century's unprecedented migration of religions. Moreover, all who profess and express religious belief find they have to retain or refashion a supportive community of those who share a fundamental understanding of reality. In practice there is no really private religion, however personal the choice of faith may seem to be.

One further point needs stressing. We shall not understand any spirituality's potential and adaptability in a time of change unless we understand its *purpose*. In general, of course, its purpose is response to a perception of ultimate reality. But its specific purpose will depend on that perception, its core insights. Here, as I understand it, there is a divergence between the Hindu and Christian traditions. At the heart of Christian faith is a vision of divinity which is supremely personal, and evokes from each individual a response of relationship, both in the present life and in a life after physical death, whatever form that may take. Resurrection, not mere survival or even reincarnation, is the corollary of this central vision and experience of relationship: but it is absent from the main streams of Hindu understanding of reality. For the Hindu reality is supremely mysterious, beyond time and beyond personhood. The goal of religion is therefore release from all transient forms and powers which are unreal or veil the mystery. For those who use the concepts of Vedanta the goal is release of *atman* and its absorption into *Brahman*; the divine essence in man returning to its source. For many, however, the earthier, short-term goal of religion is release from the natural and apparently supernatural constraints on man in this life; accretion of power over present circumstances and consequent growth in personal tranquillity. Within both traditions there have been those whose vision of reality corresponded more to that associated with the other tradition. Christian mystics like Eckhart yearned for an experience akin to release and absorption; Hindus in the *bhakti* tradition have built their lives on a loving relationship with Krishna. But the main streams of each tradition have diverged on this essential question; and this divergence profoundly affects the way in which educated Hindus and Christians perceive the issue of spirituality in the twentieth century, and the extent to which they experience it as a pressing problem.[3]

An obvious starting-point for our comparison is a cluster of issues which in the Christian setting focus on 'specifically religious' acts – namely, rites of worship and prayer. This is the most marked area of questioning among contemporary Christians, in which disquiet is more articulated and changes in practice have been clearest.

Not only has there been a general decline in church-going: even believers attend less regularly, or at least with less enthusiasm and sense of meaning. The evidence collected in Chapter 3 confirms my own observations: that although many educated Christians still pray, they find it hard to pray regularly or in words and forms traditionally taught. Nor is it insignificant that there is a steady flow of books on prayer on to the paperback market; and these have the most rapid turnover on church bookstalls. Moreover, among Manchester lecturers whose religious life had been influenced by reading, modern devotional books topped their religious reading lists after the Bible. All this suggests that acts which have been seen as central to Christian spirituality are now crucial issues. No longer are they 'givens' in the believer's religious experience; rather, they are occasions for a sense of loss and unreality, and potentially, of rediscovery and renewed faith.

Worship and prayer raise problems at two levels. The surface problem is one of religious language and symbol, and of sheer social habit. Here most clearly the changes which have refashioned British society have deeply affected the vitality and reality of traditional Christian expressions of worship; and have eroded old channels along which religious experience was transmitted. Not only is church-going no longer part of the social style of a large majority. What is done and said in churches has little meaning for many; and not only for those who are just not used to church services because their parents never took them as children. Traditional worship often fails to express or enable experience of the sacred, or to deepen awareness of the ultimate meaning of man's existence. It is not surprising that religious language and symbol has so often 'gone dead' for modern people when we consider how different is their world from that inhabited by those who wrote the New Testament or even the great English liturgies. Can modern urban man really find inspiration in such rural symbols as shepherds, wells or grains of wheat? Can educated Christians easily or profitably perceive God as Father when psychology has made us all aware of our ambivalence towards our own parents? Compounding the problem of symbol is the *language* of so many prayers and traditional Christian formulations. The musical cadences of sixteenth-century English often fail to convey contemporary meaning except to those, increasingly few, whose education has prepared them to understand and respond to it. But there is a positive side to the impact of changes in social style and communication. As church-going is no longer a social convention or obligation, those who make up the smaller congregations are probably more in earnest about their faith, and therefore more willing to see how their common worship can genuinely express it.

But at a far deeper level 'specifically religious' acts are problematic for believers. This brings us to the heart of contemporary turmoil over an authentic twentieth-century spirituality. If worship is an expression of relationship between God and man, then no amount of tinkering with forms and language will avail unless worshippers perceive afresh the nature and reality of that relationship. Here a clear and creative trend is visible among educated Christians – a craving for a renewed vision of God which is real for modern man in the world he actually inhabits, which will liberate him from a religion of credal and moral packages which he carries round with an increasing sense of guilt and dishonesty because he is unable to make them truly his own.

The evidence of this is patchy. Among Christians (as well as those outside the churches) there has been a remarkable flowering of interest in the practice of silence and meditation, and a revival of awareness that within the Christian tradition there is the resource of a deep stream of contemplation and mysticism. The popularity of Thomas Merton's works and the writing and broadcasting of Archbishop Anthony Bloom, drawing on the Russian Orthodox tradition, are two small examples. Often such interest is loosely connected with curiosity about Eastern and non-Christian traditions of mysticism, and experimentation with their techniques for self-quieting and awareness. Straws in the wind have been the eruption of TM into the world of students and businessmen; or the publication of *Return to the Centre* by Bede Griffiths, a Benedictine monk who has lived a Hindu-style contemplative life in South India, about whom, moreover, there was a BBC television programme in 1978. In the same year a BBC 'Lifelines' series was also devoted to meditation, and a morning phone-in programme, 'Tuesday Call', featured the same subject. But as one reviewer commented, many people have only the haziest ideas as to what meditation can enable. Often it is viewed as a refined and improved tranquillizer, and the serious religious implications and potential of the practice are ignored (deliberately by the proponents of TM who wish to avoid a 'religious' and particularly a Hindu label).[4] Within the major churches in the mainstream of Christian tradition further signs are evident of a craving for an authentic contemporary relationship with a God who is seen as transcendent yet supremely personal. They include the experiences of charismatic renewal, and the undocumentable evidence of individual struggles, local discussion groups and painful reconstruction from ordinary pulpits.

But the other side of the relationship is man. There is discernable a parallel quest for a renewed vision of man in his totality; not man as a shivering, naked soul so often painted in 'dooms' on the walls of mediaeval churches for the instruction of the ancestors of twentieth-century Christians, but man in his total environment, the product of the past and the pressures of the present which sociologists and psychologists now help us to understand. This means taking seriously the subtle interactions in each person of mind and body, conscious and unconscious, of heredity and environment; and then relating the whole of this to a transcendent yet personal God. A lay Christian, by profession a psychiatrist, has put squarely the issue facing the churches and individual Christians.

> Western society has to find new values which do not fixate its citizens at the material level, and that means finding a place for the new and deeper layers of our humanity in terms of personal and inter-personal involvement. Traditionally this has meant turning towards a spiritual dimension, in fact towards God. This simple turning towards God will not in fact suffice. Man's involvement with God must take place at a level of engagement of the mind and psyche which is appropriate for a society that has immense opportunities of unravelling deeper layers of the image of God in man. That is why simplistic religious crusades just do not work. Man's spiritual longing is as strong as ever, but the level of engagement between man and God must reflect the realization of these new depths in our humanity which the social, psychological and scientific horizons have opened up. One aspect of the spiritual crisis of the age is the inability of the churches to engage man accurately at a deeper level of existential experience which will do justice to these newly opened horizons . . . we cannot pursue the spiritual . . . unless we acknowledge the new insights we have acquired in the depths of our psyche regarding our humanity.[5]

Increasingly there are signs that Christian writers and preachers are beginning to engage at this deeper level and are refusing, as so often happened in the past, to brush under ecclesiastical carpets what seems problematical and threatening. It is an enterprise which demands courage, insight and delicacy, because so often it can appear merely destructive of old patterns of what has been assumed to be Christian 'morality' and 'orthodoxy'. It involves investigation of the way symbols old and new can do justice to contemporary man's aspirations for and experience of a vision of truth: it means not ignoring some parts of man and his life, and dismissing them as sinful or secular, devoid of religious meaning and potential. It leads to the abandonment of security in 'the faith': instead of to the harder commitment to a pilgrimage of and in faith.[6] This double quest for a new understanding of the relationship between God and man is central to contemporary Christian spirituality. It lies at the heart of questioning the meaning and form of acts which are in one sense 'specifically religious'.

The practical repercussions of this I would call the quest for a new religious style: an authentic 'lay style' which expresses and enables this relationship in the sort of lives Christians actually lead. This has meant re-thinking many traditional patterns of public worship and private prayer, because so often these stemmed from clerkly practices worked out in monasteries. Often, too, they were appropriate to more leisured lives, or at least life within societies ordered by the rhythms of light and dark and the seasons of the year. In most denominations this has meant cutting down the *number* of services dedicated Christians are expected to attend and making the eucharist central to the Christian's public expression of faith and mode of common worship. It enacts not only the renewed understanding of the nature of the church which we noted in the last chapter. Supremely it demonstrates and renews the relationship between God and men as and where they actually are. Most churches have also revised their eucharistic liturgies, simplifying them and modernizing their language. This often produces yet more turmoil. Some have gone into mourning for the beauty of worship, for the security of forms and images known from childhood. Others are bemused. Still more are left mutely and vaguely dissatisfied, while acknowledging that change was needed.[7] There are no easy solutions to questions of form, language and symbol for worship: those who say there are know little of the growth and power of symbol and word in a total culture. It is impossible overnight, or even over months, to produce worship which not only makes sense but leads onward to deeper perception in a changing and increasingly un-rooted society. (Liturgical changes raise in another form, too, the issue of the laity's role in the life of the churches and the possibility of a genuine 'lay style' in spirituality. Some Hindus may envy the Christian churches their authoritative structures. But precisely because there are such structures, changes tend to be made from above by liturgical specialists and commissions. Rarely is there genuine corporate involvement in change or real understanding at local level of the reasons for and significance of changes.)

But where reformed worship has 'made sense', where specifically religious acts 'come alive', it is because they express and enable relationship between God, the believer and his total life. It is where there is no dichotomy between what is a religious part of life and what is not: where worship integrates a vision of God and of man in society being made whole. Real and living worship is found in various contexts – in small groups who cooperate in ordinary life to embody their faith and infuse and seal their effort with worship. It is visible in massive gatherings like those at the Taizé community where many young people have re-found worship and concern for the world's problems as inseparable. It occurs in the intense experience of charismatic groups which, unlike their Pentecostal predecessors, do not rest content with a 'spiritual' experience, but go on to work out the implications of the in-dwelling Spirit in ordinary life.

Simultaneously there has been much concern over the practice and content of private prayer; again in the realization that real prayer must be rooted in real life. Two streams of change flow together. There has been renewed emphasis on silence, an opening of man to relationship with God beyond words which can so often be barriers instead of channels. The popularity of Thomas Merton or Anthony Bloom marks this. There has also been a re-finding of prayer in the reality of ordinary life; making everything from the newspaper to art and natural beauty a source of prayer. Michel Quoist's *Prayers of Life* were the first in a new genre. They broke new ground in the 1960s, with their vivid and colloquial language and their starting-point in such mundane things as tractors, a five-pound note, a wire fence or a bald head! Countless others are also struggling to learn and teach the art of praying life, and one of the dominant motifs in the re-creation of Christian spirituality for the twentieth century has been a broadening of the origins of 'religious' insight. The whole world of art, literature, music as well as the beauties and eccentricities of nature is drawn into the nourishment of Christian believing, praying and living.[8] Our evidence has shown how often traditional forms of prayer have died for educated Christians. Where prayer lives again it expresses this central relationship between God and man in his totality.

When the observer begins to enquire whether special acts are the focus of similar turmoil among educated Hindus he must first distinguish between the educated who live ordinary lives, 'householders' in traditional phraseology, and those who follow specific spiritual paths or disciplines. Few follow such disciplines, *sadhanas*,[9] with the goal of realization, freedom from the veil of matter to see what truly is, in which lengthy meditation may be an essential part. This must be said, because this aspect of Hindu tradition is the image of Hinduism so often projected in the West among Christians. Not the least influential force in publicizing this strand of Hindu spirituality has been the writing of Western Christians, particularly Roman Catholic religious like Bede Griffiths, Abhishiktananda and Sister Vandana, who have immersed themselves in it and discovered how its riches can bring meaning and renewal to the Christian religious experience.

For most educated Hindus life is lived in the ordinary world without expectation of the experience of 'realization' or endeavour towards it. In this framework religious rites have a role and significance very different from that in the Christian context. They are different in form, of course, partly because their goal is different. Regular and communal temple worship is rare, and certainly not central to Hindu worship in the way that the Christian eucharist is. Private prayer is more formal and stylized than is individual Christian prayer, and seems seldom to be understood as expressing and exploring a relationship of love whose implications demand work and a new insight in a changing world. The framework of religious rites is the family and domestic round of daily, annual and occasional observances to ease the passage of that family and its members through the normal occurrences and hazards of human living; by accepting the natural and supernatural forces which are thought to influence life, and then propitiating or harnessing them. Much ordinary Hindu worship is therefore materialistic, even manipulative. It is significant that of the Bombay adolescents questioned in 1978 (who were mainly Hindus), only 10% expressed love of God through prayer, considerably less than among Manchester students. For the Bombay young people, as for many other Hindus with whom I have discussed prayer, the dominant aims are happiness and well-being – and what they called 'solace', a word which Christians rarely use about prayer.

The instrumental nature of much Hindu worship and prayer was clear in a pamphlet by Swami Sivananda which contained a *mantra* in praise of Shiva: this promised to give long life, peace, wealth, prosperity and immortality. Its material aim was most modern!

> In these days, when life is very complex and accidents are an everyday affair, this Mantra wards off deaths, fire accidents, cycle accidents, water accidents, air accidents, and accidents of all description.[10]

But despite the comprehensive assistance against modern hazards intended here, modern science and technology has made the overtly

A Spirituality for the Twentieth Century? 131

manipulative aspect of worship less real or necessary for the educated. When we try to discover what the result of this change is we find that there is nothing like the public discussion which occurs in the Christian context. Nor is there a central source which registers the influence and implications of change by organized reform or teaching. The outside observer can therefore only fit together scattered pieces of evidence, and describe elements which are part of a fragmented and complex mosaic.

For many of the educated, the round of household rites and annual festivals seems to have lost some meaning, though the social nature of many observations is still important. Enjoyment, habit and a sense of obligation still pull educated Hindus to traditional worship far more strongly than is the case with their Christian counterparts. Yet there is a marked tendency to drop some rites and curtail others. Almost everyone recognizes that many rites are now shorter, particularly for marriages, because an educated man's income and professional obligations do not permit the time off and lavish expenditure expected of his parents and grandparents. The ceremonies marking major life crises – birth, puberty, marriage and death – remain, if attenuated. But lesser ones are quietly dropped. However, even where this trend occurs, many religious symbols of Hindu tradition almost certainly retain a vitality for the educated far stronger than in the Christian context. This persistence is due largely to the close interweaving of Hindu tradition and Indian culture and to the fact that massive social change has not torn Indian society up from its roots.

Although there is no central authority to control change in Hindu worship, there *are* instances of public and formal attempts to make sense of worship and adapt it to the circumstances of a changing world. Some voluntary bodies produce new rites, re-design or translate from Sanskrit old ones. One such is the Dharma Nirnaya Mandal in Maharashtra. This aims to *re-establish dharma* in the contemporary world. One of its exercises has been a new sacred thread ceremony. Old and now irrelevant parts of the ceremony are discarded, such as the mother's leave-taking of her son. The child now promises to study truth as a schoolboy and a student, recognizing that books and even nature rather than a specific person will be his *guru*.

Individual religious leaders are also trying to reintegrate worship and modern life, often laying new stress on personal prayer rather than ritual observance. Swami Chidananda, for example, urges people to let their daily work be a song of divine praise, whatever work it is that modern India's economic structure demands of them.[11] One science teacher, deeply influenced by her Shankara-charya in South India, said simply, 'The school laboratory is my *mandir* (temple)'. He exhorts his followers to pray briefly each day, then treat work as prayer, no longer believing that lengthy prayer, impractical in modern life, is obligatory. But discussion of the nature and purpose of prayer does not appear as widespread and personally crucial as it is among Christians. For some, however, prayer is a contemporary and vital experience, leading to a sense of personal relationship with the divine with which Christians can sympathize deeply. Gandhi was an obvious example, conducting prayer meetings and drawing for their content on many religious traditions. In 1931 he even held such a prayer group at the Palace of Westminster, to the surprise of British observers! In his personal life he prayed daily; not in formal rite, but attentive to what he experienced as an 'inner voice'.

Other influences in the world of the educated tend to devalue traditional ritual, only sometimes replacing it with other forms or a renewed understanding of worship. The increased popularity of many devotional cults suggests that they fill a vacuum in the lives of educated Hindus. Some are well established in Hindu tradition such as the India-wide Krishna cults, or regional ones such as those which draw on Maharashtra's tradition of popular saints. Yet others are new, even bizarre; like the cult of Santoshi Ma, popular among women and adolescent girls, which originated in a film. (Devotional films are also increasing, though we do not know who actually attends them or what, if anything, they contribute to the audience's religious awareness.) The 'invented Hinduism' of so many of the educated does not stress or encourage acts of worship and prayer. It leaves the individual free to do as he pleases. But its tendency is to draw attention away from the traditional and ma-terial worship which was the framework of much Hindu religious experience.

Overall, the evidence suggests that there is here no turmoil simi-lar to that which educated Christians are experiencing. In part this is because the great range and flexibility of Hindu traditions enables personal and piecemeal adjustment with less sense of strain, of being pressed into old and now unreal moulds. More fundamen-tally, worship is not a central problem for most Hindus because it does not, as for the Christian, express a relationship between God and man which is both heart and goal of the religious experience.

We have seen that the nature and place of worship in any religious tradition depends partly on the value placed by that trad-ition on life in this present world. How do our two traditions perceive the significance of this world, of man, his social and natural environment, and what influence does this perception have on their spirituality? I suggest that a marked feature of the religious experience of the educated in *both* traditions in this century has been a 're-finding of the religious significance of the world'.

Christians have always been tempted to 'flee from the world' – either literally in a separated or enclosed community with its own life-style, or, more subtly, by treating ordinary life (with all its necessities, its pains as well as its joys) as irrelevant or at least peripheral to their relationship with God. This tendency has roots in the Jewish apprehension of an awesome God apart from his world, who demands holiness from man. It was reinforced by the Christian stress on personal salvation and the supreme importance of each individual's response to God. The result has been the constant danger of a dichotomy between the religious and the ordinary, protecting the sacred by insulating it from human living. In Britain Christians have faced another danger – that of complaisance because they live in a so-called Christian society. Because the churches and the faith were so visible, so 'established', it was fatally easy for Christians in the past to rely on social convention as their right religious response to the world, and in so doing to refuse to see that the gospel might demand changes in society and life-style.

In every age and place there have been Christians who have redressed the balance, have resisted the separation of religion into a Sunday compartment, have spoken out against social habits and assumptions. But among Christians in post-war Britain there seems to be a growing awareness that an authentic modern spirituality, a genuine response of modern man to God, must be thoroughly grounded in real life. It is no coincidence that those who struggle publicly and articulately with this issue are not just religious professionals, priests and theologians, but lay Christians – psychiatrists, broadcasters, teachers and the like – whose professional knowledge and involvement is so real and important that they are forced to integrate them afresh with their faith.

Theologically this is expressed in two themes which are stressed in contemporary Christian writing of many kinds and are seeping through via pulpits and religious broadcasting to those who read little. These are the themes of incarnation and the kingdom of God. The concept of incarnation is expanded beyond the belief that God clothed himself in the flesh of one man at a particular point in time. It sees all life as the material of incarnation, the fleshing out of God's presence. Following from this is a re-emphasis on corporate salvation. Although this was central to Pauline writ-

ing in the New Testament, contemporary Christians are understanding afresh and therefore more forcefully that life in its totality
must be redeemed and restored to its true status – as the place of
divine revelation, and of man's relationship with God. Not the
least influential in this renewal of realization that the whole of life
must be taken up into the religious vision was the scientist and
mystic, Teilhard de Chardin, who wrote of the totality of humanity
caught up in and transformed into the body of Christ.[12] Inextric-
able from this wider understanding is the stress that the core of
Jesus' teaching was not a simple message of personal salvation
from sin and its consequences but the proclamation of the kingdom
of God, coming on earth here and now, to which men cannot
avoid response. All life is the material of this kingdom. (To emphasize that this includes all that appears modern and worldly and
is a corporate experience, preachers have seized on the image of
the city. They note that scripture begins with a story set in a
garden, but ends with a vision of a city made new.)

Just as salvation is seen to include society and the natural order,
so its component of personal salvation is re-expressed in ways
which make sense of, and in, the lives of contemporary men and
women. An image popular in the past was of the divine shepherd
rescuing the frail and trembling sheep from the waste land of sin.
Now, in ways not uninfluenced by modern psychology, personal
salvation is gradually being understood as a wider process of learning what it means to be truly human, made in the image of God.
This still includes recognition of sin and the need for forgiveness.
But it sees with fresh understanding and compassion where men
are wounded and incapable of responding to God in love. It recognizes the dark side of human personality and experience, the
many contradictions within each individual. It cries out that people
in their *totality* must be saved, that these aspects of existence
should not be denied, but re-integrated in a process of making
anew whole human beings. Such redeemed, renewed men and
women will then individually and corporately become part of the
body of Christ – Christ who is seen as the archetypal figure of man
journeying towards wholeness in relationship with God.[13]

In trying to interpret the ways in which educated Christians are
refinding the religious significance of the world I speak as an
insider. I cannot do this for the Hindu tradition. To one outside
that tradition it seems that one of its dominant aspects has been to
devalue both the individual and the material world as modes of
divine disclosure, as of true significance in the perception of reality.
The individual could rarely choose in religious matters: he was

expected to conform to *dharma*, because this was the way society as a whole could act in harmonious conjunction with reality. Even the man who 'renounced' society for the solitary pursuit of realization conformed to an accepted pattern which helped to conserve the fundamental shape of society. After death individual personhood was understood to end. Similarly, matter was thought to veil reality rather than being vested with religious significance as the fleshing out of reality. But, on the other hand, Hindus have not been as inclined as some Christians to operate with a gulf, a disjuncture, between faith and real life. Religion and ordinary living have been virtually co-terminous through the mechanism of social structure, the total provision for the ordering of human activity through individual and caste *dharma*, and the enfolding web of group ceremonial. The refinding of the religious significance of the world has therefore taken a rather different form from the one we have discerned in the Christian context.

In the Hindu process of rediscovery the pioneers have generally not been traditional authority figures. Some *swamis* have been significant innovators; but educated Hindus immersed in politics, education and business have been equally articulate. There seems to be a distinct trend towards re-thinking the religious significance of life in this world even among those who preach what I have called 'invented Hinduism', with its stress on the ultimate release of the divine essence in each man. Swami Chidananda, for example, whose teaching on new forms of prayer in today's world we have noted, persistently urges men to pursue truth in and through life as it now is rather than devaluing it. Similarly Swami Muktananda Paramahansa has stressed the reality of the material world and its religious significance. As one of his pamphlets says, 'Swamiji holds that the world is not an illusion but a manifestation of the Divine Consciousness. . . . This whole world is . . . Brahman revealed before our eyes in manifoldness.'[14]

One theme long established among others in Hindu tradition is enabling this process of rediscovery – action in the world while renouncing the fruits of action. A religious man need not take the way of knowledge or of total renunciation. He may participate in ordinary life in a spirit of non-attachment, of calm selflessness: thereby he will seek truth through and by means of the material world without being overwhelmed or ensnared by it. Among educated lay Hindus, Gandhi, supremely, preached that this way of renouncing the fruits of action was the solution to the Hindu tendency to devalue action in this world. For him religion was the whole of life: not in the sense of conformity to patterns of a society identified with Hindu tradition, but as a search for truth through every human activity, from prayer to politics or public hygiene. Only non-attachment could, he believed, protect the religious man from corruption in a life of immersion in ordinariness. Not surprisingly he took the *Bhagavad Gita* as his key text in this respect. The *Gita* is now the best-known and best-loved portion of scripture among educated Hindus – in part perhaps because its message helps many, besides Gandhi, to make sense of modern life *within* their religious inheritance.

The *Gita* is the 'gospel' of those educated who increasingly detach themselves from the prescriptions of *dharma*, and define their tradition as 'a religion', based on a creed which is independent of Indian society and culture. The creed maintains that the divine nature is latent in every man; and this has, I judge, enabled many to find a religious significance in the individual apart from his membership of family and caste. Vivekananda laid particular stress on the divinity of all humanity. The Ramakrishna Mission continues to do so; and it is one of the most influential all-India religious organizations among the educated. For Gandhi too, the individual was crucial: not just because he saw religion as each man's quest for truth, but because he felt that only individual reformation could be the base for a radical transformation of the social and political order.

But what difference does all this make? If there are signs in the Hindu and Christian traditions that the educated are re-finding in different ways that their real world has religious meaning, does it affect the way they act? I have suggested that 'spirituality' includes a life-style, a general and practical expression of man's response to his vision of truth, his awareness of the sacred, just as much as it involves overtly religious acts. Is there evidence among our two groups of changes in life-style attributable to new religious understanding of this world?

The first area to examine is the educated believer's reaction to the prevailing social order and style. Here the Christian has the dilemma of living in a society in which Christianity was for so long 'established', a society which buttressed belief as an outer ring of religious authority. Practical Christian life was for many synonymous with decorous conformity to accepted social norms and standards. So easily Christians' response to present change can be to stick to old conventions, to refuse to question social divisions. Or more energetically and stridently they may respond by railing at changes which have eroded religious authority, weakened the churches and corrupted what they see as Christian morals. Both responses are visible in Britain today.[15] But there are also signs of serious Christian thought on this matter; of attempts to work out the social implications of faith, to prize it loose from mere acceptance of the prevailing social order or hankering after social styles which are fast dying. The involvement of churches and individual Christians in social justice for a range of under-privileged groups, for harmonious industrial and race relations, are examples. Many, too, as individuals or corporately, are re-thinking personal ethics in the light of social change, new medical knowledge and psychological insight, and the new understanding of personal wholeness noted earlier. Cases in point are such highly charged issues as abortion, homosexuality or divorce. Here previously there was general agreement on what was Christian morality. Now older standards are seen – at least by some – to have been as much influenced by social convention as by religious truth.[16]

But there has been little serious thought about whether the faith demands a particular life-style, markedly different from that prevailing in the surrounding society. Christian stewardship of time, talents and money is a beginning: but often its object has been to muster resources for specifically church work rather than to re-fashion a Christian style for the whole of life. Some groups have taken salvation of the natural order seriously and urged fellow-Christians to heed the ecologists' warnings and change their patterns of consumption. In general, however, Christians have preferred not to ask such radical questions: they remain undistinctive in society, living on a legacy of what is acceptable social behaviour for believers.

Hindus have graver problems in working out what social order and style of life is appropriate in response to their religious vision because for so long the issue has been unequivocally resolved in the institution of caste, and in patterns of duty prescribed for each social group and individual at particular stages of life. Now changes in so many of the assumptions and priorities of the educated re-open the issue. Can 'a religion' of Hinduism be cut loose from caste-ordered society? Or can India's social order be reformed to accommodate and express both what is valued from tradition and the new insights and values of twentieth-century Indians?

Some have replied by founding or joining reformed sects which denounce caste and renounce its patterns of life. Most have refused to break so radically with tradition. Among these was Gandhi, who nonetheless worked out and preached a new style of life which was strikingly novel in its priorities and implications. It was based on fraternity and mutual recognition of equal human worth across all social divisions: on economic sufficiency rather than competitive consumption. He was deeply influenced by Ruskin and Tolstoy, and sought for a social order which would preclude individual, organized and institutional violence. Consequently his ideal was a rural society whose members limited their wants and produced whatever they could to satisfy their basic needs without having to enter into wide scale economic relations or industrial means of production. In his own ashram communities he ordained a life of poverty, simplicity and manual labour in which each member had to be prepared to do even the most menial and undignified of household tasks. This enacted his concern that older Hindu attitudes to purity and pollution should go, that untouchability should be abolished, and that caste groups should cease to see themselves in a hierarchy of status and worth.[17]

Few have accepted Gandhi's principles or adopted his life-style.[18] But change there has been among educated Hindus. Some will tell the foreigner that caste has been abolished. But though this is manifestly not so, it is true that many older practices of social separation and discrimination have quietly and thankfully been dropped. In a way the availability of an imported, semi-Western style among the educated has allowed them to shelve if not solve the problem. Because it is so widely acceptable it permits change without demanding that the educated Hindu makes a religious issue of new patterns of personal behaviour and social relationships. If a religious rationale is required, then 'invented Hinduism' is to hand, implicitly denying many social aspects of the Hindu religious inheritance.

There is another aspect of contemporary spirituality among both educated Hindus and Christians which suggests that practical change is happening in response to religious re-evaluation of the world. This could be called an ethic of public involvement. It is clearest in the Christian setting. For centuries in Britain the churches and Christians as individuals have been involved in social welfare – health, education, care for the weak – consciously following the example of Christ's compassion for all men as children of God. Often *politics* and religion were separate compartments of life, and Britain has had no tradition of religious political parties, as has continental Europe. However, it is now far rarer to find Christians lapsing into political quietism, assuming that faith does not have political implications. Here is a practical working out of a renewed understanding of incarnation and the kingdom of God. Churches do not dictate political attitudes to members. But they *encourage* them to become politically involved. On major issues they sometimes suggest guiding principles, and most have special boards responsible for studying complicated public issues. Considerable numbers of ministers and priests of all denominations are active in public life at different levels, although there is a residual antipathy still in Britain to 'meddling clerics' in politics. (Political activity by Anglican parsons was more acceptable because of the background they shared with the governing class, and their recognized position in the political system through episcopal representation in the House of Lords.) Even now there tends to be controversy when religious professionals are politically outspoken, as in the case of Mervyn Stockwood, who retired in 1980 from being Bishop of Southwark. He had long been known as a protagonist of the underprivileged, ministering in a diocese which contains some of London's poorest housing and worst social problems. Such men have not been trying to re-establish episcopal or clerical power in politics: but have urged on all Christians a religious duty of political involvement.

Among educated Christians a growing integration of faith and public action seems clear. Certainly this is the theme of many contemporary books which work out for Christians some of the implications of current economic and social structures. It is not insignificant that many books on prayer deal with such matters; following the understanding that an authentic modern spirituality can accept no divorce between 'spiritual' and 'social' or 'political' thinking and action. Some ephemeral contributions to religious debate which appear in *The Times* on Saturdays also reflect this deeper public involvement.[19] More local evidence suggests the same trend. In my Manchester survey nearly three-quarters of believing staff thought that religious leaders should be active in public life, while just over three-quarters said that their faith actually influenced their attitude to public life, including politics. But involvement brings controversy – because there is rarely an obvious Christian response to an issue. Christian principles have to be discerned painfully and applied to problems; and in this process believers differ. Some of the most obvious recent examples are Christians' debates among themselves over legal changes relating to abortion or homosexuality; over grants to the World Council of Churches; and over the implications of Edward Norman's 1978 Reith Lectures, which dealt with the linkages between Christianity and current political ideologies and cast doubt on their propriety.[20]

The situation of the educated Hindu is almost diametrically the opposite. Political participation in defence of Hindu *dharma* in specifically Hindu parties is almost coeval with the development of modern politics in India. But events leading up to Partition, and Gandhi's assassination, not only stopped for the time all such action, but warned many that overtly religious politics was fraught with danger in a plural society. Now 'communal' parties are permitted, but are not strongly supported. It is still a delicate matter for Hindus to pursue a specifically Hindu programme in a country where there remain significant religious minorities, and where inter-communal violence is a grim and constant possibility. For Hindus, moreover, the precise form of government is 'theologically' irrelevant: what matters – and always has mattered in Hindu political theory – is that government should permit the functioning of Hindu society. Consequently it is on matters of law and social policy which touch caste and family matters in particular that India's secular governments have faced overt 'Hindu' opposition. But that has been a minority opposition. Even *sadhus* appear to be politically ignorant and indifferent; and certainly not committed to revivalist Hindu politics.[21]

On the other hand, Hindus in this century have been exploring other aspects of an ethic of public involvement and obligation as a result of their beliefs. Compassion for others because of their humanity has not been a dominant feature of Hindu tradition, as it has been of Christian faith. Charity has certainly been a religious obligation, but often valued for its effect on the spiritual state and social prestige of the donor. But there seems to be a real change in this area – a new affirmation of human solidarity and fraternity which is expressed in public welfare. The origins of this change are debatable. Some ascribe it to the example of Christian missions from the nineteenth century, others trace its source in the strand of Hindu tradition which emphasizes the divine latent in every man. But the evidence of change is there – the welfare work of the Ramakrishna Mission, the donations to welfare and education by trustees of some major Hindu temples and the countless private individuals who without payment give of their time and expertise in such fields as health and workers' cooperatives. Among major leaders in public life the most influential in promoting new attitudes of fraternity and new patterns of humanitarian work was Gandhi. He preached and acted out a vision of religious truth in which response to the divine demanded not only prayer and worship but active service of all mankind. He castigated those who thought that religion could be separated from the rest of life and insisted that politics, social service and care for individuals were as 'religious' as meditation, and that those who tried to divorce and compartmentalize them did not know the meaning of true religion.

His ideals are partially carried on in contemporary India by the *sarvodaya* movement, dedicated to 'the welfare of all'. It is not insignificant that even some *sadhus* realize that something more is required of them than renunciation of society. Of a group studied in north India in the 1960s nearly 20% were involved in some form of social work.[22]

There is another aspect of the reaching after an authentic spirituality for twentieth-century man – the response of educated men and women to the experience of other faiths, in a world where migration of religions now occurs on a major scale. This has caused more change for our Christian group. India's Hindus have long lived in a religiously plural society. Their religious tradition equips them to cope with this by the social mechanism of separation and does so by its flexibility towards beliefs and patterns of devotion, because variations here do not threaten it as a whole. The insights and practices of other religions cause Hindus no major problems. When attractive they can today, as they have for centuries, be grafted on to the existing stock, as groups and individuals choose. Partly because of the credal flexibility within Hindu tradition, and the absence of any central revelation, and partly because of the close interweaving of Hindu religious experience with Indian society, there was and still is very little incentive in the tradition for missionary activity. (The Arya Samaj is a recent exception, and about one fifth of the branches of the Ramakrishna Mission are now outside India.)

Eclecticism and tolerance have been a major part of the Hindu response to other faiths; they are the hallmarks of the response of the educated today. Gandhi was a striking example of this. He drew almost promiscuously on every source he could find for inspiration and expression of religious truth, and preached the essential unity of all believers in every religious tradition. He saw religions as a search for truth and consequently in his view there were as many religions as there were seekers. Truth as perceived in this life would always be relative, and therefore no man could claim to have the truth; and no man or institution should presume to denigrate another's vision or attempt (other than by love and example) to persuade him to change it. Among living Hindu teachers Swami Chidananda, for example, also preaches religious tolerance. For him the rationale for tolerance is the unity of all religions, claiming that all pursue the same goal of realizing that all men are part of the divine, of the Supreme Consciousness. 'All faiths are one and all prophets have lived the same life of ethical perfection, divine compassion, goodness and awareness of the oneness of mankind.'[23] There are countless other educated Hindus, hidden and unknown in the public sphere, who gain comfort from the Bible; or at another level stand pictures of Jesus or the Virgin alongside those of Krishna, without any sense of incongruity or disloyalty. This attitude takes us back to the goal of Hindu spirituality and the Hindu understanding of revelation which have already concerned us.

By contrast other faiths are a major problem for Christians. If the goal of Christian spirituality, the believer's total response to its central vision, is relationship, then it matters supremely to perceive aright the God to whom that relationship tends, to find the right paths to knowledge of him. Furthermore Christians in Britain are now faced for the first time with the experience of religious pluralism at home. No one can fail to see the vitality of Asian, African and West Indian religions among our migrant communities or the jet-age *gurus* who set up religious shop among us. Radio and television bring other traditions right into our own homes. In universities student notice boards are as likely to advertise classes in Buddhist or Transcendental Meditation as cricket fixtures or the next disco.

Within the churches, too, other forces are breaking down older attitudes. One is the collapse of dogmatism noted in the previous chapter. Another is the renewed perception of the believer's life as one of a search, a pilgrimage towards a constantly renewed vision of truth, rather than of possession of faith. Furthermore, the felt poverty of much traditional Christian worship prompts many to interest in the style of worship and techniques of prayer of other religions. Few educated Christians can now with integrity view other faiths in the way their grandparents or even their parents did. The nineteenth-century image of the benighted heathen, fit objects for charity and conversion, sturdily buttressed by imperial assumptions of the supremacy of Western culture and the white man's duty to civilize and guard the inhabitants of European empires, no longer fits political, cultural or religious reality. Growing familiarity with the vitality and riches of other faiths raises radical questions, moreover, about the nature of revelation and of religious knowledge itself.

The implications of religious pluralism have caused some Christians to retreat in fear and revert to fundamentalism. Others seem so eager to borrow to make up for their own deficiencies that they plunge headlong into a syncretistic gallop; with little regard for basic questions about the nature of religious experience, symbol and style and its social conditioning, or about religious authority and truth. The churches have officially responded with cautious exploration, sharing and listening across religious barriers, a response known as 'dialogue'. Often this is the work of professionals who have the time and expertise to engage in it; and in ordinary congregations it is an enterprise in its infancy, if it happens at all. A major problem in dialogue, however, is one which is a main concern of this book: that although understanding and comparison of beliefs at an intellectual level is important, every religion is intricately connected to the society in which it exists, and consequently has an ambience and flavour which cannot be grasped by discussion and description. Real 'dialogue' must be grounded in shared experience, and this is impractical for many ordinary Christians in Britain.[24]

Yet the experience of religious pluralism, of the migration of religious leaders, ideas and actions, is beginning to influence Christian spirituality. It underlines the wider meaning of incarnation – the action of God in all men, at all times, in many ways. Christians are learning that they cannot, as was once thought, 'take Christ into' other religious traditions. They must find him already there, just as they are learning to find the divine presence in music, art, literature and nature. The contemporary situation also suggests to some over-cerebral and rational Western Christians that their faculties of intuition and of contemplative awareness need recognition and deliberate cherishing. These, too, are roads to religious experience and knowledge. They are open to every man, and indeed are vital if the whole man is to enter into relationship with God.

Our enquiry into the possibility of an authentic twentieth-century spirituality for educated Hindus and Christians has shown how great are the differences between the world's great religious traditions, and even within those traditions, in the way people understand the meaning and implications of religious belief. Spirituality, the believer's total response to a vision and so to the whole of life, is profoundly important for anyone seeking to understand a religious tradition, but it is almost impossible to describe and document. Our investigations also suggest that both Hindu and Christian traditions are living through a period of stress, though there seems to be less of a crisis for religion in the Hindu experience. A dominant strand in the response of educated Hindus to their religious heritage is a sense of its *potentiality*. Many with whom I have talked have spoken with great conviction of its vision of truth, not just for twentieth-century Indians, but for the whole world; and see it as a particularly fitting religion for the contem-

porary world, not least because of its flexibility and credal tolerance.[25] The Christian sense of crisis, by contrast, stems in part
from the tendency in the past for Christians to perceive their
religious heritage and experience in more static terms of 'the faith'.

However, both traditions clearly have resources with which to
deal with the stress and questions which change provokes – resources of ideas, institutions and people; and almost for the first
time on a significant scale the resources of example and inspiration
across old religious barriers. The process of creative response to
change is often slow and halting. It is almost always painful and
disruptive, eliciting hostility and defensiveness from others within
the same tradition. But amongst many educated Hindus and Christians there are signs of recognition that creative change is essential,
that received truth, whether formulated in creeds or embodied in
praxis, is not enough; that truth must be discovered by living it
and in a sense experimenting with it. The very threats to older,
received truths in fact lead to the uncovering of new truth and the
revitalizing or rediscovery of old truth. Men's perception of ultimate meaning, their visualization of the gods, and the response to
life which this demands, can never be static. In religion stasis means
death. This century, as a time of unprecedented change, consequently has experienced in acute form both the death of religions
and their renewal. For both educated Christians and Hindus some
experience of death and loss is the precondition for the birth of an
authentic religious vision and response to the contemporary world.

Epilogue

=

Thus far our study of men and gods in the changing worlds of Britain and India has been analytical and empirical. It has dealt with the facts of the contemporary experience of educated Christians and Hindus, in as much as they can be observed, measured or assessed in relation to three central features of all religious traditions, namely their power and viability as total world views, their authority structures and networks of communication, and their spirituality in response to life, all of which are open to question in a time of rapid change. This approach and style springs from my training; historians see religions as phenomena embedded in time and place, and therefore deeply influenced by changes in their surrounding contexts. But I also write from this angle of vision out of conviction that the Greeks' ancient injunction, 'know thyself', lies at the heart of understanding across boundaries of space, time, culture and religious tradition. For those who choose or are thrust into relationships of encounter and dialogue with people of other faiths, one way forward in such understanding is to start from the pressure points where social change is forcing religious traditions to make new responses: areas of potential decay and renewal; experiences where change makes religious tension inevitable, and can be met either in the spirit of expectancy and hope or of frightened withdrawal and ossification. Whereas 'dialogue' has often tended to mean sharing the riches and strength of one's inheritance, empathy and mutual perception may in a time of change spring more from honest sharing of one's perceived weaknesses and dangers.

I have deliberately avoided an attempt to abstract a 'Hindu Spirituality' for Western Christian consumption, or any prescription for Christian problems of authority and contemporary spirituality from the Hindu experience, because no deep and lasting influence across religious boundaries is possible without honest understanding of some of the differences of the religious traditions concerned, and of their historical and contemporary setting. Our study has been such a ground-clearing exercise. But it may be fitting to conclude it with a more personal note of reflection on how involvement with India, her peoples and traditions, has influenced one Western Christian.

Each individual can only speak for himself or herself in this matter, because there are only personal 'passages to India', and many different experiences of Hindu tradition, philosophy and worship. Those who know northern India more intimately will not, for example, understand the significance and power of southern India's temple tradition. The Westerner who has journeyed to Hindu ashrams and experienced their austere sprituality of disciplined study and meditation, waiting for illumination at the feet of a *guru*, may well know little of the domestic and social round of the householder Hindu's religious experience; or the joyous abandonment of the *bhakti* sect or group of pilgrims. Therefore my conclusions reflect my experience: they cannot pretend to be a prescription for others or presume to be a recipe for reformation in areas of contemporary Christian disquiet.

In yet another sense it can be misleading to speak of 'the influence of India'. For many people the manner and mechanics of that influence may well be indirect – by highlighting or bringing new meaning to existent but submerged or little stressed aspects of their own religious traditions and inheritance. For some, whose own tradition with its language and formulation has 'died' and now fails to communicate to them an experience of the numinous or to nourish qualities of inner awareness, it may be necessary to go away, even physically, to another continent and culture, to learn to see what they actually have at home, to experience re-illumination of the riches of their own inheritance from the light of another religious tradition. The twentieth-century world of transreligious experience gives new meaning to St John's prologue unfolding the mystery of the Word that is the light of all men, and the enlightenment of all who seek for truth.

In the Hindu world there is at one level a refreshing mundaneness for a visitor who comes from a culture where increasingly religion has been shut away in special buildings, at particular times, in distinctive segments of life, however much this is at variance with the heart of the Christian vision springing from the first disciples' experience of incarnation in the ordinary. The practice of caste and the prescriptions of individual and group *dharma* have acute dangers which contemporary Hindus clearly perceive. But their anchoring of religious experience and expression firmly in the everyday, reinforced by the social and festive nature of much religious pilgrimage and religious observance, is an infinitely valuable reminder to the Western Christian that where religion is compartmentalized, divorced from daily life, it ultimately dies as a living religious tradition and becomes the cultic hobby of the few. (Nearer home for the Western Christian, of course, the Jewish tradition in a similar way witnesses to the religious meaning and potential of the thoroughly ordinary.)

The mundane quality of much Hindu religious activity and teaching is particularly striking as it complements the deep Hindu strand of spirituality which expects or acknowledges an experience of a transcendent mystery of the divine. Here is much which can tell Christians of the need and possibility of a new integration of the sense of the numinous and the routine, the growth of a sense of the holy from within the lives of ordinary men and women who have neither time nor inclination for indulgence in a special 'religious culture'. Furthermore, the Indian ability to talk freely without embarrassment about religion, and the expectation that most people will have something personal and experimental to share in this area of life, should encourage fearful and silent Christians to speak aloud their fears and doubts, as well as their hopes and convictions. For until honesty and openness are accepted as natural the churches will never be communities of pilgrims, but increasingly restrictive and deadening structures.

Sheer physical encounter with India can also affect the Western visitor powerfully. In a strange way I find that the slower pace of life, the pressures and hassles of daily existence, as well as the physical closeness to birth, sickness and death, and the daily and seasonal rhythms of light and dark, of searing heat or driving dust and rain, disturb European perceptions of time and space, of presence and absence. I think particularly of that quality of light at dawn and sunset when there is a strange incandescence and transparency. When the sky gradually lights from cold black to pearl grey and through to sunrise, or fades from vivid blue through a hazy dun to final dark, there is almost an imperative to give way to wonder and awe. It is no coincidence that these times of vivid division and transition from one state of natural being to another have long been considered holy in India, and times most fitting for prayer.

For me not only the natural surroundings of the Hindu world, but also the stark contrasts of its society and the strands within its religious tradition heighten a sense of the forces of good and evil, dark and light, joy and sorrow, which are masked in the easier environment of the West. Sometimes this sense is deeply disturbing, as in encounter with worship of the destroyer goddess, Kali, or the inhuman austerities of some ascetics. But these jolt the foreigner out of the blandness and more monochrome quality of life in a technologically streamlined society. For many Hindus what seem to the outsider demonstrable opposites and contrasts find resolution in the Upanishadic teaching that beyond and beneath what is visible is a mystery of being too deep for words, for mental experience and rational explanation. The rediscovery of interior awe, of the reality of non-material forces, of the mystery at the heart of all religious experience, is a crying need for Western Christians. (Its absence in so many of the churches and their members have, as we have already seen, proved an insurmountable barrier between them and many of those who either have or crave for experience of the numinous.) But this is *rediscovery*, as within Christian tradition that deep awareness of fundamental mystery is present in the perception that sorrow and joy are inseparable, that destruction precedes all renewal, that life only comes through pain and death, and that emptiness opens the way for the experience of fulfilment.

It is perhaps the mutability, mobility and variety of religious experience in the Hindu world which can most surprise and help the Christian observer. The individual Hindu can wander through many avenues of philosophy and theology, and can take numerous paths of observance. Indeed in different stages of his life (as student, householder or retired person) he has different religious duties and priorities allotted to him. This suggests that the Western concept, reflected in the use of language, of 'having' or 'losing' faith, does violence to the reality of religious experience. Many now powerfully – and rightly – reject the notion of Christianity as a package deal of faith and morals, a notion which has done much to shut many young people off from the resources of their own religious inheritance. The Hindu perception can help point Westerners back to the truth that religious belief and experience is not something to be grasped, found or lost but a deepening capacity for a new quality of awareness, a pilgrimage towards deeper and more inward truth. Early Christianity was of course described as 'the Way', followed by a community bound by love. For the individual this means persistent change; willingness to leave behind old habits, practices, perceptions, to experiment and grow into new truths and experiences at different stages of his life and as his external circumstances alter. Whereas the truth that *all* Christians must change and grow continually in religious experience has at times been obscured by technical manuals of the spiritual life for the holy few, the Hindu notion of rightful stages of growth for all men can liberate Christians from false fears about 'losing faith'. Faith is a matter of vision and trust, not of possession: it has a provisional quality. It must change with the individual and his environment. In a real sense, if Christians do not persistently and chronically 'lose' and 'refind' faith as their lives change, their religion will become a cultic hobby rather than a living pilgrimage.

But how is this quality of awareness to be deepened and sustained, and pilgrimage towards vision facilitated? Such awareness, though present in all men, can so easily be dampened down or extinguished. It needs persistent renewal, just as a lamp's flame depends on oil to feed the wick. Contemporary searching for answers to this question among educated Christians became clear in the last chapter of this enquiry. My own passage to India, particularly my experience of Christian ashrams which explore the riches of Hindu traditions for the renewal of Christian worship, have re-illuminated for me the role both of silence and of symbol in this process of deepening and sustaining.

Symbol and silence are both deeply embedded in Christian traditions. But much Christian spirituality is predominantly verbal, reflecting its cultural context; and ordinary Christian worship is not only encased in words, but is also noisy. One strand in Hindu experience lays paramount stress on silence and attentiveness, an opening to truth through intuition and illumination at a level of experience and personality beyond words. The Christian mystics have long known the need for and power of silence in the religious experience. But for lay Christians it has often not been a living possibility, but rather seen as a practice reserved for those enclosed from the ordinary world. I am convinced that the contrary is true, that it is precisely Christians immersed in ordinary life who most need to rediscover the resources of silence. By the way of patient and wordless stillness, the religious experience can again spring up from the place where each individual is; not poured into a particular mould of worship, not constricted by patterns of devotion and language of prayer which for so many have 'gone dead'. This way needs courage, for both laity and their pastors, brought up in traditions which have emphasized 'going to church' and 'saying one's prayers' as the external marks of the believing Christian.

The use of symbols, a vital part still of Hindu culture, similarly demands deeper consideration by Western Christians. A symbol recollects the worshipper, concentrates him upon a single point, illuminates through its association with the past, and leads onwards to fresh realizations. As we saw, so many symbols of traditional Christian worship now seem to fail to do this, as they spring from experiences and commonplaces which ordinary people in industrial society no longer share. But symbols are almost essential for public, if not private worship, for the same reason as silence – that the mystery which worship approaches is too deep to be evoked and acknowledged in words alone. The churches cannot evade this problem. Nor can they solve it by a casual borrowing of symbols from other cultures. Only as each Christian community investigates the potency and potential of old and new symbols can forms of worship emerge which convey and express the experience of the numinous for twentieth-century man. Shepherds, wells, or candle-light, images of sacrifice and expiation, may well now be non-starters as symbolic carriers of religious experience and men's re-sponse to it. But light, fire, wind, flowers, water, wine, food, cel-ebration and festivity are parts of life which with imaginative reflection may still have the meaning and illuminative power of living symbols. They *may*: but the process is not automatic, not least because as such general aspects of life they can so easily fail to carry specific religious insight and degenerate into signs of wool-ly and perhaps facile aspiration. But in an age and culture of lost symbols it is essential that Christians should investigate what they have lost, and what riches are still at their disposal for the renewal of worship.

Hindu attitudes towards 'orthodoxy', in particular Hindu flexi-bility in matters of right belief, also influence my response to the contemporary problems of how in a world of rapid social and intellectual change to prevent the thought forms and language of Christian theology inherited from the past becoming a barrier to truly contemporary Christian experience and spirituality and a wall of division between those who genuinely seek for religious vision but find themselves outside the churches, and those for whom older orthodoxies still carry conviction. Perhaps the churches must re-think their ideas of 'belonging' and be prepared to become far more 'fuzzy at the edges'.

Often in the past lack of clearly defined boundaries, as in the case of the Church of England, has been decried on the grounds that it weighs down a church with nominal members whose peri-pheral attachment dilutes the efforts of the organization and brings it into disrepute. I have in mind a blurred edge with a much more positive meaning and function, and a great potential for shared exploration of religious experience. It would mean accepting as genuine participants in the pilgrim community people at many different stages of religious perception and articulation, including and positively welcoming without prior conditions of commitment to particular orthodoxies and the practice of specific rites many who now feel that their personal pilgrimage is hindered by churchly practices and ecclesiastical formulations. New patterns of acceptance and looser association for some imply new styles of pastoral care, to give people the encouragement, and at certain times and stages the instruction, they need at their particular point upon the pilgrimage. They also make more urgent a re-thinking of the varieties of worship and prayer suitable to such an open-ended community, particularly as in Britain's rapidly changing and diverse society it would draw on people of many religious backgrounds or of none, unlike the days when Christendom and European society were coterminous and men shared patterns of thought and symbol, even when they did not as individuals accept many of the tenets assumed to compose Christian faith and morals. Eucharistic worship clearly could not be the sole form of public celebration of faith and community. It would have to be complemented by experiments in communal silence, for example; by forms of active service which are seen directly and interpreted as part of the pilgrim community's expression of and growth in faith; and perhaps celebration of common concern and mutual care in festive meals. Such styles might have meaning for many who could not with integrity participate in a eucharist and for whom there is now little alternative.

Such 'open-endedness' for the churches and the care implicit in it for the needs of individuals raises vast problems of ministry in ecclesiastical structures already stretched to breaking-point by shortage of pastors. It demands an even more radical re-thinking of the *nature* of ministry than is actually occurring, a renewed vision of ministry far deeper than consideration of part-time ministers, worker-priests, or even the ordination of women. Here the Hindu experience of the *diffusion* of religious authority and ministry may shed light on possible ways forward. As we have seen, a wide range of Hindus have particular religious functions, and authority pertaining to those functions – whether it is in teaching, praying, leading public or private worship, in healing, or in social regulation. My observation of this pattern in India makes me ask whether the churches are not now being called to recognize in new forms the early Christians' understanding that there were many ministries. Perhaps particular people should be set apart by the local community of faith for different functions, rather than agglomerating most of these in one special ministerial order. Local congregations could begin to experiment on these lines, setting apart those of their members (now of course called 'laity' without a recognized ministry), who seemed particularly called to and fitted for certain types of ministry – prayer, healing, counselling, teaching, organization, as well as officiating at public worship. As well as radical involvement of the 'laity' at the heart of the church's life and work, lack of which is a problem we noted in Chapter 4, this would mean, too, a way of bridging the contemporary gulf between much of the professional life of educated Christians and their role and experience in the context of organized religion. But perhaps only continuing inflation and social change will ultimately bring about such changes at the level of whole churches, as they break down vested interests and render impossible traditional patterns of ministry.

But far more important than the logistics of reform or of organization is the underlying sense of those dimensions of human existence which are almost indefinable, but at which such words as 'numinous' and 'transcendent' begin to hint: the sense of the mystery which lies at the heart of all religious experience. When this sense is shallow, then tinkering with symbols, organization and doctrinal formulations is little more than shuffling a pack of cards. I have found in journeys to India not only a deepening awareness of such mystery but its clear crystallization in the person of Jesus, as I have become more aware of the riches and strivings within the Hindu inheritance, and as I have been forced to understand him in a universe of faiths and diversities of revelation. He increasingly becomes the transparency of God in the world of men. His life enacts the contradictions of light and dark, humanity and inhumanity, grief and joy. His way of dereliction and death points to their resolution in fullness and resurrection and in so doing becomes the incandescence of the mystery beyond words at the heart of being. St Paul wrote of 'the fellowship of the mystery' open to all men. It is a sense of this mystery which is without price, particularly in times of rapid change, whatever one's particular religious inheritance. It provides the resources with which to face the implications of change for one's own religious tradition without fear, but with exhilaration. The Christian disciple experienced this, though exiled on Patmos, and was compelled to articulate its renewing power: 'Behold, I make all things new.' Out of the contemporary turmoil of Hindu tradition Rabindranath Tagore wrote of the same mysterious sources of renewal:[1]

I thought that my voyage had come to its end
at the last limit of my power – that the
path before me was closed, that provisions
were exhausted and the time come to take
shelter in a silent obscurity.

But I find that thy will knows no end in me.
And when old words die out on the tongue,
new melodies break forth from the heart;
and where the old tracks are lost,
new country is revealed with its wonders.

Notes

Introduction

1. W. M. Teape, *The Secret Lore of India and The One Perfect Life for All being A Few Main Passages from the Upanishads*, 1932.

2. India's regional variations in culture and religion are a major problem in this sort of work, as is noted in Chapter 1. It was impossible to study towns representing every region; so I chose places representative of different historical experiences and aspects of Hindu tradition, and deliberately avoided the South, which is discussed in the works of Milton Singer, one of the few scholars who has observed how urban Hindus actually live their religious inheritance today. (His works are referred to in the text and in the bibliography.)

1. The Religious Experience: Problems of Comparison

1. Changes in the study of religion since the eighteenth century are surveyed in R. N. Bellah, *Beyond Belief*, 1970.

2. See, for example, F. F. Conlon, *A Caste in a Changing World*, 1977, which deals with social adaptation; M. Lederle, *Philosophical Trends in Modern Maharashtra*, 1976, which describes ideological responses to change, as does D. H. Killingley, 'Vedanta and Modernity', *Indian Society and the Beginnings of Modernization c. 1830–1850*, ed. C. H. Philips and M. D. Wainwright, 1976, pp. 127–40. A case study of the ability of Hinduism to change and develop new emphases is C. Parvathamma's work on the Lingayats of Karnataka, 'Religion and Social Change: A Study of Tradition and Change in Virasaivism', *Dimensions of Social Change in India*, ed. M. N. Srinivas, S. Seshaiah and V. S. Parthasarathy, 1977, pp. 243–52.

3. For example, O. Chadwick, *The Secularization of the European Mind in the Nineteenth Century*, 1975; D. L. Edwards, *Religion and Change*, 1969. See also L. K. Pritchard, 'Religious Change in Nineteenth-Century America', *The New Religious Consciousness*, ed. C. Y. Glock and R. N. Bellah, 1976, pp. 297–330.

4. Among the most accessible are those presented in M. Argyle and B. Beit-Hallahmi, *The Social Psychology of Religion*, 1975; D. Martin, *A Sociology of English Religion*, 1967; D. Perman, *Change and the Churches*, 1977; L. Paul, *The Deployment and Payment of the Clergy*, 1964; R. J. Rees, *Background and Belief*, 1967; *National Survey on Religious Attitudes of Young People*, 1978. See also the *Church of England Year Books*.

5. P. Ashby, *Modern Trends in Hinduism*, 1974, pp. 49–70; V. G. Pundlik, 'Religion in the Life of College Teachers', 1970, which apart

from the statistics gathered by the author also cites other unpublished surveys in Appendix I; unpublished figures collected by students at Sophia College, Bombay, 1978; G. Poitevin, 'Quelle sécularisation? des dieux ou des hommes?', *Spiritus*, 64, XVII, September 1976, pp. 229–64.

6. Martin, *A Sociology of English Religion*, pp. 34–5.

7. U. King, 'Indian Spirituality, Western Materialism: An Image and its Function in the Reinterpretation of Modern Hinduism', *Social Action*, 28, 1, January-March 1978, pp. 62–86; M. Singer, *When a Great Tradition Modernizes*, 1972, pp. 27–37. For the work of Max Muller, one of the foremost European scholars in the nineteenth century who made Hindu texts available to the West, see N. C. Chaudhuri, *Scholar Extraordinary*, 1974.

8. *Indian Opinion*, 2 October 1909, *The Collected Works of Mahatma Gandhi*, Vol. IX, 1963, p. 389. One of Gandhi's most forthright assertions of the contrast between spiritual India and the material West is in his booklet, *Hind Swaraj*, published in 1909, now available in *The Collected Works*, Vol. X, 1963, pp. 6–68.

9. D. Martin, *The Religious and the Secular*, 1969. Others share his unease. For example, Peter L. Berger, *The Social Reality of Religion*, 1973; A. M. Greeley, *Unsecular Man*, 1972; Peter E. Glasner, *The Sociology of Secularization*, 1977, where he calls secularization a 'social myth'.

10. For a rather different definition and use of 'secularization' by an Indian scholar examining his own society, see M. N. Srinivas, *Social Change in Modern India*, 1966, pp. 118–46.

11. P. Laslett, *The World we have Lost*, 1965, especially pp. 139–46.

12. See B. R. Wilson, *Religion in Secular Society*, 1966, and *Contemporary Transformations of Religion*, 1976; Edwards, *Religion and Change*; Chadwick, *The Secularization of the European Mind*.

13. This is the definition most commonly used by educated Hindus with whom I discussed the problem. For academic discussion about definitions and the precise nature of the Indian state see D. E. Smith, *India as a Secular State*, 1963; V. P. Luthera, *The Concept of the Secular State and India*, 1964; V. K. Sinha (ed.), *Secularism in India*, 1968; A. S. Ayyub, 'Secularism', *Change and Conflict in India*, ed. R. Thapar, 1978, pp. 106–18.

14. R. Panikkar, *The Unknown Christ of Hinduism*, 1964, pp. 25–6; S. Weil, *Waiting on God*, 1959, pp. 137–8. The same point is forcibly made by academic writers in the concept of each religion having its particular 'mood', created by the emergence of its institutions and thought forms within a particular socio-cultural matrix. See Robert F. Spencer's introduction, 'Religion in Asian Society', in a volume edited by him, *Religion and Change in Contemporary Asia*, 1971; C. Geertz, 'Religion as a Cultural System', *Anthropological Approaches to the Study of Religion*, ed. M. Banton, 1966, pp. 1–46.

15. These major philosophical themes have been called a 'thematic cluster': Ashby, *Modern Trends in Hinduism*, p. 14. Two convenient paperback introductions to Hindu ideas and practices and their evolution over time, are K. M. Sen, *Hinduism*, 1961; R. C. Zaehner, *Hinduism*, 1962. It is not insignificant that Zaehner, a Roman Catholic, approached

the subject 'theologically' through an analysis of these concepts; while Sen, a Hindu, started with the practical expressions of the Hindu religious experience and their historical growth.

16. Zaehner, *Hinduism*, pp. 2–3, 102–24. Two studies of particular regions and the religious attitudes and practices of their inhabitants independently underline the difficulty of using the English word 'religion' of the Hindu experience, because it carries the connotation of two separate spheres, belief and life, which is utterly alien to the Hindu perception. See D. F. Pocock, *Mind, Body and Wealth*, 1973; L. A. Babb, *The Divine Hierarchy*, 1975.

17. For a survey of six major systems of Hindu philosophy see Sen, *Hinduism*, pp. 78–85.

18. For a glimpse into the distinctive regional religious experience of Hindus see, for example, Lederle, *Philosophical Trends in Modern Maharashtra*, particularly ch. 1; K. W. Jones, *Arya Dharm*, 1976.

19. Babb, *The Divine Hierarchy*, particularly ch. 6. Pocock in *Mind, Body and Wealth* makes a similar observation from Gujarat. He notes the interweaving of the worship of *Mata*, the most powerful spirit in the village pantheon, with that of Shiva and Parvati, deities in the wider Hindu pantheon. For a more academic discussion of the interaction of the Great and Little Traditions to make up the totality and variety of the Hindu experience, see M. Marriott, 'Changing Channels of Cultural Transmission in Indian Civilization', *Aspects of Religion in Indian Society*, ed. L. P. Vidyarthi, 1961, pp. 13–25; Singer, *When a Great Tradition Modernizes*, pp. 43–8.

20. Singer, loc. cit. M. N. Srinivas is one of the main proponents of the idea of a normative, Sanskritic core of Hinduism. This is disputed by Singer himself, and L. A. Babb, for example.

21. Speech by Mahatma Gandhi on 1 May 1915, reported in *The Hindu*, 3 May 1915, *The Collected Works*, Vol. XIII, 1964, p. 69. Among Radhakrishnan's best known work is *The Hindu View of Life*, 1960. K. M. Pannikar's arguments are cited in A. B. Creel, 'Secularization and Hindu Tradition', *Religion and Society*, vol. XXII, no. 4, December 1975, pp. 77–92; and in T. Ling, *A History of Religion East and West*, 1968, p. 375.

22. D. H. Killingley, 'Vedanta and Modernity', *Indian Society*, ed. Philips and Wainwright, pp. 127–40.

23. W. G. Neevel, 'The Transformation of Sri Ramakrishna', and C. R. Pangbourn, 'The Ramakrishna Math and Mission: A Case Study of a Revitalizing Movement', *Hinduism*, ed. B. L. Smith, 1976, pp. 53–97, 98–119.

24. A Bharati, 'The Hindu Renaissance and its Apologetic Patterns', *Journal of Asian Studies*, vol. XXIX, no. 2, February 1970, pp. 267–87.

25. A readable and readily available introduction to Indian society and discussion of major problems of evidence and interpretation like the origins of caste is B. S. Cohn, *India*, 1971. A major modern analysis of the ideas supporting caste is L. Dumont, *Homo Hierarchicus*, 1972.

26. A good survey of major trends in twentieth-century British society is A. Marwick, *Britain in the Century of Total War*, 1968. See also the

interpretation of the changing face of British society in A. H. Halsey, *Change in British Society*, 1978.
27. A recent survey of some of the main trends in Indian society is S. C. Dube (ed.), *India since Independence*, 1972. See also Srinivas, *Social Change in Modern India*.
28. See Srinivas, op. cit., pp. 1–45; J. Silverberg (ed.), *Social Mobility in the Caste System in India*, 1968.
29. See D. Martin, *A General Theory of Secularization*, 1978, particularly ch. 2.
30. Berger, *The Social Reality of Religion*, pp. 116–30.
31. The phrase is Abhishiktananda's in his *Hindu-Christian Meeting Point*, revised English edition 1976. Panikkar makes a similar point in *The Unknown Christ of Hinduism*, pp. 96–8. Extracts from the Upanishads can be found in Zaehner (tr. and ed.), *Hindu Scriptures*, 1966.
32. For a discussion of this see Bellah, *Beyond Belief*, pp. 216–29.

2. *How Dead are the Gods? The Hindu World*

1. According to the census there are very few atheists in India. In 1961 only two areas recorded any sizeable number – over 34,000 in Tamil Nadu and over 44,000 in Nagaland: in both assertion of atheism was linked to an assertion of regional identity which the central government was reluctant to countenance. In other Hindu areas not more than 100 claimed to be atheists. In a small South Indian town 12% of a sample questioned had 'no belief in religion'. A. M. A. Ayrookuzhiel, 'A Study of the Religion of the Hindu People of Chirakkal (Kerala)', *Religion and Society*, vol. XXIV, no. 1, March 1977, pp. 5–54.
2. V. G. Pundlik, 'Religion in the Life of College Teachers'. (It is noteworthy that over 90% of respondents were men; this, given the known conservatism of women's religious attitudes in most societies, would tend to depress the number of believers. The strength of the believing groups is thus particularly interesting.)
3. M. Zaveri, 'The Religious Beliefs and Practices of College Teachers', unpublished paper 1969, cited in Appendix I, Pundlik, op. cit.
4. E. Shils, *The Intellectual Between Tradition and Modernity*, 1961, p. 64.
5. Evidence of the attitudes of the younger age group is drawn from the following: G. Poitevin, 'Quelle sécularisation? des dieux ou des hommes?', *Spiritus*, 64, XVII, p. 252. Findings of research among 300 Pune students, over 90% of them Hindu, 1970–71, by Professor Y. B. Damlé, cited in unpublished version of Poitevin, op. cit., lent to me by the latter. Findings of a questionnaire to 60 young adults in Bombay (mostly Hindu) in February 1978, by 3 Sophia College students (unpublished). Research into the attitudes of Hindu students of a South Indian university, P. H. Ashby, *Modern Trends in Hinduism*, pp. 49–70.
6. Paul C. Wiebe, 'Religious Change in South India', *Religion and Society*, vol. XXII, no. 4, December 1975, pp. 26–46; Ayrookuzhiel, *Religion and Society*, vol. XXIV, no. 1.
7. R. Mehta, *The Western Educated Hindu Woman*, 1970, pp. 49–73.

8. Y. B. Damlé, 'Perception of Modernization by College Youth in India', UNICEF *Assignment Children*, no. 27, July-September 1974, pp. 33–4, and 'Students and Modernization', cited in Pundlik, op. cit., Appendix I.

9. D. L. Gosling, *Science and Religion in India*, 1976, p. 96.

10. Mehta, *The Western Educated Hindu Woman*, pp. 56, 68. See also Pundlik, op. cit.; S. Kirtane, 'The Religious Practices of the Educated Women in Poona', cited in Pundlik, Appendix I; Gosling, *Science and Religion in India*, p. 108.

11. Again in the Bombay sample the boys' attitudes differed markedly from those of the girls. 33.3% of boys felt that religion had an important place in their lives, compared with 63.3% of the girls.

The figures for scientists questioned at selected academic institutions are not exactly comparable because of the mixed religious identity of the samples: but in Delhi and Bangalore, where Hindus predominated, the following results were obtained.

Religion important	*Delhi*	*Bangalore*
	%	%
At all times	48	56.6
Family occasions	21	16.8
When I need help	22.3	11
Never	15.8	21

See Gosling, op. cit., p. 101.

12. For evidence of abbreviated morning prayer among businessmen, see M. Singer, *When a Great Tradition Modernizes*, pp. 315–18, 331–3. M. R. Wood studied twelve educated working women in Ahmedabad (Gujarat), and found that only three of their husbands did lengthy morning prayer; while the evening prayer which was traditionally the women's had become less regular. 'Employment and Family Change', *Women in Contemporary India*, ed. A. de Souza, 1975, pp. 37–53.

13. Wood, op. cit.

14. B. D. Varadachar, 'Socialisation and Social Change', *Dimensions of Social Change in India*, ed. Srinivas, Seshaiah and Parthasarathy, p. 387. Wood, op. cit.; S. Vatuk, *Kinship and Urbanization*, 1972, pp. 105, 179–80; survey of abbreviations of rituals in M. Srinivas, *Social Change in Modern India*, pp. 125–6.

15. Social pressure to maintain ritual is clear in Pundlik's study. Many of the college lecturers he questioned felt that some rites and rituals should be maintained because they were a necessary part of Indian (rather than specifically religious) identity (83.5% of believers; 68.8% of agnostics; 44.2% of atheists). Pundlik, op. cit. See also Mehta, *The Western Educated Hindu Woman*, p. 54.

16. A total of 26.6% felt that dogma and ritual still held meaning for them; but 70% felt that it did not (80% of boys and 60% of girls in the sample).

17. For this phenomenon of the growing homogeneity of the Hindu religious experience and the 'democratization' of Sanskritic Hinduism

enshrined in the Great Tradition, see P. C. Wiebe, 'Religious Change in South India', *Religion and Society*, vol. XXII, no. 4, pp. 26–46; M. Marriott, 'Changing Channels of Cultural Transmission in Indian Civilization', *Aspects of Religion in Indian Society*, ed. Vidyarthi, pp. 13–25; Singer, *When a Great Tradition Modernizes*, pp. 187–8.

18. Singer, op. cit., pp. 148–241; K. S. Nair, *Ethnicity and Urbanization*, 1978, pp. 71, 75–6; Vatuk, *Kinship and Urbanization*, pp. 177–8; M. Holmström, 'Religious Change in and Industrial City of South India', *Journal of the Royal Asiatic Society*, 1971, 1, pp. 28–40.

19. In 1961 2 out of 303 films were classified as 'devotional', in 1966 1 out of 316, in 1971 8 out of 433, in 1972 6 out of 414: Y. Atala, 'Communication', *India since Independence*, ed. S. C. Dube, p. 283. *Bhakti* in films as a money-spinner is considered by Singer, op. cit., pp. 162–4.

20. I owe this information to R. W. Taylor of the Christian Institute for the Study of Religion and Society, Bangalore.

21. Srinivas, *Social Change in Modern India*, pp. 138–9; G. Kurian, 'The Indian Family in Transition: Some Regional Variations', *Family and Social Change in Modern India*, ed. G. R. Gupta, 1976, pp. 3–18.

22. Surveys of recent research in this field are P. Kapur, 'Studies of the Urban Women in India' and A. D. Ross, 'Changing Aspirations and Roles', *Family and Social Change in Modern India*, ed. Gupta, pp. 65–102, 103–132.

23. A. B. Creel, 'Secularisation and Hindu Tradition', *Religion and Society*, vol. XXII, no. 4, pp. 77–92.

24. See the enquiries of Singer into the world of South Indian businessmen, op. cit., pp. 320–331.

25. Numbers of cases of violence against person or property, and cases of insult and indignity against 'Scheduled Castes' were reported to the Upper House of the Indian Parliament in 1972 as 2339 in 1967; 2241 in 1968; 2253 in 1969; 2701 in 1970; 3136 in 1971; 3316 in 1972. B. Venkataraman and D. Venugopal, 'Public Order', *India Since Independence*, ed. Dube, p. 462. The best work on the contemporary position of the ex-untouchables is J. Michael Mahar (ed.), *The Untouchables in Contemporary India*, 1972.

26. T. Ling, *A History of Religion East and West*, pp. 374–5.

27. This is the main outcome of the researches of G. Poitevin recorded in 'Quelle sécularisation? des dieux ou des hommes?', *Spiritus*, 64, XVII, pp. 229–64.

28. M. N. Srinivas discusses this phenomenon of the Indian acceptance of contradiction in a sensitive article, 'Modernization', *Change and Conflict in India*, ed. R. Thapar, pp. 125–9.

29. A. Bharati, 'The Hindu Renaissance and its Apologetic Patterns', *Journal of Asian Studies*, XXIX, 2, p. 268.

30. S. N. Eisenstadt, 'Prologue: Some Remarks on Patterns of Change in Traditional and Modern India', *Change and Continuity in India's Villages*, ed. K. Ishwaran, 1970, pp. 21–35. Creel, 'Secularization and Hindu Tradition', *Religion and Society*, Vol. XXII, no. 4, pp. 77–92.

31. See Chapter 1 n. 13 above; also J. Duncan M. Derrett, *Religion, Law and the State in India*, 1968; R. D. Baird, 'Religion and the Secular',

in *Religion and Social Conflict in South Asia*, ed. B. L. Smith, 1976. pp. 47–63.

32. On state norms discussed in this paragraph, see A. K. Saran, 'Secular-Sacred Confrontation: A Historical Analysis', *Religion and Society*, vol. XVIII, no. 3, September 1971, pp. 9–35; Creel, 'Secularization'; M. Galanter, 'Secularism, East and West', *Secularism in India*, ed. V. K. Sinha, pp. 159–91, and 'The Religious Aspects of Caste: A Legal View', in D. E. Smith, *South Asian Politics and Religion*, 1966, pp. 277–310.

33. K. Subramaniam, *Brahmin Priest of Tamil Nadu*, 1974; R. H. Hooker, 'Voices of Varanasi', unpublished manuscript lent to me by the author, which describes some of the Sanskrit Pandits in the conservative university city of Varanasi (1978).

34. For example, the writings of the philosopher, Radhakrishnan; or a recent work by a prominent social analyst, B. Kuppuswamy, *Dharma and Society*, 1977.

3. How Dead are the Gods? The Christian Experience

1. For a survey of later nineteenth-century Christianity in Britain, see D. Martin, *A Sociology of English Religion*, pp. 19–29.

2. This paragraph is based on Martin, op. cit., pp. 36–41; M. Argyle and B. Beit-Hallahmi, *The Social Psychology of Religion*, pp. 8–10; L. Paul, *The Deployment and Payment of the Clergy*, pp. 17, 19.

3. R. J. Rees, *Background and Belief*, pp. 38, 122.

4. Martin, op. cit., p. 43; Argyle and Beit-Hallahmi, op. cit., p. 11; D. Perman, *Change and the Churches*, p. 34. Attendance varies in regularity among the members of the different churches. 4/10 Roman Catholics attend Mass on Sundays, about 1/13 Anglicans attend church on Sundays, while 1/4 Free Church members attend each Sunday. Martin, op. cit., pp. 39–40.

5. Rees, op. cit., pp. 33, 121; *National Survey on Religious Attitudes of Young People 1978*, Table 29, p. 38.

6. Martin, op. cit., p. 37; Paul, op. cit., p. 20; Manchester Lecturers' Survey 1978. The number of infant baptisms per 1000 live births rose from 623 in 1885 to 717 in 1927 but dropped to 554 in 1960. Paul, op. cit., p. 19.

7. Argyle and Beit-Hallahmi, op. cit., p. 12. I owe much of the information in this and the following paragraph to the Rev. Michael Mayne, formerly Head of BBC Radio's Religious Programmes.

8. This paragraph is based on Argyle and Beit-Hallahmi, op. cit., p. 13; Perman, op. cit, p. 35; Rees, op. cit., pp. 30, 33, 34; *National Survey 1978*, Table 20, p. 23; Manchester Surveys 1978; Rees, op. cit., p. 34 quotes the following table from F. Zweig, *The Student in the Age of Anxiety*, Heinemann 1963, p. 52, giving the results of a small survey among students at Oxford and Manchester:

	Oxford Sample (102)	Manchester Sample (103)
Believer	32.35%	66.01% ('practising' – 53.39%)
'Groping'	18.62%	12.62%
Agnostic	35.29%	16.5%
Atheist	13.72%	4.85%

9. Argyle and Beit-Hallahmi, op. cit., p. 13.

10. Rees, op. cit., pp. 48–58.

11. *National Survey 1978*, Table 20, p. 23.

12. Argyle and Beit-Hallahmi, op. cit., p. 12; Rees, op. cit., p. 123.

13. Argyle and Beit-Hallahmi, op. cit., p. 12; *National Survey 1978*, Table 32, p. 41.

14. Rees, op. cit., p. 63.

15. This is amply demonstrated in O. Chadwick, *The Secularization of the European Mind in the Nineteenth Century*

16. Perhaps the best introduction to the detail and complexity of this subject is Martin, *A Sociology of English Religion*.

17. In 1851 there had been 1 Anglican parson for every 1043 people; by 1951 there were only 2000 more Anglican clergy to minister to a population which had more than doubled – 1 parson for every 2271 people. Paul, op. cit., p. 21.

18. For a discussion of the trends noted in this and the following paragraphs see Martin's work in his *A Sociology of English Religion, The Religious and the Secular*, and *A General Theory of Secularization*. Also relevant for working class attitudes in the nineteenth century is Chadwick, op. cit., ch. 4, 'The Attitudes of the Worker', pp. 88–106 (1977 edition).

19. Martin discusses 'Superstitions and Subterranean Theologies' in *A Sociology of English Religion*, pp. 74–6, and *The Religious and the Secular*, p. 109. He draws heavily from G. Gorer, *Exploring English Character*, 1955. Particularly interesting is Gorer's chapter 14, 'Religion and Other Beliefs', pp. 237–77. See also the more recent evidence from *National Survey 1978*, Tables 23 and 24, pp. 28–9, 73–4. For religion in twentieth-century America, see Martin, *A General Theory of Secularization*, particularly chapter 2; C. Y. Glock and R. N. Bellah, *The New Religious Consciousness*.

20. For a discussion of these trends see B. R. Wilson, *Religion in Secular Society*, pp. 36–85; Martin, *The Religious and the Secular*, pp. 115–16.

21. This is dealt with in some detail by D. L. Edwards, *Religion and Change*, ch. 3, 'The Psychological Impact of the Secular Century', pp. 109–57.

22. This is the useful concept employed by P. L. Berger, *A Rumour of Angels*, 1971 edition, pp. 13–42.

23. Chadwick, op. cit., ch. 3, 'Science and Religion', pp. 161–88.

24. *National Survey 1978*, Table 27, pp. 34–5. 14% felt that only Christianity should be taught; 35% felt that several religions should be taught and the central place given to Christianity; 43% felt that all major religions should be taught; 41% felt that moral education should be given.

25. Martin, *A General Theory of Secularization*, pp. 63–4.

26. E. R. Norman, 'Christianity and the World', Reith Lectures broad-

cast in November-December 1978, published in *The Listener*, 2, 9, 16, 23, and 30 November, 7 December 1978 (e.g. Lecture 1, 'The Political Christ'). Based on these lectures is Dr Norman's *Christianity and the World Order*, 1979. See also Martin, *A General Theory of Secularization*, pp. 63–4; *A Sociology of English Religion*, pp. 58–67.

27. Paul, op. cit., p. 11.

28. For this debate which followed the 1958 publication of the report by the Committee on Homosexual Offences and Prostitution (*The Wolfenden Report*), see B. Mitchell, *Law, Morality and Religion in a Secular Society*, 1970 edition. *The Wolfenden Report* and Professor Hart asserted that certain areas of life were the individual's private concern in which the state should not as a rule intervene; while Lord Devlin held that any society must protect not only its outer boundaries and visible frameworks but also its inner core of assumptions, which in the British case he assumed to be Christian. See H. L. A. Hart, *Law, Liberty and Morality*, 1963, and P. Devlin, *The Enforcement of Morals*, 1965.

29. F. Zweig, *The Student in the Age of Anxiety*, p. 205, cited in Rees, op. cit., p. 35. Rees says that his later findings strongly support Zweig's conclusions.

30. D. Hay, 'The Spiritual Experiences of the British', *New Society*, 12 April 1979.

31. For an introduction to some of the 'extra-ecclesial' manifestations of religious attitudes and longings, see Glock and Bellah (eds), *The New Religious Consciousness*, on American evidence; 'Religion and the Sacred' in Greeley, *Unsecular Man*; Perman, *Change and the Churches*, ch. 4; B. R. Wilson, 'New Missions to Old Believers' in *Contemporary Transformations of Religion*; K. Leech, 'Spirituality and the Present Climate', *Soul Friend*, 1977; M. Furlong, *The End of Our Exploring*, 1973, ch. 5, 'Seventies' Journey'; J. Bowden, *Voices in the Wilderness*, 1977, pp. 22–7.

32. *National Survey 1978*, Tables 21 and 22, pp. 24–7.

33. The Saturday religious articles in *The Times*, contributed by a wide range of clergy and laity, are a fascinating barometer of trends in educated Christian concerns, fears and hopes. Many indicate extreme disquiet at aspects of change (or lack of it) in the churches. See for example, 'Challenge of a Religion "Without Strings" ', 18 November 1978, in which Bishop R. P. C. Hanson considered the revival of interest in religion, but the divorce between this revival and religion as supplied by the churches; also 'Keeping up the Fight for English in the Church', 17 June 1978, in which David Martin casts doubts on the utility of and reasoning behind Anglican liturgical reform.

4. Gurus and Gospels: Religious Authority and Communication in a Changing World

1. Don Cupitt in John Hick (ed.), *The Myth of God Incarnate*, 1977, p. 133. For examples of this process, see pp. 2, 133–4, and also for the general point, p. x.

2. Another study which badly needs doing is to compare what happens

when these positions are more or less reversed, when Christians live in an environment moulded by another religion, as in India: and when Hindus find themselves in an encompassing society which is totally distinct from their religious tradition and unsupportive of it, as in the case of Hindu migrants in contemporary Britain.

3. The importance of parents as the major influence in the formation of religious attitudes has been demonstrated by other twentieth-century studies, although the nature of this influence varies across denominations, and according to the type of relationship established between parent and child. Argyle and Beit-Hallahmi, *The Social Psychology of Religion*, pp. 30–33. For further evidence of the relegation of RE to a minor status in the experience of particular groups of young people, and for their dissatisfaction with the way in which it was taught, see Rees, *Background and Belief*, pp. 29, 71; *National Survey 1978*, Table 26, pp. 32–3, 77.

4. For evidence of the national decline in Sunday school attendance in this century see Paul, *The Deployment and Payment of the Clergy*, p. 20; Argyle and Beit-Hallahmi, op. cit., p. 12; Martin, *A Sociology of English Religion*, pp. 41–2.

5. A Western-style doctor in Pune commented to me on the mixture of Western and traditional medicine favoured among many of her patients, including the educated. Another study showed how even educated and high caste Hindus in the rural area surveyed still believed in the power of irrational forces over material affliction and illness, and consulted not only 'modern' doctors, but some of the 23 local 'healers' who were presumed to be in touch with these forces. Of those exhibiting symptoms of illness, 59% had consulted some healing agency; and of those 40% had consulted only a Western-style doctor, while 46% had consulted traditional and modern healers, and only 14% had been solely to a traditional healer. G. M. Carstairs and R. L. Kapur, *The Great Universe of Kota*, 1976, p. 116. Damlé, questioning Pune students in 1970–71, however, found that a large majority would only consult doctors, not priests or magicians, in case of illness but did not indicate whether 'doctors' in this case included ayurvedic practitioners. Y. B. Damlé, UNICEF *Assignment Children*, No. 27, 1974, p. 39.

6. 'Vedic Counter to Pollution', *The Times of India*, 26 April 1978. See also A. Bharati, 'Hinduism and Modernization', *Religion and Change in Contemporary Asia*, ed. Spencer, pp. 95–6. The Arya Samaj made similar claims in the later nineteenth century, and also claimed that the Vedas were the basis of all science. K. S. Jones, *Arya Dharm*, pp. 45, 67, 141 n. 63, 163–4.

7. S. Radhakrishnan, 'The Voice of India in the Spiritual Crisis of Our Time', *The Hibbert Journal*, 44, July 1946, cited in U. King, *Social Action*, 28, 1, 1978, p. 81. Lecture by Vivekananda in Lahore, 12 November 1879, published in *Advaita Vedanta. The Scientific Religion*, Advaita Ashrama, Calcutta 1952, ⁴1974.

8. Educated Hindu mothers are painfully aware of their inability to bring up their children with traditional religious influences: R. Mehta, *The Western Educated Hindu Woman*, pp. 55, 70. *Amar Chitra Katha* is a series of Hindu myths retold in comic strip form for children, published

by India Book House Education Trust, Bombay. Over 160 titles were available in 1978.

9. Two sensitive attempts to convey this attitude to those outside the Hindu tradition are Abhishiktananda, *Hindu-Christian Meeting Point*, e.g., pp. 5, 19, 91; R. Panikkar, *The Unknown Christ of Hinduism*. R. Thapar disputes the point sometimes made that Hindus have no sense of history. In analysing the Indian sense of history this prominent historian notes that the basic difference between it and, for example, the Greek sense of history is that the former stresses moral causal connections, whereas the latter emphasizes a rational analysis of cause and effect in which conscious human behaviour is crucial. R. Thapar, 'A Sense of History', *Change and Conflict in India*, ed. Thapar, pp. 1–7.

10. I owe much of this to Sister Sara Grant of the Christa Prema Seva Ashram, Pune. Particularly helpful is her article, 'Hindu Religious Experience', *The Way*, vol. 18, no. 1, January 1978, pp. 13–24.

11. D. L. Edwards, *Religion and Change*, p. 165. His brief section on 'The Authority of the Bible' (pp. 161–65) is a good historical introduction to the problem, his footnotes providing a useful guide to further reading.

12. For discussion of this dimension of the contemporary crisis in the use and understanding of the Bible see D. E. Jenkins, *The Contradiction of Christianity*, 1976, e.g., pp. 85–8; Edwards, op. cit., p. 164; Bowden, *Voices in the Wilderness*, pp. 38–41; F. Wright, *The Pastoral Nature of the Ministry*, 1980, pp. 17–19. See also the controversy on the role of scholars in relation to the assumptions of ordinary Christians, between two Anglican scholar-bishops: R. P. C. Hanson, 'The Unexamined Assumption of Most Christian Believers', *The Times*, 10 June 1978; J. A. T. Robinson, 'Unexamined Assumption of Christian Scholars', *The Times*, 24 June 1978.

13. Baba Padmanji quoted in M. Lederle, *Philosophical Trends in Modern Maharashtra*, p. 189.

14. R. Hooker, 'Voices of Varanasi'.

15. Of the 204 South Indian students interviewed in Ashby's study, 19 had had formal instruction in the Vedas, 20 in the Upanishads, 138 in the *Gita*, and 160 in the Epics. When asked what books they read *now*, only 2 mentioned the Upanishads, while 53 read the *Gita*, and 21 mentioned works by Vivekananda and/or Gandhi. P. H. Ashby, *Modern Trends in Hinduism*, pp. 63–4.

16. Speech by Mahatma Gandhi, 1 May 1915, *The Hindu*, 3 May 1915, *The Collected Works of Mahatma Gandhi*, Vol. XIII, 1964, p. 69.

17. Cited in A. Bharati, 'Gandhi's Interpretation of the Gita', *Gandhi India and the World*, 1970, ed. S. Ray, pp. 57–70. See also ibid., pp. 39–56, J. Jordens, 'Gandhi's Religion and the Hindu Heritage', and R. C. Zaehner, *Hinduism*, pp. 170–3. For Gandhi's attitude to Hinduism, to scripture as authority, and his own position, see *Young India*, 6 October 1921, *The Collected Works of Mahatma Gandhi*, Vol. XXI, 1966, pp. 245–50. He explained what he meant by the overriding authority of the 'inner voice' in letters to K. Natarajan (16 November 1932) and N. Khargiwale (9 January 1933), *Collected Works*, Vol. LII, 1972, pp. 6, 410–11.

Gandhi's main writings and teachings on the *Gita* are ashram discourses, 1926, *Collected Works*, Vol. XXXII, 1969, pp. 94–376; his translation of the *Gita* and commentary, 1929, ibid., Vol. XLI, 1970, pp. 90–133; letters to the ashram on the *Gita*, 1930 and 1931, ibid., Vol. XLIX, 1972, pp. 111–49.

18. Evidence of the problem of the Christian ministry is in L. Paul, *The Deployment and Payment of the Clergy*; Edwards, *Religion and Change*, particularly chs 3 and 4; Martin, *A General Theory of Secularization*, pp. 278–303, 'Crisis amongst the Professional Guardians of the Sacred'; Greeley, *The Persistence of Religion*, particularly the chapter entitled 'Religious Leadership'; Perman, *Change and the Churches*, ch. 8, 'Ministerial Malaise'.

A personal account of the crisis in one Anglican priest and his resolution of it within the ministry is W. H. Vanstone, *Love's Endeavour, Love's Expense*, 1977.

19. Professor David Jenkins, academic theologian and director of the William Temple Foundation, is an example; or the lay writer and broadcaster, Monica Furlong. Among J. Dominian's writings are *Proposals for a New Sexual Ethic*, 1977, e.g. p. 12; *Authority*, 1976. Perhaps Hans Küng's most influential book in Britain is his *On Being a Christian*, (1974) ET 1977.

20. G. Sale, 'The Ministry of the Laity's Vital Role in the Church', *The Times*, 12 November 1977; see also M. Batten, 'Developing the Role of the Layman in the Church', *The Times*, 8 July 1978, and her 'The Three Main Tasks for Lay Christians', *The Times*, 17 November 1979.

21. Daniel Jenkins, 'Diminishing the Power of the Ecclesiastical Bureaucracy', *The Times*, 23 September 1978.

22. One of the most serious studies of the sociology as well as the theology of the charismatic movement is R. A. Quebedeaux, 'Charismatic Renewal. The Origins, Development and Significance of Neo-Pentecostalism as a Religious Movement in the United States and Great Britain 1901–74', unpublished thesis, 1975.

23. See, for example, the activities of Madras pandits when asked for opinions on problems of pollution within the family caused by death or menstruation when important rituals had to be performed. Singer, *When a Great Tradition Modernizes*, pp. 94–9, 194–5.

24. K. W. Jones, *Arya Dharm*, p. 110.

25. R. Mehta, *The Western Educated Hindu Woman*, p. 69.

26. This assessment of the decline in the status and economic condition of Brahmin priests is based on the following sources of which the first is the most important: K. Subramaniam, *Brahmin Priest of Tamil Nadu*; S. Vatuk, *Kinship and Urbanization*, e.g., p. 160; P. C. Wiebe, 'Religious Change in South India', *Religion and Society*, vol. XXII, no. 4, pp. 26–46; P. Brent, *Godmen of India*, 1972, pp. 47–9.

27. I owe considerable information on this to Dr V. V. Pendse, Director of the Jnana Prabodhini, which cooperates with the Dharma Nirnaya Mandal in producing and publishing new rites. An example of the changes which are made is the removal from the Thread Ceremony of the mother's leave-taking of her child, which stems from the idea that boys went away

to the forest to study with a *guru*. The new rite does not suggest that the boy should follow a particular *guru*; but that books and even nature will be his educators.

28. An investigation of the agents of the reformulation of Hindu tradition on the basis of Vedanta is in A. Bharati, 'The Hindu Renaissance and its Apologetic Patterns', *Journal of Asian Studies*, XXIV, 2, pp. 277–81.

29. For some account of the life and activities of Swami Shankaracharya see Singer, *When a Great Tradition Modernizes*, pp. 84–9; Subramaniam, *Brahmin Priest of Tamil Nadu*, pp. 31, 96, 99, 109, 110. Another example of active caste spiritual leaders helping in the processes of adaptation to a changing world is F. F. Conlon, *A Caste in a Changing World*, pp. 202–12.

30. There is a considerable literature on *gurus*, past and present. Among useful surveys are Brent, *Godmen of India*; K. Singh, *Gurus, Godmen and Good People*, 1975; V. Mangalwadi, *The World of Gurus*, 1977; Sister Vandana, *Gurus, Ashrams and Christians*, 1978; C. S. J. White, 'The Sai Baba Movement', *Journal of Asian Studies*, Vol. XXXI, no. 4, August 1972, pp. 863–78; D. F. Pocock, *Mind, Body and Wealth*, particularly ch, 7.

31. Some of Gandhi's most important exposition on the role of experience and the inner voice are: Gandhi to boys and girls, 21 March 1932, *Collected Works*, Vol. XLIX, 1972, p. 223; Gandhi to K. Natarajan, 16 November 1932, ibid., Vol. LII, 1972, p. 6; Gandhi to N. Khargiwale, 9 January 1933, ibid., Vol. LII, 1972, pp. 410–11.

32. For a study of such a 'market place situation' in Bangalore, South India, see M. Holmström, 'Religious Change in an Industrial City of South India', *Journal of the Royal Asiatic Society*, 1971, 1, pp. 28–40.

33. D. Martin captures this 'mood' in *A General Theory of Secularization*, p. 93, and *A Sociology of English Religion*, pp. 64–7. For a discussion of contemporary understanding of modes of knowledge in religious matters see R. N. Bellah, *Beyond Belief*, pp. 39–44, 194; L. A. Reid, *Ways of Knowledge and Experience*, 1961, pp. 103–93, section entitled 'Knowledge and Religion'.

5. A Spirituality for the Twentieth Century?

1. Two attempts by Western Christians to live within the Hindu tradition are described in K. Klostermaier, *Hindu and Christian in Vrindaban*, 1969; J. Moffitt, *Journey to Gorakhpur*, 1973. Another problem is that in few religious traditions is there just *one* spirituality: this is particularly true of the Hindu tradition which embraces many distinctive regional, caste and sectarian spiritualities.

2. D. Hay, 'The Spiritual Experience of the British', *New Society*, 12 April 1979, for example. See also C. Armstrong, 'A Return to the Nursery of Spiritual Discipleship', *The Times*, 20 August 1977; R. P. C. Hanson, 'Challenge of a Religion "Without Strings" ', *The Times*, 18 November 1978.

3. The Hindu stress on power over constraints and release from these

is examined in N. Chaudhuri, *Hinduism*, particularly in the epilogue, 'Hindu Spirituality', pp. 311–29. The Christian vision of a relationship with God is at the heart of the witness of the New Testament writers. It is no coincidence that although the churches are taught that the whole church rather than the individual is the 'Bride of Christ' of the Revelation vision, many Christians have seen and expressed their individual relationship with God in the metaphor of human, sexual love. St John of the Cross and John Donne are two examples from very different spiritual traditions.

The problem of a fundamentally divergent vision and its damaging effect on both Hindus and Christians if neither draws on the insights of the other is at the centre of the discussion by my distinguished predecessor in the Teape Lecture series, J. A. T. Robinson, now published as *Truth is Two-Eyed*, 1979.

4. See for example, T. Merton, *Seeds of Contemplation*, revised edition 1960; *Contemplation in a World of Action*, 1971; Bede Griffiths, *Return to the Centre*, 1978; A. Bloom, *Living Prayer*, 1966; U. Kroll, *T. M. A Signpost for the World*, 1974; D. Wade, 'A Question of Meditation', *The Times*, 9 September 1978.

5. J. Dominian, *Proposals for a New Sexual Ethic*, pp. 68–9.

6. See for example, H. A. Williams, *The True Wilderness*, 1965; *True Resurrection*, 1972, *Tensions*, 1976; M. Furlong, *The End of Our Exploring*, and also *Travelling In*, 1973 edition; J. Drury, *The Pot and the Knife*, 1979.

7. D. Martin, 'Keeping up the Fight for English in the Church', *The Times*, 17 June 1978. See also M. Higham, 'Against the Modernization of the Lord's Prayer', *The Times*, 26 November 1977; P. Hebblethwaite, *The Runaway Church*, 1975, pp. 25–41.

It is not coincidence that it has often been left to the sociologists to point out the depth of deprivation which flows from the loss of the old liturgies. This loss must of course be weighed against the positive gains for authentic modern Christian faith which comes from the use of everyday language and experimental forms of worship; but liturgical reformers have much to learn about the dynamics of people's awareness and expression of the numinous from students of society who may well be agnostics. Some of the stranger liturgical experiments have occurred in America, of which Bryan Wilson has noted caustically: 'Modern communications have produced a new liturgical emporium, from which all items may be carelessly and mindlessly brought together, not to represent an appreciation of the accumulated inheritance of past culture, but merely so that a few people may be *high* for an hour or two,' *Contemporary Transformations of Religion*, p. 95.

8. A powerful plea for this approach to the resources for Christian spirituality is A. Ecclestone, *Yes to God*, 1975. See also on the question of authentic contemporary prayer his *A Staircase for Silence*, 1977; J. H. Churchill, *Finding Prayer*, 1978; A. Bloom, *Living Prayer*; M. Furlong, *Contemplating Now*, 1971; A. Squire, *Asking the Fathers*, 1973; R. Harries, *Turning to Prayer*, 1978; H. A. Williams, *Becoming What I Am*, 1977; M. Quoist, *Prayers of Life*, 1966 edition.

9. *Sadhana* is the nearest translation of the English word 'spirituality', but it denotes a particular spiritual discipline or path, and is therefore a narrower concept than the one used in this chapter. For the variety of such *sadhanas* in the Hindu tradition see K. Klostermaier, 'Sadhana. A Sketch of Indian Spirituality', *Religion and Society*, vol. XVI, no. 2, June 1969, pp. 36–50.

10. *Message of Swami Sivananda*, 1974.

11. Swami Chidananda, *A Guide to Noble Living*, 1973, e.g., pp. 103, 105.

12. See, for example, P. Teilhard de Chardin, *The Phenomenon of Man*, 1959; *Le Milieu Divin*, 1960.

13. See for example, the writings already cited by such authors as H. A. Williams and M. Furlong. The influence of Jung is marked in the attempts of many contemporary Christians to reach a new understanding of personal salvation.

14. *Swami Muktananda Paramahansa*, 1969, p. 60; *Swami Muktananda Paramhansa. Adept Master of Siddha Yoga*, 1969; Swami Chidananda, *A Guide to Noble Living*.

15. For a discussion of those who have taken on the defence of traditional Christian ethics see Perman, *Change and the Churches*, ch. 11, 'The Moral Watchdogs', pp. 169–90.

16. This was one of the elements in the debate following the publication of J. A. T. Robinson's *Honest to God*, 1963. Chapter 6 was entitled 'The New Morality'. More recent discussions include, for example, Dominion, *Proposals for a New Sexual Ethic*; Ecclestone, *Yes to God*, ch. 6.

17. For the evolution of Gandhi's life-style see his *Autobiography*; also J. M. Brown, *Gandhi's Rise to Power*, 1972. Gandhi's attitude to caste and untouchability is explained in his *Varnashramadharma*, 1962, and *The Removal of Untouchability*, 1959. His attitudes and their influence are also considered in D. Dalton, 'The Gandhian View of Caste, and Caste after Gandhi', *India and Ceylon: Unity and Diversity*, 1967, ed. P. Mason, pp. 167–76.

18. For some remaining Gandhians see V. Mehta, *Mahatma Gandhi and his Apostles*, 1977.

19. See for example. D. E. Jenkins, *The Contradiction of Christianity*; Ecclestone, *Yes to God*, pp. 70–86, and *A Staircase for Silence*, pp. 84–99; Churchill, *Finding Prayer*, p. 72; K. Leech, 'Christianity as an Instrument of Radical Renewal', *The Times*, 9 September 1978, and *Soul Friend*, pp. 191–3; Harries, *Turning to Prayer*, pp. 119–26. Among the Saturday articles in *The Times* in recent months on a religious response to major public issues have been M. Batten, 'Work-sharing as a Christian Response to Unemployment', 27 August 1977, and 'Towards a Christian Philosophy of Money', 28 May 1977; R. Holloway, 'The Ironies of the Christian Attitudes to Power', 29 January 1977; P. Oestreicher, 'Taking the Non-violent Demands of the Gospel Seriously', 21 October 1978.

20. E. R. Norman, *Christianity and the World Order*.

21. B. D. Tripathi, *Sadhus of India*, 1978, pp. 148–52. See also 'Hindu Religion and Culture in Indian Politics', Ashby, *Modern Trends in Hinduism*, pp. 91–115.

22. Tripathi, op. cit., pp. 206–8. For Gandhi's attitudes and practice see his *Autobiography*; also R. N. Iyer, *The Moral and Political Thought of Mahatma Gandhi*, 1972; J. M. Brown, *Gandhi and Civil Disobedience*, 1977, pp. 14–15, 25–6.

23. Swami Chidananda, *A Guide to Noble Living*, pp. 52–3.

24. The problems involved in 'dialogue' cause heated controversy. For recent discussions see J. Hick, *God and the Universe of Faiths*, 1973, and his 'Jesus and the World Religions' in Hick (ed.), *The Myth of God Incarnate*, 167–85; for criticisms of his approach see M. Green (ed.), *The Truth of God Incarnate*, 1977, pp. 114–19. An important scholarly assessment of the present position is H. Küng, *On Being a Christian*, 'The Challenge of the World Religions', pp. 89–116. A useful survey of changes in the Christian attitude to Hinduism is E. J. Sharpe, *Faith Meets Faith*, 1977.

25. See also R. Mehta, *The Western Educated Hindu Woman*, pp. 72–3; and an address by S. C. Thakur, Professor of Philosophy at Surrey University, 'Hinduism in a Post-Industrial Society', 8 April 1978, at a London seminar on 'The Nature of Religious Man'.

Epilogue

1. R. Tagore, *Gitanjali*, 1917, No. 37, p. 29. See also Revelation 21.5.

Bibliography

Abhishiktananda, *Hindu-Christian Meeting Point. Within the Cave of the Heart*, Revised English edition, Delhi 1976.

Argyle, M. and Beit-Hallahmi, B., *The Social Psychology of Religion* Routledge & Kegan Paul, London and Boston 1975 edition.

Armstrong, C., 'A Return to the Nursery of Spiritual Discipleship?', *The Times*, 20 August 1977.

Ashby, P., *Modern Trends in Hinduism*, Columbia University Press, New York and London 1974.

Ayrookuzhiel, A. M. A., 'A Study Of The Religion Of The Hindu People Of Chirakkal (Kerala)', *Religion and Society*, Vol. XXIV, No. 1 (March 1977), pp. 5–54.

Ayyub, A. S., 'Secularism', R. Thapar (ed.), *Change and Conflict in India*, Macmillan, Madras 1978, pp. 106–118.

Babb, L. A., *The Divine Hierarchy: Popular Hinduism in Central India*, Columbia University Press, New York and London 1975.

Baird, R. D., 'Religion and the Secular: Categories for Religious Conflict and Religious Change in Independent India', B. L. Smith (ed.), *Religion and Social Conflict in South Asia*, Brill, Leiden 1976, pp. 47–63.

Batten, M., 'Developing the Role of the Layman in the Church', *The Times*, 8 July 1978.

'Work-sharing as a Christian Response to Unemployment', *The Times*, 27 August 1977.

'Towards a Christian Philosophy of Money', *The Times*, 28 May 1977.

'The Three Main Tasks for Lay Christians', *The Times*, 17 November 1979.

Bellah, R. N., *Beyond Belief. Essays on Religion in a Post-Traditional World*, Harper & Row, New York, Evanston and London 1970.

Berger, P. L., *A Rumour of Angels. Modern Society and the Rediscovery of the Supernatural*, Penguin Books, Harmondsworth 1971.

The Social Reality of Religion, first published 1967, Penguin edition, Harmondsworth 1973.

Bharati, A., 'The Hindu Renaissance and its Apologetic Patterns', *Journal of Asian Studies*, Vol. XXIX, No. 2 (February 1970), pp. 267–287.

'Hinduism and Modernization', in R. F. Spencer (ed.), *Religion and Change in Contemporary Asia*, University of Minnesota Press, Minneapolis 1971, pp. 67–104.

'Gandhi's Interpretation of the Gita. An Anthropological Analysis', S. Ray (ed.), *Gandhi India and the World. An International Symposium*, Temple University Press, Philadelphia 1970, pp. 57–70.

Bloom, A., *Living Prayer*, Darton, Longman & Todd, London 1966.

Bombay Survey (unpublished) of religious and social attitudes of young adults, conducted by three Sophia College students, February 1978.

Bowden, J., *Voices in the Wilderness*, SCM Press, London 1977.

Brent, P., *Godmen of India*, Allen Lane, The Penguin Press, London 1972.

Brown, J. M., *Gandhi's Rise to Power. Indian Politics 1915–22*, CUP, Cambridge 1972.
 Gandhi and Civil Disobedience. The Mahatma in Indian Politics, 1928–34, CUP, Cambridge 1977.

Carstairs, G. M., and Kapur, R. L., *The Great Universe of Kota. Stress, Change and Mental Disorder in an Indian Village*, Hogarth Press, London 1976.

Chadwick, O., *The Secularization of the European Mind in the Nineteenth Century*, CUP, Cambridge 1975. Paperback edition CUP, 1977.

Chaudhuri, N. C., *Scholar Extraordinary. The Life of Friedrich Max Muller*, Chatto & Windus, London 1974.
 Hinduism. A Religion to Live By, Chatto & Windus, London 1979.

Chidananda (Swami), *A Guide to Noble Living*, Divine Life Society, Sivanandanagar 1973.

Church of England Year Books.

Churchill, J. H., *Finding Prayer*, SCM Press, London 1978.

Cohn, B. S., *India: The Social Anthropology of a Civilization*, Prentice-Hall, Englewood Cliffs 1971.

Conlon, F. F., *A Caste in a Changing World. The Chitrapur Saraswat Brahmans, 1700–1935*, Thomson Press, Indian edition, New Delhi 1977.

Creel, A. B., 'Secularisation and Hindu Tradition', *Religion and Society*, Vol. XXII, No. 4 (December 1975), pp. 77–92.

Dalton, D., 'The Gandhian View of Caste, and Caste after Gandhi', in P. Mason (ed.), *India and Ceylon: Unity and Diversity*, OUP, London 1967

Damlé, Y. B., 'Perception of Modernization by College Youth in India', UNICEF *Assignment Children*, No. 27 (July-September 1974), pp. 33–43.

Derrett, J. Duncan M., *Religion, Law and the State in India*, Faber, London 1968.

Devlin, P., *The Enforcement of Morals*, OUP, London 1965.

Dominian, J., *Authority: A Christian Interpretation*, Burns & Oates, London 1976.
 Proposals for a New Sexual Ethic, Darton, Longman & Todd, London 1977.

Drury, J., *The Pot and the Knife*, SCM Press, London 1979.

Dube, S. C., (ed.), *India since Independence. Social Report on India 1947–1972*, Vikas, New Delhi 1972.

Dumont, L., *Homo Hierarchicus*, Paladin English edition, London 1972.
 'World Renunciation in Indian Religions', *Contributions To Indian Sociology*, No. IV (April 1960), pp. 33–62.

Ecclestone, A., *Yes to God*, Darton, Longman & Todd, London 1975.
A Staircase for Silence, Darton, Longman & Todd, London 1977.
Edwards, D. L., *Religion and Change*, Hodder & Stoughton, London 1969
Eisenstadt, S. N., 'Prologue: Some Remarks on Patterns of Change in Traditional and Modern India', K. Ishwaran (ed.), *Change and Continuity in India's Villages*, Columbia University Press, New York 1970, pp. 21–35.
Contemplating Now, Hodder & Stoughton, London 1973 ed.

Furlong, M., *The End of our Exploring*, Hodder & Stoughton, London 1973.
Travelling In, Hodder & Stoughton, London 1973 ed.

Galanter, M., 'The Religious Aspects of Caste: A Legal View', D. E. Smith, *South Asian Politics and Religion*, Princeton University Press, Princeton 1966, pp. 277–310.
'Secularism, East and West', V. K. Sinha (ed.), *Secularism in India*, Lalvani Publishing House, Bombay 1968, pp. 159–191.
Gandhi, M. K., *The Collected Works of Mahatma Gandhi*, The Government of India, Delhi, 1958f.
An Autobiography. The Story of My Experiments with Truth, Jonathan Cape, London 1966 ed.
Varnashramadharma, Navajivan Press, Ahmedabad 1962.
The Removal of Untouchability, Navajivan Press, Ahmedabad 1959.
Geertz, C., 'Religion as a Cultural System', M. Banton (ed.), *Anthropological Approaches to the Study of Religion*, Tavistock Publications, London 1966, pp. 1–46.
Glasner, Peter E., *The Sociology of Secularisation. A Critique of a Concept*, Routledge & Kegan Paul, London 1977.
Glock, C. Y., and Bellah, R. N., (ed.), *The New Religious Consciousness*, University of California Press, Berkeley, Los Angeles and London 1976.
Gorer, G., *Exploring English Character*, Cresset Press, London 1955.
Gosling, D. L., *Science and Religion in India*, Christian Literature Society, Madras 1976, C.I.S.R.S. Series on Religion, No. 21.
Grant, Sr. Sara, 'Hindu Religious Experience', *The Way*, Vol. 18, No. 1 (January 1978), pp. 13–24.
Greeley, A. M., *The Persistence of Religion*, SCM Press, London 1972.
Green, M. (ed.), *The Truth of God Incarnate*, Hodder & Stoughton, London 1977.
Griffiths, Bede, *Return to the Centre*, Fount, Collins, Glasgow 1978. (First published 1976.)
Gupta, G. R. (ed.), *Family and Social Change in Modern India*, Vikas, New Delhi 1976.

Halsey, A. H., *Change in British Society. Based on the Reith Lectures*, OUP, Oxford 1978.
Hanson, R. P. C., 'Challenge of a Religion "Without Strings" ', *The Times*, 18 November 1978.

'The Unexamined Assumption of Most Christian Believers', *The Times*, 10 June 1978.

Harries, R., *Turning to Prayer*, Mowbray & Co., London and Oxford 1978.

Hart, H. L. A., *Law, Liberty and Morality*, OUP, London 1963.

Hay, D., 'The Spiritual Experiences of the British', *New Society*, 12 April 1979.

Hebblethwaite, P., *The Runaway Church*, Collins, London 1975.

Hick, J., *God and the Universe of Faiths*, Macmillan, London 1973.

Hick, J. (ed.), *The Myth of God Incarnate*, SCM Press, London 1977.

Higham, M., 'Against the Modernization of the Lord's Prayer', *The Times*, 26 November 1977.

Holloway, R., 'The Ironies of the Christian Attitudes to Power', *The Times*, 29 January 1977.

Holmström, M., 'Religious Change in an Industrial City of South India', *Journal of the Royal Asiatic Society*, 1971, 1, pp. 28–40.

Hooker, R., 'Voices of Varanasi', unpublished manuscript. (This is now published as *Voices of Varanasi*, CMS, London 1979.)

Iyer, R. N., *The Moral and Political Thought of Mahatma Gandhi*, OUP, New York 1972.

Jenkins, Daniel, 'Diminishing the Power of the Ecclesiastical Bureaucracy', *The Times*, 23 September 1978.

Jenkins, David E., *The Contradiction of Christianity*, SCM Press, London 1976.

Jones, K. W., *Arya Dharm. Hindu Consciousness in 19th-century Punjab*, Indian edition, Manohar, Delhi 1976.

Jordens, J., 'Gandhi's Religion and the Hindu Heritage', in S. Ray (ed.), *Gandhi India and the World. An International Symposium*, Temple University Press, Philadelphia 1970, pp. 39–56.

Killingley, D. H., 'Vedanta and Modernity', in C. H. Philips and M. D. Wainwright (ed.), *Indian Society and the Beginnings of Modernization c. 1830–1850*, SOAS, London 1976.

King, U., 'Indian Spirituality, Western Materialism: An Image and its Function in the Reinterpretation of Modern Hinduism', *Social Action*, 28, 1 (January-March, 1978), pp. 62–86.

Klostermaier, K., 'Sadhana. A Sketch of Indian Spirituality', *Religion and Society*, Vol. XVI. No. 2 (June 1969), pp. 36–50.

Hindu and Christian in Vrindaban, SCM Press, London 1969.

Kroll, U., *T.M. A Signpost for the World*, Darton, Longman & Todd, London 1974.

Küng, H., *On Being a Christian*, Collins, London 1977. (Original German edition, 1974.)

Kuppuswamy, B., *Dharma and Society. A Study in Social Values*, Macmillan, Madras 1977.

Kurian, G., 'The Indian Family in Transition: Some Regional Variations',

G. R. Gupta (ed.), *Family and Change in Modern India*, Vikas, New Delhi 1976, pp. 3–18.

Laslett, P., *The World we have Lost*, Methuen, London 1965.
Lederle, M., *Philosophical Trends in Modern Maharashtra*, Popular Prakashan, Bombay 1976.
Leech, K., *Soul Friend. A Study of Spirituality*, Sheldon Press, London 1977.
'Christianity as an Instrument of Radical Renewal', *The Times*, 9 September 1978.
Ling, T., *A History of Religion East and West. An Introduction and Interpretation*, Paperback edition, Macmillan, London 1968.
Luthera, V. P., *The Concept of The Secular State and India*, OUP, Calcutta 1964.

Mahar, J. Michael, *The Untouchables in Contemporary India*, University of Arizona Press, Tucson, Arizona 1972.
Mangalwadi, V., *The World of Gurus*, Vikas, New Delhi 1977.
Marriott, M., 'Changing Channels of Cultural Transmission in Indian Civilization', L. P. Vidyarthi (ed.), *Aspects of Religion in Indian Society*, Meerut, *c.* 1961.
Martin, D., *A Sociology of English Religion*, SCM Press, London 1967.
The Religious and the Secular. Studies in Secularization, Routledge & Kegan Paul, London 1969.
A General Theory of Secularization, Basil Blackwell, Oxford 1978.
'Keeping up the Fight for English in the Church', *The Times*, 17 June 1978.
Marwick, A., *Britain in the Century of Total War. War, Peace and Social Change 1900–1967*, The Bodley Head, London 1968.
Mehta, R., *The Western Educated Hindu Woman*, Asia Publishing House, Bombay 1970.
Mehta, V., *Mahatma Gandhi and His Apostles*, Viking Press, New York 1977.
Merton, T., *Seeds of Contemplation*, revised ed., Burns & Oates, London 1960.
Contemplation in a World of Action, Allen & Unwin, London 1971.
Mitchell, B., *Law, Morality, and Religion in a Secular Society*, OUP, London 1970, paperback edition.
Moffitt, J., *Journey To Gorakhpur. Reflections on Hindu Spirituality*, Sheldon Press, London 1973.
Muktananda Paramahansa, Swami, *Swami Muktananda Paramahansa*, Shree Gurudev Ashram, Ganeshpuri 1969.
Swami Muktananda Paramahansa. Adept Master of Siddha Yoga, Shree Gurudev Ashram, Ganeshpuri 1969.

Nair, K. S., *Ethnicity And Urbanization*, Ajanta Publications, Delhi 1978.
National Survey on Religious Attitudes of Young People, London 1978.
Neevel, W. G., 'The Transformation Of Sri Ramakrishna', B. L. Smith

(ed.), *Hinduism. New Essays In The History Of Religions*, Brill, Leiden 1976, pp. 53–97.

Norman, E. R., *Christianity and the World Order*, OUP, Oxford 1979. (Based on 1978 Reith Lectures, first published in *The Listener*, November-December 1978.)

Oestreicher, P., 'Taking the non-violent demands of the Gospel seriously', *The Times*, 21 October 1978.

Pangbourn, C. R., 'The Ramakrishna Math and Mission: A Case Study of a Revitalising Movement', B. L. Smith (ed.), *Hinduism. New Essays in the History of Religions*, Brill, Leiden 1976.

Panikkar, R., *The Unknown Christ of Hinduism*, Darton, Longman & Todd, London 1964.

Parvathamma, C., 'Religion and Social Change: A Study of Tradition and Change in Virasaivism', in M. N. Srinivas, S. Seshaiah and V. S. Parthasarathy (ed.), *Dimensions of Social Change in India*, Allied Publishers, New Delhi 1977.

Paul, L., *The Deployment and Payment of the Clergy*, Church Information Office, London 1964.

Perman, D., *Change and the Churches. An Anatomy of Religion in Britain*, The Bodley Head, London, Sydney and Toronto 1977.

Pocock, D. F., *Mind, Body and Wealth. A Study of Belief and Practice in an Indian Village*, Blackwell, Oxford 1973.

Poitevin, G., 'Quelle sécularisation? des dieux ou des hommes?' *Spiritus*, 64, XVII (September 1976), pp. 229–64.

Pritchard, L. K., 'Religious Change in Nineteenth-Century America', C. Y. Glock and R. N. Bellah (ed.), *The New Religious Consciousness*, University of California Press, Berkeley, Los Angeles and London 1976.

Pundlik, V. P., 'Religion in the Life of College Teachers', Unpublished PhD Thesis, Poona University 1970.

Quebedeaux, R. A., 'Charismatic Renewal. The Origins, Development, and Significance of Neo-Pentecostalism as a Religious Movement in the United States and Great Britain 1901–74'. Oxford DPhil thesis 1975.

Quoist, M., *Prayers Of Life*, Gill & Son, Dublin and Melbourne 1966 ed.

Radhakrishnan, *The Hindu View of Life*, Paperback edition, Unwin, London 1960.

Rees, R. J., *Background and Belief. A Study of Religion and Religious Education as seen by Third-Year Students at Oxford, Cambridge and Bangor*, SCM Press, London 1967.

Reid, L. A., *Ways of Knowledge and Experience*, George Allen & Unwin, London 1961.

Robinson, J. A. T., 'Unexamined Assumption of Christian Scholars', *The Times*, 24 June 1978.

Truth is Two-Eyed, SCM Press, London 1979. *Honest to God*, SCM Press, London 1963.

Ross, A. D., 'Changing Aspirations and Roles: Middle and Upper Class Indian Women Enter the Business World', G. R. Gupta (ed.), *Family and Social Change in Modern India*, Vikas, New Delhi 1976, pp. 103–132.

Sale, G., 'The Ministry of the Laity's Vital Role in the Church', *The Times*, 12 November 1977.

Saran, A. K., 'Secular-Sacred Confrontation: A Historical Analysis', *Religion and Society*, Vol. XVIII, No. 3 (September 1971), pp. 9–35.

Sen, K. M., *Hinduism*, Penguin, Harmondsworth 1961.

Sharpe, E. J., *Faith Meets Faith. Some Christian Attitudes to Hinduism in the Nineteenth and Twentieth Centuries*, SCM Press, London 1977.

Shils, E., *The Intellectual between Tradition and Modernity: The Indian Situation*, Mouton & Co., The Hague 1961.

Silverberg, J. (ed.), *Social Mobility in the Caste System in India. An Introductory Symposium*, Mouton, The Hague 1968.

Singer, M., *When a Great Tradition Modernizes. An Anthropological Approach to Indian Civilization*, Pall Mall, London 1972.

Singh, K., *Gurus, Godmen and Good People*, Orient Longman, Bombay 1975.

Sinha, V. K. (ed.), *Secularism In India*, Lalvani Publishing House, Bombay 1968.

Sivananda, Swami, *Message of Swami Sivananda*, Divine Life Society 1974.

Smith, D. E., *India as a Secular State*, Princeton University Press, Princeton 1963.
    South Asian Politics and Religion, Princeton University Press, Princeton 1966.

Spencer, Robert F., *Religion and Change in Contemporary Asia*, University of Minnesota Press, Minneapolis 1971.

Squire, A., *Asking The Fathers*, SPCK, London 1973.

Srinivas, M. N., *Social Change In Modern India*, University of California Press, Berkeley & Los Angeles 1966.
    'Modernisation', R. Thapar (ed.), *Change and Conflict in India*, Macmillan, Madras, 1978, pp. 125–9.

Subramaniam, K., *Brahmin Priest of Tamil Nadu*, Wiley Eastern, New Delhi 1974.

Tagore, R., *Gitanjali*, Macmillan, London 1917.

Teape, W. M., *The Secret Lore of India and The One Perfect Life for All being A Few Main Passages from the Upanishads*, W. Heffer, Cambridge 1932.

Teilhard de Chardin, P., *The Phenomenon of Man*, Collins, London 1959.
    Le Milieu Divin. An essay on the interior Life, Collins, London 1960.

Thakur, S. C., 'Hinduism in a Post-Industrial Society' (Unpublished paper given in London on 8 April 1978).

Thapar, R., 'A Sense of History', R. Thapar (ed.), *Change and Conflict in India*, Macmillan, Madras 1978, pp. 1–7.

The Times of India, 26 April 1978.

Tripathi, B. D., *Sadhus of India. The Sociological View*, Popular Prakashan, Bombay 1978.

Vandana, *Gurus, Ashrams and Christians*, Darton, Longman & Todd, London, 1978.
Vanstone, W. H., *Love's Endeavour, Love's Expense. The Response of Being to the Love of God*, Darton, Longman & Todd, London, 1977.
Varadachar, B. D., 'Socialisation And Social Change', M. N. Srinivas, S. Seshaiah & V. S. Parthasarathy (ed.), *Dimensions Of Social Change In India*, Allied Publishers, New Delhi, 1977.
Vatuk, S., *Kinship and Urbanization. White Collar Migrants in North India*, University of California Press, Berkeley, Los Angeles & London, 1972.
Vivekananda, *Advaita Vedanta. The Scientific Religion* (1897), Advaita Ashrama, Calcutta, 1952, 4th Impression 1974.

Wade, D., 'A question of meditation', *The Times*, 9 September 1978.
Weil S., *Waiting on God*, Collins, Fontana Books, London 1959.
White, C. S. J., The Sai Baba Movement: Approaches to the Study of Indian Saints', *Journal of Asian Studies*, Vol. XXXI, No. 4 (August 1972), pp. 863–78.
Wiebe, Paul C., 'Religious Change In South India: Perspectives From A Small Town', *Religion and Society*, Vol. XXII, No. 4 (December 1975), pp. 26–46.
Williams, H. A., *The True Wilderness*, Constable, London, 1965.
True Resurrection, Mitchell Beazley, London, 1972.
Tensions. Necessary Conflicts in Life and Love, Mitchell Beazley, London 1976.
Becoming What I Am. A Discussion of the Methods and Results of Christian Prayer, Darton, Longman & Todd, London 1977.
Wilson, B. R., *Religion in Secular Society. A Sociological Comment*, Watts, London 1966.
Contemporary Transformation of Religion, OUP, London 1976.
Wood, M. R., 'Employment and Family Change: A Study of Middle Class Women in Urban Gujarat', A. de Souza (ed.), *Women In Contemporary India*, Manohar, Delhi 1975, pp. 37–53.
Wright, F., *The Pastoral Nature of the Ministry*, SCM Press, London 1980.

Zaehner, R. C., *Hinduism*, OUP, Oxford, London and New York 1962.
Zaehner (trans. & ed.), *Hindu Scriptures*, Dent, London 1966.

Index